D1599979

Transforming History

Transforming History

A Guide to Effective, Inclusive,
and Evidence-Based Teaching

MARY JO FESTLE

The University of Wisconsin Press

The University of Wisconsin Press
728 State Street, Suite 443
Madison, Wisconsin 53706
uwpress.wisc.edu

Gray's Inn House, 127 Clerkenwell Road
London EC1R 5DB, United Kingdom
eurospanbookstore.com

Printed in the United States of America

This book may be available in a digital edition.

Library of Congress Cataloging-in-Publication Data
Names: Festle, Mary Jo, author.
Title: Transforming history : a guide to effective, inclusive, and
    evidence-based teaching / Mary Jo Festle.
Description: Madison : The University of Wisconsin Press, [2020] |
Includes bibliographical references and index.
Identifiers: LCCN 2019039070 | ISBN 9780299326807 (cloth)
Subjects: LCSH: History—Study and teaching (Higher)—United States.
Classification: LCC D16.3 .F47 2020 | DDC 907.1/173—dc23
LC record available at https://lccn.loc.gov/2019039070

Contents

List of Illustrations   VII

Introduction   3

1   What We Teach   13

2   Who We Teach   47

3   How We Teach   87

4   How We Assess   142

5   Who We Are   192

Conclusion   227

Acknowledgments   233
Notes   237
Index   291

Illustrations

Figures

Figure 1   Intentional and effective teaching   11
Figure 2   Components and timing of good discussions   124

Tables

Table 1   Traditional Course Planning versus Backward
           Design   16
Table 2   Types of Questions   89
Table 3   Relationship between Inside and Outside of
           Class Activities   108

Examples

Example 1   Transparent Assignment   42
Example 2   Course Alignment Diagram   104
Example 3   Unit Plan   111
Example 4   Matrix Graphic Organizer   136
Example 5   Class Participation Rubric   147
Example 6   Essay Rubric A   151
Example 7   Essay Rubric B   152
Example 8   Website Rubric   155
Example 9   Wrapper for a Take-Home Essay   167
Example 10   Ethnographic Peer Observation Form, Part A   180
Example 11   Ethnographic Peer Observation Form, Part B   181

Transforming History

Introduction

To be a historian is to be a teacher.
JAMES GROSSMAN

When I was in graduate school, some busy fellow students—who were trying to finish their dissertations and simultaneously teach their first courses independently—shared a survival strategy: get two good textbooks, one for the students and one to use for writing lectures. While I strongly endorse surviving stressful situations, I am grateful that some wiser mentors gave me different advice, because there is a lot of evidence that teaching can be done better than that, and there are many reasons to do it better.

Some people mistakenly think that effective teaching results primarily from knowing a lot of content and being dedicated, or they believe that great teachers are charismatic "naturals."[1] Unfortunately, a deep knowledge of history doesn't tell us how to teach students to ask good questions, make sense of a complicated topic, analyze a primary source, read scholarly monographs intelligently, or conduct research. Our dedication doesn't automatically help students see the relevance of what they're studying. Instructors aren't born knowing how to create engaging assignments or the most effective ways to grade them. Few people are "naturals" at designing a coherent course where the work done inside and outside of class time are tightly aligned. Although most of us know that facilitating a discussion or delivering a lecture are skills that can be improved, fewer are familiar with the evidence about how to go about it.

This book starts from a few assumptions. First, people are enriched by understanding the past, so teaching history matters. As James Grossman, executive director of the American Historical Association, put it, "To be a historian is to be a teacher."[2] Historians teach in books, articles, historic sites, museums, archives, news media, films, conversations, and especially in classrooms. Another assumption is that teaching is a

3

complex endeavor. Teaching requires integrating one's content knowledge with a host of different skills, and doing this well is challenging. Finally, the ability to teach history effectively is learnable. There is not just one right way of doing it well, but there is scholarship that points us toward ways to do justice to both our content and students.

This book is written for history faculty who are committed to the vocation of teaching—those who are willing to work hard and conscientiously in order to transform students' minds and who hope to work intelligently and effectively so they remain healthy and satisfied over long careers. We increase the odds of achieving those goals by being reflective students of our craft and being motivated to improve.

Why Now? Our Teaching Context

We are teaching in challenging times. Not everyone understands what we do. Periodic exposés blame instructors for how few historical facts citizens remember.[3] Remarks from people I've just met about how it must be nice to teach only a few courses and have my summers off inevitably come in the midst of a sixty-hour work week when I'm hopelessly behind in grading. Even colleagues may not get it. During one of my first faculty job interviews, I was nervously discussing the challenges of teaching history with a dean, who remarked, "I don't understand the problem. After all, history doesn't change, does it?" I wasn't sure if he was joking or didn't understand the interpretive nature of history. We historians know that although what has already happened in the past remains unchanged, our understanding of the past and interpretations of it are always evolving, and this "threshold concept" is tricky for many of our students, too.[4]

Our teaching context continually changes. Every term, we encounter new students, a collection of unique individuals. They grew up in a rapidly changing world, which contributes to a shifting landscape in our departments and in higher education more broadly. Ideas about the best ways to teach result from new research. It's always a good time to think carefully about our teaching, but given recent occurrences, it is especially important now.

The number of students enrolling in history courses and majoring in history has been declining in the United States.[5] Some students do not see the relevance of our discipline. That may be because they don't see it enough in political leaders or popular media, or because we haven't demonstrated the historical roots of current dilemmas or the value of how historians use evidence to inform decisions and practice fair-minded analysis and respectful discourse. The value of the liberal arts is not always apparent to students (or their parents) who wonder whether degrees in the humanities will pay off after graduation—an understandable concern in difficult economic times. Perhaps we have done a poor job of showing students the varied kinds of rewarding careers that history majors enjoy and the ways history graduates use skills honed in our courses to contribute to workplaces, communities, and the world.

"Why do history professors make history boring?" asked that same dean. That was a pretty tough interview question for a newly minted PhD, but one we should consider. For decades, history has ranked near the bottom of subjects high school students like because it is perceived as boring.[6] Although African American, Native American, and Latino high school students were especially unengaged in the study of U.S. history, male children from affluent white families were also uninspired. Interest in the past does not appear to be the problem. Interviews demonstrated that people regularly engaged with history, through books, films, family memories and materials, hobbies, and public history sites, and that these activities often had great personal meaning, but they did not remember their history classes in elementary or high school fondly. "Boring" was the single most common word offered to describe their experiences.[7] That means our students frequently come to college with negative preconceptions about history.

Troubling data suggests that some history instructors are not sufficiently serving their students once they make it to college. A recent Gardner Institute study of 28,000 students in introductory U.S. history courses at thirty-two institutions of higher education found thousands of students who failed, withdrew, or took incompletes, and most of them had good academic standing overall and cannot be easily dismissed as "bad students." The study found that race, family income levels, gender, and status as a first-generation college student were the best predictors of who would not succeed in introductory history courses. Even worse, doing poorly in history courses had significant implications, as it was highly correlated with the decision to drop out of college. The report concluded that the ways we are currently teaching introductory history may well be "subtly but effectively promoting inequity."[8] "It is very appealing to imagine that the history classroom is a level playing field, where students' willingness to work hard determines their level of success," David Pace observes, but instead "our courses can be a one-way ticket to a life of marginality and one more step in the creation of a society in which inequality undermines the foundations of democracy."[9] Most historians I know would be appalled if their courses simply benefited already privileged students, and most of them believe in the potential of historical knowledge and skills to help prepare an educated and empowered citizenry. Can't we do better?

Many individual faculty members are dedicated to high-quality teaching, but our profession has been slow to demonstrate a similar commitment. History is not alone, of course; many critics have pointed out that the majority of college faculty are "woefully unprepared" to teach because graduate programs too often assumed that if you know content, you can teach it.[10] As David Pace points out, history graduate programs prepare budding professionals for their research careers through "careful training, access to the writings of others in the field, and careful evaluation and feedback by peers. In the process, evidence is systematically gathered, assumptions are carefully examined, and competing interpretations are weighed against one another. And the entire enterprise is infused with a commitment to rigor and collective responsibility."[11]

Most graduate students have not received the same quantity or quality of training for teaching, and this reveals our profession's traditional priorities. For years, our most prestigious professional journals and conferences marginalized the scholarship of and discussions about teaching. Many faculty members began their careers ill-prepared to implement a huge portion of their job description and were forced to reinvent the wheel, mimic what a favorite professor did, or rely on "haphazardly shared folk wisdom" that would not meet professional standards for research about history but was considered acceptable for teaching young minds.[12]

Signs of change, however, suggest that we are now teaching in a period of great opportunity. Over the past twenty to thirty years, in higher education there has been a revolution in scholarship of teaching and learning (SOTL), which has sparked a "pedagogical turn" in the field of history as well.[13] Scholars have explored our discipline-specific modes of thinking and "decoded" precisely what is challenging for students.[14] We are borrowing insights from SOTL in other fields to see if they are applicable to history. We are having more discussions about our fundamental goals and how they should be reflected in our surveys, upper-level courses, and capstone seminars. As we consider our teaching methods, we treat student work as evidence to be analyzed, and our conversations are more grounded in theory, research, and shared values instead of speculation or folk wisdom. As the American Historical Association Tuning Project illustrates, the history profession as a whole seems to be taking teaching more seriously.[15] Prestigious journals and annual meetings dedicate a bit more time and space to teaching. More graduate programs offer teaching workshops, courses, or certificates. It is rarer to hear pedagogy dismissed as a lesser concern; indeed, more institutions value high-quality teaching and welcome SOTL in the criteria for promotion and tenure.

The digital revolution has transformed history teaching. In a generation, an astonishing amount of historical information has appeared on the Internet. Twenty years ago, faculty planning a course only had a few books of collected documents to choose from, none of which fully met their individual course goals, but now we have free access to over 20 million primary sources. Undergraduate students can access a host of scholarly articles in a fraction of the time it used to take graduate students working in a research library. It seems like the dark ages when students had to retype an entire essay every time they made revisions. Thankfully, we all can write better now, partly because it is so quick and easy to edit our work.

Technological advances have brought many benefits, but it means teaching has to keep pace. Students have many sources of information beyond their professors and textbooks, but being exposed to information is not the same as knowing how to think like a historian. Students urgently need help learning how to critically evaluate and interpret the reliability and significance of the information out there. "With a cheap Web template and no professional training to speak of, any scoundrel can create a site that calculatingly misleads," observed Sam Wineburg, who illustrated this with the example of a persistent, patently false narrative about thousands of Southern blacks volunteering to fight for the Confederacy that fooled many people.[16] In addition, instructors must grapple with the new problem of abundance by selecting materials for well-designed courses that engage students, recognizing that if we don't, those students might be distracted by technology at their fingertips. If we are wise, we will make optimal use of the many new ways to communicate history in the digital age.[17]

7

History instructors benefit from access to sound multi-institutional research about students' learning experiences. For example, the Wabash Institute's National Study of Liberal Arts Education assessed students at nineteen institutions as they entered college, at the end of their first year, and at the end of their fourth year. The study explored the effects of teaching techniques, campus interactions, and experiences on critical thinking skills and deep learning.[18] Another large study, the Transparency in Teaching and Learning Project, surveyed more than 25,000 students in hundreds of courses at more than forty institutions to look for changes in their metacognition, academic confidence, and skill mastery. The study suggests there are concrete practical things faculty can do to promote their students' learning, including that of students from traditionally marginalized groups. We now know much more about high-impact practices.[19]

At the same time, psychologists and others who study the science of learning have made great advances. They know more about how the brain works, what factors impede student learning, what increases motivation, how to improve metacognition, which practices help develop mastery, variations in orientation toward learning, and the effect of classroom climate and stereotypes, to mention a few important topics. Fortunately, these insights have begun to be shared more widely and in language accessible for nonspecialists.[20] Many campuses now have centers for teaching and learning staffed by committed professionals whose job is to keep up with the scholarship about teaching and learning and support faculty in their specific course contexts.

What Is an "Effective" Teacher?

This book synthesizes and applies scholarship and theory about teaching in general—and teaching history specifically—for those who want to be effective instructors. By "effective," I mean instructors whose students learn significant ideas, concepts, and skills that are valued by our discipline and whose learning lasts (rather than disappearing a few weeks after the term ends). Effective teaching also means that students' learning was due (in part) to their instructor's actions to facilitate it. I also argue that effective teaching is scholarly, inclusive, and intentional.

"Scholarly teachers" approach teaching in the same manner they conduct research: curious, analytical, scrupulous, smart about methods, and focused on evidence. To be scholarly teachers, we don't need to conduct and publish formal research about the effectiveness of our pedagogical strategies (although we could). Scholarly teaching means something simple but powerful: using the scholarship and theory that already exists about effective teaching, thinking carefully about what we are doing, and continuously considering the evidence available about how well we're teaching and how well our students are learning.

By "inclusive," I mean we teach in a way that provides the opportunity for all students (who work hard and in the right direction) to learn successfully. Inclusive teaching does not mean that all students end up performing equally well, but that the instructor has taken evidence-based steps so that those who excel aren't just the ones who get an A in every class or went to a great high school. Inclusive instructors understand that the class climate can contribute to or inhibit a student's learning and that our actions (as well as our attitudes and course content) contribute to the climate. Inclusive teachers understand the challenges that various students face and try to create a class environment where all feel they belong. Students see this sort of instructor as fair and approachable, someone who respects them both as individuals and members of cultural groups.

By "intentional," I mean that we have clear and good reasons for how we decide to teach and that we cultivate the habit of being reflective about our teaching. Adapting a framework used by pioneers in multicultural teaching, I maintain that intentional teachers ask themselves fundamental questions: "What do I want to teach, and why?" "Who are my students?" and "Who am I?" The answers to these questions feed into the larger question of "How do I teach?"[21] Convinced by experts in course development, I propose that instructors should use a deliberate process known as backward course design, in which they start by carefully selecting their overall end-of-course goals for student learning and only then choose readings, assignments, and instructional strategies that align with those goals.[22] Finally, I believe intentional history teachers will regularly ask the assessment questions, "How are we doing?" and "How do I know?" That is, they are smart about how to evaluate their students' performances and their own, in part so they can continually improve as teachers and so they can demonstrate their effectiveness to department chairs, deans, and hiring and tenure and promotion committees.

Although history faculty work in very different circumstances and differ in their areas of expertise, identities, and teaching styles, one thing most of us have in common is that we tend to work long and hard. Teaching can be quite rewarding, but many faculty are unsure about whether they are effective and feel a lot of stress. The framework in this book will improve our effectiveness and efficiency in teaching, but we also need to pay attention to our well-being. Fortunately, a growing body of scholarship about thriving faculty and career development offers advice about how to be successful and stay motivated, satisfied, and healthy over the long term.

How to Use This Book

The book is organized around five areas we need to think carefully about: our content, our students, our methods, ourselves, and how to assess learning and teaching. Even though these topics are interrelated, each chapter takes on one of them. Chapter 1 focuses on what we teach—history content goals and how to design a coherent course with clear and engaging assignments that ask students to meet those goals. Chapter 2 argues for the importance of knowing who our students are—their prior knowledge and assumptions related to history, what they find challenging about learning history, and their motivation, identities, and mindsets—in order to teach inclusively and improve the odds of all of them learning well. Chapter 3 examines how we teach, providing both general principles and evidence-based suggestions for when and how to use specific strategies. Chapter 4 considers assessment, including how we evaluate student work and how we evaluate the quality of our teaching and make the case to others that we are effective instructors. Finally, the last chapter discusses who we are as faculty, including our individual contexts, interests, identities, and assumptions, and what the research tells us about how to be successful and remain "sane." Figure 1 illustrates the framework.

The principles, practices, and framework described here work in a variety of face-to-face classroom settings (and many online, too, although that is not my focus)—large classes with hundreds of students, small seminars, and those at any level.[23] They work whether we are introverts or extroverts, teach ancient history or modern, political history or social, or any region of the world. I imagine the book may speak to early career instructors wanting to develop their skills using proven practices, mid- or late career faculty looking for new ways to reenergize their teaching, community college veterans aiming to empower their students, graduate students and part-time instructors looking for a leg

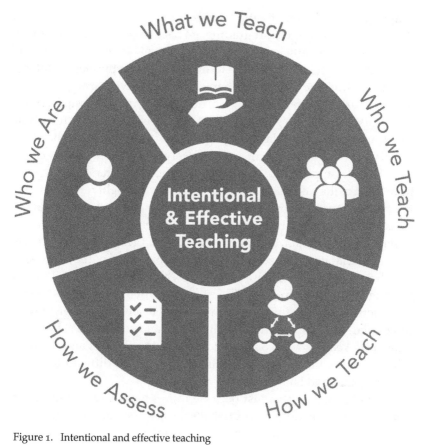

Figure 1. Intentional and effective teaching

up in a depressingly competitive job market, and anyone in the humanities who enjoys thinking about teaching and learning. It contains concepts and suggestions that I wish I had known when I began teaching and ones I regularly need to remind myself of as a seasoned veteran.

I would like readers to read the whole book from cover to cover, but I recognize that for a subject as complex as teaching, there's a lot to take in. Feel free to treat this book as a resource and come back when you want to ponder specific topics. When you're getting ready to plan a new course, reread chapter 1, which will remind you of the importance of seeing the course as a whole and designing your major assignments while creating the syllabus and unit plans. (The section on unit plans is in chapter 3.) Before the first few days of class, review the sections in chapter 2 on student motivation and building community and norms. When you are ready to start grading, go back to chapter 4 and remind yourself of tips for efficiency and getting students to actually read your feedback. If in the middle of the term you're afraid the class is falling into a rut, check the sections in chapter 3 about active learning or interactive lecturing. If a few students are dominating the discussions, chapter 3 is also the place to go. If you want to get feedback from students or a colleague about how class is going, look at chapter 4. If, on the other hand, you yourself are in a rut, or if you feel overwhelmed, review chapter 5. If you're applying for a new job or a promotion, chapter 4 suggests how to make the case that you deserve it, and you might reread chapter 5, which encourages you to reflect on your personal style and assumptions about teaching. The index provides further guidance.

Historian Ken Bain, author of *What the Best College Teachers Do*, has remarked that he is amazed "that some people who say they value research never consider to use any of the research findings when it comes to designing their own classes."[24] I'm not surprised because most historians don't have time to immerse themselves in a whole new field with unfamiliar journals, terminology, methods, and conferences. It's hard enough to keep up with our day-to-day responsibilities and the new scholarship in our areas of specialization. It can be difficult to know where to start, and I hope this book will help.

Historians know that just because things have traditionally been done a certain way doesn't mean that's the best way to do them.[25] I believe most of us can improve our teaching—and our students' learning—in practical and important ways. I know that history matters, and I am certain that it doesn't have to be boring for our students. There are many smart, creative, and dedicated history instructors, and now is a good time for us to apply recent scholarship and new insights and benefit from one another's and our students' experiences, so that (to paraphrase Bain) history teaching is no longer "one of those human endeavors that seldom benefits from its past."[26]

1   What We Teach

Our most important choice is what we try to teach.

DAVID PERKINS

Determining our content should be the easy part of teaching, shouldn't it? After all, we are historians; we're passionate about the past and know a lot about it. Even if we're going to teach a course outside our specialties, we know how to find and analyze sources and connect and organize what we learn. We certainly know more than our students—not just about the content but also about "doing history." We ask good questions about historically significant concepts. It may take time, but we are capable of evaluating others' arguments and building our own. The scholarship on learning refers to us as "experts," not in an arrogant sense but to point out that we're professionally trained and knowledgeable.[1] We have internalized the discipline's methods and ways of thinking and now perform them almost automatically.

Unfortunately, our content knowledge is not always enough as we teach students. Sometimes students don't take away what we hope they will. Their work may be shallow, confused, or simply repeat back what we said. Some never understand what we are trying to accomplish or grasp the course's relevance. In the worst-case scenario, students leave our courses unchanged.

On the other hand, some students rave to their friends about their history class, do all the readings, energetically discuss the ideas, improve their historical skills, and generally do work that warms our hearts. It surely is easier to put time and effort into teaching with such good students and experiences.

Like history itself, teaching is complex, so it's difficult to pinpoint the specific causes when things go really well or just so-so. If our courses don't achieve what we hoped, some of the blame may reside in students' effort, intellect, or preparation. Part of it may result from our readings, assignments, or day-to-day teaching methods. When it goes well, we might wonder if we were simply lucky. Was success due to the students? Our subject matter? Our teaching style? The organization of the course? It makes sense to try to isolate and analyze the various components of teaching and use scholarship about course design, history, and learning to inform the tentative conclusions we draw.

This chapter starts with what David Perkins and other experts in course design assert should be a central concern: our choice about what to teach.[2] It argues that choosing meaningful, historically significant goals is a crucial step in the process of designing an effective, well-integrated course in which students learn well. This step might prove difficult; it requires that we become conscious of our discipline's conventions, select from among many possible worthy goals, and resist some temptations. In the approach of backward design, deciding and articulating exactly what we want to teach is the step from which all other decisions flow, including the nature of our assignments. Assignments signal to students what matters and constitute the way they accomplish our goals, so they deserve special attention. Thus, articulating our goals is not a step to be rushed. Clarity about them energizes and guides us—so we may engage our students and teach them meaningful lessons about how to analyze, investigate, and communicate about the past.

Backward (but Wise) Course Design

When we describe what we teach, we sometimes think of our course content in shorthand ways, such as "medieval Europe," or "Latin American independence movements," "the Ming dynasty," or "the United States since 1865," which describe a time period, geographic region, or event(s). This surface level description obscures our goals and content. It implies we will cover everything about the topic—or at least everything we can cram into the term. However, we cannot teach everything about everyone who lived in medieval Europe, so we must decide which people or historic phenomena students will be focusing on. (Institutions, and if so, which kind? Long-term changes, or continuities? People's daily lives? Their worldviews? Their rulers?) If we're teaching about Latin American independence movements, we have to choose which movements to focus on (typical ones? unusual ones?) and consider exactly what we want students to learn about them: their causes, supporters and opponents, methods, results, implications? Will we teach our interpretations of the movements, or show students how historians differ, or ask them to make their own interpretations? In teaching history, as in writing it, we must be selective.

The decision about which specific historical content, ideas, and skills to focus on is the first and fundamental decision in the course design process often called backward design or understanding by design.[3] Backward course design differs from the way many instructors tend to plan their courses. Typically, before the semester begins, the instructor chooses readings and the main topics to cover. Then the bulk of the planning work occurs throughout the semester, where before each class meeting, the instructor decides what will happen (lectures, discussions, or other learning activities). Similarly, the instructor waits to decide the specific content of the assessments (exams, major assignments, projects) until shortly before they are given.

In the process of backward design, instructors proceed in a different order. They begin by contemplating and deciding where they want students to be at the end of the course, describing the main (big-picture) components of what they should be able to understand and do.

Second, once they have decided their specific, higher-level learning goals, instructors work backward to consider how students will demonstrate that they have achieved those goals, determining what kind of work (exams, projects, major assignments, etc.) best serves that (assessment) purpose.

After making those decisions (and still before the semester begins) instructors consider the nitty-gritty details of the course. In this third stage, faculty sketch out what needs to happen on a unit and day-to-day level; they decide on which matters (topics and skills) they will need to offer instruction and what students will need to read, think about, and do inside and outside of class to perform well on the assessment activities.

Table 1 contrasts the different order of steps that instructors use in traditional course planning and backward design.[4]

The order of tasks and their timing are done differently with backward design. The main components of the course are all mapped out (in broad strokes, but as much as possible) in conjunction with one another before the semester begins. This front loading means that backward course design is more difficult for instructors before the term

Table I. Traditional Course Planning versus Backward Design

Traditional Course Planning	Backward Design
1. Choose topics and readings.	1. Decide outcomes/specific goals (i.e., the main things students will learn).
2. Plan instruction and experiences for each class meeting.	2. Determine what will serve as evidence of students' learning and design the main assessments and their grading criteria.
3. Design assessments to evaluate students' learning.	3. Identify the main learning experiences, materials, and key instruction that students will need to perform well.

starts but makes life easier throughout the duration of the course. If we have sketched out unit plans and already know our main goals for individual class meetings before the semester starts, we won't be starting from scratch (in a panic) shortly before class, wondering what to do. Instead we simply implement a plan and fill in the details. Similarly, we are more efficient when the time comes time to assess, because we mainly administer (or tinker a little with) already-designed exams and projects and grade from already-established criteria.

Although the workload certainly matters, backward design is even more beneficial because it ensures that the basic components—goals, assessment, and teaching and learning activities—are integrated and mutually reinforcing. This integration makes it far more likely that we will accomplish our goals for students' understanding and retention of important ideas and skills. For some instructors, starting by thinking about the end of the course feels a bit foreign at first, but most come to realize its value. After all, it is much easier to map a route when we know our final destination.

Research on learning tells us that for the majority of students, significant learning doesn't happen just by being exposed to information; it needs to be intentionally planned for and practiced, and this is especially true for historical ways of thinking that do not come "naturally" for students.[5] Articulating our priorities turns out to be important for metacognition, too, for us and our students. Keeping our eyes on our big-picture learning goals helps us make those many and difficult decisions about which material is most important to include. In addition, clearly (and regularly) articulating these goals to students helps them understand how the course holds together. They are less likely to get lost in the myriad details they encounter and more likely to understand how each class day contributes to the purposes of the course.[6]

Backward Course Design,
Part I: Starting with Worthy End Goals

As we begin the first step of backward design, deciding on the end-of-course goals/desired results, it helps to consider four key questions.

How do we want students to be different as a result of taking our course?

Significant learning means that our students change in ways that are not superficial or temporary. As Dee Fink put it, "We want that which students learn to become part of how they think, what they can and want to do, what they believe is true about life, and what they value—and we want it to increase their capability for living fully and meaningfully."[7]

Historians believe history has the potential for making a long-term difference in students' lives. The study of history expands our sense of possibilities, allowing us "to go beyond the fleeting moment in human history into which we've been born."[8] History provides insights into the human condition, meaning making, and justice. It provides perspective. History reveals the forces acting on us and equips us to consider our choices.[9] History preserves collective memory and informs our understanding of identities. It forces us to face uncertainty and complexity.[10]

Studying history contributes to many goals of the Association of American Colleges and Universities (AAC&U), including students developing knowledge of the wider world, a sense of social responsibility, and skills related to communication, analysis, complexity, and diversity.[11] History students encounter people from other places and times, and as a result, they often develop curiosity, openness, and empathy—all characteristics of intercultural knowledge and competence.[12]

The world needs leaders who understand the roots of contemporary problems, appreciate the value and limitations of evidence, consider the likely consequences of decisions, and communicate clearly and with integrity. We also need voters who can weigh alternatives, listen to multiple perspectives, and evaluate arguments before they reach decisions. As Leah Shopkow and her colleagues put it, "We need citizens who can parse the political rhetoric and consumers who can read the subtexts of the advertisements aimed at them."[13] Reasoned judgment, respectful engagement with differences, and deliberation for the common good are useful for anyone: people involved in charitable organizations, workplace and athletic teams, school boards, unions, religious groups, self-help associations, professional societies, cooperatives, identity and interest groups, people pushing for social change, and our friends and neighbors.[14] For anyone in the digital age, the ability to sift through and make sense of a massive amount of information is a very valuable skill.

How will taking our course enrich the students—as thinkers, workers, citizens, and humans? Research on transformative learning suggests that faculty can change students in profound and lasting ways by posing "productive challenges" that affect them as people and prompt them to consider their identities, assumptions, and values.[15] We promote significant learning by looking into our hearts and pondering what we want our students to say about how the course changed them years after they finished it.

What are the specific ideas we want students to understand?

At the end of the course, which are the "essential understandings" we want students to take with them? We should distinguish these essential ideas from things that would merely be "good to know" or even lower priority information that would be "nice to be familiar with."[16] Examples of key ideas might be: "Independence movements didn't always result in much independence"; "Majority rule can be really hard for minorities"; "War is hell"; "The medieval Church was more powerful than the political rulers"; "Slavery alone didn't cause the Civil War, but slavery was at its heart."

One way to promote significant ideas is to design a course that asks big questions. Excellent teachers often embed the skills, habits, attitudes, and information they want students to learn in intriguing questions that attract them and require them to reason from evidence.[17] Big questions aim not to entertain students but to spark their curiosity for sustained thinking on a challenging topic. Questions worth grappling with are relevant, are enduring, get at significant quandaries or mysteries, make us consider basic issues of human nature, or include ethical dilemmas and trade-offs. "Generative topics," as David Perkins called them, figure centrally in our discipline and resonate with students' interests and our own. Indeed, Ken Bain advises faculty to remember the sort of big questions that first motivated their own fascination with their field.[18]

Big questions might be ones like the following:[19]

- How could the Holocaust have happened?
- Who was responsible for slavery?
- Why did some societies set up empires and others get colonized?
- Was immigration a good thing?
- Has the United Nations made the world a better place?
- What does it mean to be Chinese (or Afro-Caribbean, Jewish, British)?
- Is capitalism, communism, or socialism best?
- Have women always been oppressed?
- Can significant change occur nonviolently?
- Which societies have successfully negotiated multiculturalism?
- Has there ever really been much social mobility?
- Can there be benevolent dictators?
- Why do religious groups go to war with one another?
- What convinces people to risk their lives in war? Under what circumstances would you be willing to do the same?
- Was World War II (or any war) a "good war"?
- Why did the events of September 11, 2001, occur?
- Were medieval people fundamentally different from us? Would you be "you" if you lived in a different time period?
- What are the prerequisites for and limitations of democracy?
- What has worked to decrease poverty?
- During what period was X country most "just"?
- Is terrorism ever justified?
- What does the past have to do with the present, anyway?

Historians know that ideas matter, but sometimes—perhaps because we know the biggest questions cannot be answered definitively (or because scholars sometimes debate narrower, subtler, historiographical questions)—we pose smaller questions about which undergraduates have less curiosity. Research on the best instructors suggests that it is better to focus on the larger, engaging, meaningful questions in our course's content. Undergraduates may not be able to supply authoritative answers to big questions, but we aren't asking them to earn a doctorate. Instead, we're hoping that engaging big questions may inspire them to study history more deeply, learn how historians approach complex questions, or give them valuable perspectives for their lives.[20]

Which concepts about history do we consider most important for students to grapple with?

To decide which historical concepts or ways of thinking we want our students to learn, we need to be aware of them ourselves. Sam Wineburg and David Pace have observed that historians have been overly reticent about their distinctive disciplinary assumptions and intellectual processes.[21] Years of graduate training and experience mean that professors perform our discipline's analytical practices unconsciously, making it difficult to remember what it's like to be (and effectively teach) a novice. "If we are to help students make a successful transition into the realm of history," Pace asserted, "we must have a very firm and conscious understanding of what makes our discipline special and what kinds of mental operations and procedures students must master to succeed in it."[22]

In recent years, there have been important efforts to describe these mental operations and procedures. The American Historical Association (AHA) brought together hundreds of historians to discuss our "disciplinary core and learning outcomes." Participants in the "Tuning the Discipline" project asked: When students complete a history program of study or major, what should they know, understand, and be able to do?[23] Other historians, independent of the Tuning Project, have made helpful clarifying observations on this question.[24]

Most historians find certain overarching concepts to be worthy of investigation and analysis. These include how people were affected by their specific context; the multifaceted causes and consequences of change; periodization; continuities; contingency; agency; power and oppression; complexity; identity; and the difficulty of making interpretations, generalizations, and judgments. SOTL research has shown that the interpretive nature of history is one of the discipline's threshold concepts. A threshold concept is a fundamental idea that must be grasped—an epistemological shift, a different way of looking at the world—that is necessary before a novice can progress in a discipline.[25]

Do we hope our students will learn more about context, agency, the interpretive nature of history, the foreignness of the past, the ways the past speaks to us today, or something else in our course? Do we want them to recognize that they already use historical tools/concepts (on Facebook and Instagram, for example) like chronology, argumentation, archiving, and narrative?[26] Although not a fan of writing learning objectives, Josh Ashenmiller wrote eloquently about some concepts he wanted students to engage with. "I want them to sit in front of a keyboard paralyzed by doubt, struggling with the epistemological questions 'How do I really know what happened?' and 'What exactly is a fact?' . . . I want them to hesitate for the rest of their lives before ever using the word 'inevitable.'"[27]

Examples of conceptual outcomes include "History isn't just names and dates but an interpretive endeavor"; "There are more than two sides to a story"; "The past actually rarely repeats itself"; "History isn't just written by the victors"; "There's a lot of history besides political history"; "Race is a construct, but one with powerful ramifications."

Which specific skills do we want students to become better at doing?

Some historians prefer the terms "competencies," "habits of mind," or "cognitive habits," over the word "skills," but in any case, what I refer to are historians' methods—what historians *do*, related to ways of thinking, analyzing, researching, or communicating. Analytical skills include interpreting primary sources, where our complex heuristic involves sourcing (considering provenance, authorship, audience, and motivation), contextualizing, asking questions about what sources say and their silences, connecting and comparing them to other sources, and corroborating.[28] Analysis also includes examining issues from multiple perspectives and examining secondary sources for patterns, relationships, disagreements, gaps, and changed interpretations over time. Some competencies involve arguments—identifying, summarizing, constructing, and marshaling evidence for them. Research skills include finding articles, evaluating the credibility of information, and citing sources.[29] Communication skills include writing topic sentences, outlines, or captions for photos; revising one's writing; and participating in civil discussions.

Learning to "do history" builds skills (in close reading, analysis, research, synthesis, and communication) that are useful in other fields and endeavors. When we initiate students into the discipline's ways of thinking, they consider how knowledge is created, which is a foundation for deep learning and transferring knowledge to other contexts. As Grant Wiggins and Jay McTighe put it, "When we are helped to ask certain questions—Why is that so? Why do we think that? What justifies such a view? What's the evidence? What's the argument? What is being assumed?—we learn a different kind of powerful transfer: the ability to grasp what makes knowledge *knowledge* rather than mere belief, hence putting us in a far better position to increase our knowledge and understanding."[30]

The Tuning Project describes many key competencies that every history major should develop, and students do this by taking a dozen or so courses. Achieving conceptual understanding and developing skills takes time, and history SOTL has uncovered many common bottlenecks where students tend to get stuck. With focused instruction, practice, and feedback, students certainly can make substantial progress in one semester, but only on a few skills and concepts at a time.[31] Which few should we focus on?

The teaching context affects our choices. Some departments prescribe certain competencies/goals for different course levels, and some courses are prerequisites for others. If our course serves an institution's general education program, we may be asked to achieve interdisciplinary goals related to global awareness, citizenship, ethical development, writing, learning how to learn, or critical thinking.[32] Even with no external expectations, however, we should consider which ideas and skills are most appropriate for our students, be they upper-level history majors, potential history majors, or reluctant nonmajors taking a course to fulfill a requirement. For example, perspective taking or primary source analysis may be suitable for an introductory course; historiographic mapping may be a skill for a methods course; and because writing a lengthy research essay involves integrating many skills, it may be more suited for a capstone seminar.

Resisting the "Coverage" Temptation

We must choose from many worthwhile goals. Research suggests that to teach effectively we must resist the temptation to do too much and reject the false promises of "coverage." In the conventional coverage model, faculty expose students to as much information about the past as possible, often providing an authoritative, fact-filled narrative that they ask students to repeat back on exams, ID questions, or essays. (Critics refer to this approach as "bulimic."[33]) This traditional model often assumes that students must know certain fundamental facts (usually about history of the U.S. or Western civilization), so we must cover them all, or that students must accumulate a large body of facts before they can do any meaningful analysis of them.[34]

The "cover everything" approach does not result in long-term learning. It assumes what Sam Wineburg, a psychologist who has extensively studied how people learn history, called the attic theory of cognition, the idea that people collect facts like they do furniture, storing them in the attic, so they can use them later when they need them. Unfortunately, the brain doesn't work that way. "Light rail excursions through mounds of factual information may be entertaining," noted Wineburg, "but such dizzying tours leave few traces in memory."[35] In addition to quickly forgetting most facts, without understanding the idea-based connections between them, students have difficulty discerning which ones are most important. An "information transmission" approach to teaching leads to surface approaches to learning and confuses what the professor talks about with actual student understanding.[36]

Speeding through content tends to cast faculty into a role of dispensers of information (rather than sophisticated interpreters and constructors of history) and casts students as consumers of historical knowledge (rather than independent thinkers).[37] As a result, the coverage model unintentionally reinforces the novice's misconception that history is simply a series of uncontested facts to be received (rather than analyzed).[38] As Lendol Calder observed, historians' tendency to quickly cover many topics actually "covers up" (that is, conceals) the fundamental nature of the discipline of history.[39] So do high school textbooks. Overly packed with facts (one has 840 "main ideas"!) and characterized by an authoritative narrative voice, the textbooks leave students unaware that there is much historians are unsure about, that historians disagree with one another, and that events might have turned out differently.[40] Instead of "covering," then, effective teachers should "uncover" the many ways historians go about trying to make sense of the complex, uncertain, and contested past and give students practice evaluating arguments and evidence on their own.[41]

Learning is not something done to students, but something students themselves must do. Learning results from "what the student does and thinks," explained cognitive science pioneer Herbert Simon, "and only from what the student does and thinks." To develop mastery of content, SOTL tells us that students must acquire component intellectual skills, practice integrating them, and know when to apply what they have learned.[42] Common sense also suggests that students should do the types of activities historians do rather than simply watching their professor do them. As David Pace and Joan Middendorf pointed out, "We need only imagine ourselves in a learning situation that is unfamiliar to us—a first lesson in knitting, a new computer program, or the grammar of a foreign language—to realize that simply hearing a lecture on a complex process is rarely sufficient to permit us to actually perform the task and to integrate it with dozens of other new procedures."[43] Not surprisingly, the AHA's Statement on Excellent Classroom Teaching of History asserts that courses should provide students with "multiple opportunities to do the work of the historian."[44]

Historical facts matter, of course. Historians agree that good history is built on a foundation of extensive and reliable evidence, but simply asking students to remember facts, a low-level cognitive skill, is inconsistent with the goal of challenging them. Facts do not speak for themselves. It is quite possible for a student to know some facts but not understand their implications. There is an enormous difference between being able to repeat a few facts and being able to assess how well a historian used facts as evidence for an argument. It requires even deeper understanding to select the most relevant facts to back up one's own argument. Analysis and synthesis are much higher-level goals than simply learning facts.[45] Analytical skills are needed more urgently than ever in the digital age, where there is an abundance of information to sift through and neo-Nazis can create an online "Hitler Historical Museum" purporting to be "nonbiased" and "educational."[46] In *The New Education*, Cathy Davidson asserted that every educated person needs certain skills. "For our era, the ability to search and research—sorting, evaluating, verifying, analyzing, and synthesizing abundant information—is an incredibly valuable skill."[47] Happily, those search and research skills are ones that students of history need, too. Not surprisingly, the AHA Statement on Excellent Classroom Teaching states that facts should not be treated as "the final goal of historical study."[48] If we want to teach for understanding, instead of leading with a large body of facts, we put big questions, ideas, or concepts (which require understanding information) at the center of our courses.

When we emphasize understanding ideas rather than facts, students learn better. They are more motivated to learn the facts they need to understand, and research on brains shows that they are more likely to retain and use their knowledge.[49] The gold standard of teaching is that students become capable of independently using their knowledge in contexts outside our classrooms, a concept known as "transfer."[50] Transfer means that students can analyze a specific document that we discussed in our class and also intelligently interpret one from a different time period in a different course. Transfer means that years after graduating, even if they can't remember the dates of the New Deal, alumni can reason contextually so that they know it occurred in response to the Great Depression and can draw connections to contemporary political discussions about the role of the federal government.

In sum, resisting the "coverage" temptation means that we don't design a course guided by the question: "How much information can I expose students to during the semester about subject X?" If we're aiming for quality instead of quantity, we should focus on better questions, such as, "Which foundational ideas do I want students to deeply understand?" and "Which higher-level historical thinking goals do I want to prioritize?"[51] If we ask those questions, we will be a step closer to teaching in ways that ensure our students' takeaways from our history courses will be lasting and significant.

Spelling Out Student Learning Outcomes/Goals

When writing our student learning objectives (SLOs), we focus on what students will be able to *do* as a result of taking the course. As Charles Bonwell observed, we often use the phrase "critical thinking" imprecisely, and over the years it has become a more generic term like "Kleenex" or "Coke."[52] Focusing on the verbs clarifies which specific intellectual tasks students will be doing (e.g., identifying a scholar's argument is different from comparing two scholars' arguments). This specificity will focus and improve our daily teaching. It also helps prevent us from posing low-level tasks solely related to memorizing or repeating facts. Our goals should be measurable, meaning that there is a way we can see that students have achieved them. (It's hard for us to see "understanding" in students' brains, but we can see whether they have accurately "compared" or "summarized" in an essay.) Finally, our goals should be realistic for the subject matter, length of the course, and level of students.[53] The sample SLOs below include examples in parentheses for purposes of illustrating possibilities, but they are adaptable for different subject matter.

By the end of the semester, you will be able to:

- *Identify* the argument in a scholarly source.
- *Compare* multiple historians' arguments (on the causes of the French Revolution) and the main evidence they used to support their arguments.
- *Evaluate* the persuasiveness of historians' arguments (on the causes of the French Revolution).
- *Defend and refute* the idea (that World War II was a "good war") using effective evidence.
- *Compare and contrast* (the Allies' military strategy in the three major theaters during World War II or Germany's experiences in World War I and World War II).
- *Write* an evidence-based argument (about whether the state or local activists deserve more credit for the successes of the civil rights movement).
- *Create* an exhibit that illustrates the experiences and perspectives of three different groups of people (during industrialization).
- *Synthesize* the main causative forces (that affected African Americans in the twentieth century and the strategies African American leaders developed to cope with them).
- *Describe* (at least three realistic options available to people imprisoned in concentration camps and the potential risks and benefits of each option).
- *Find* relevant scholarly articles by historians (on a topic of your choice related to the history of disease in Europe).
- *Create* an annotated bibliography (on a topic of your choice related to colonial West African history).
- *Explain* (the difference between primary and secondary sources or the challenges historians face in uncovering the "truth" or the significance of the Civil War for conceptions of nationalism).

- *Analyze* primary sources the way historians do.
- *Assess* the credibility of information on a website.
- *Transcribe* an interview (for the Smithsonian Digital Volunteers project) using oral history best practices.
- *Conduct* an oral history interview (with a woman who participated in sports before Title IX).
- *Draw sensible conclusions* (from interviews with the players from the All American Girls Professional Baseball League about how gender expectations influenced them).
- *Transcribe* three primary sources (for the University of Iowa DIY History project) and *teach* your classmates about their context and significance.
- *Recognize* key events (in Western civilization before 1660) and *place them in the period* when they occurred (or in chronological order).
- *Summarize* characteristics (of Confucianism at the time when it became state ideology).
- *Find* examples (that show how gender expectations changed for men between 1880 and 1920).
- *Critique* a recent popular culture portrayal (of ancient Greece) for how accurately it portrays the historic context.
- *Connect* what we learned about (U.S. foreign policy) to a contemporary situation.
- *Evaluate* (which Latin American nation best met the needs of its citizens in the century after independence).
- *Investigate* and then *describe* the main consequences of (mass-produced automobiles on U.S. society).
- *Practice* the process of deliberative dialogue and *consider* its relevance for contemporary society.
- *Reflect on* (how learning about soldiers' experiences has influenced your thinking about willingness to participate in a war).
- *Observe* ways in the present (that contemporary French people make allusions to their history and identity).
- *Apply* leadership theories (to decide who was the most effective national leader during the Cold War).
- *Assess* (how well Karl Marx's predictions proved true in the Russian Revolution).
- *Narrate* (the Pullman strike) in a way that incorporates its root causes, workers' and management's positions and strategies, turning points, and outcomes.
- *Narrate* (the origins of the Cold War) from the perspective of (the

leaders of the Soviet Union) and then narrate it from the perspective
of (the leaders of the United States).

- *Show an appreciation and empathy for* cultures and perspectives
  different from your own.
- *Articulate* how you will use the knowledge and skills acquired in
  this course in your future academic endeavors.[54]
- *Answer the question*: Who (from the period 1850–1880) deserves to
  be honored with a statue?
- *Recognize* how you personally have been influenced by history.
- *Create* a portion of a class website analyzing a key event (in
  LGBTQIA) history.

Peter Stearns provided an example of the power of backward design
when he described how using the process dramatically improved his
revised world history course. Although he always had course goals,
Stearns realized that he had not articulated them specifically and
clearly. Choosing a discrete number of ideas and analytical skills—not
too many—helped him focus his instructional efforts and resulted in
concrete improvements in students' performances, confirmed by two
years of pre- and post- testing. Students acquired the desired intellectual skills without compromising his content goals, and this teaching
success was "immensely satisfying." He concluded, "Explicit identifi-
cation of analytical goals, with equally explicit exercises that reinforce
methods of thinking, works."[55]

Backward Design,
Part 2: Deciding Major Assignments

Courses are what students do in them.

JOHN MCCLYMER

Our assessments should assess what we value, engage students, be rigorous, reveal something about the tasks and vir-
tues at the heart of our subject, give students a meaningful
encounter with essential ideas.

GRANT WIGGINS

After we decide on our specific goals for students' learning, the second phase of backward design is deciding how students will

show us they have accomplished them. Assignments serve as evidence of the degree to which students have learned. Major assignments—whether essays, research projects, exams, wikis, presentations, or a host of other possibilities—are among the greatest tools faculty have. If we assign it as a course requirement, students do it, and as John McClymer suggested, what students *do* is what most influences their learning.[56] As Grant Wiggins suggests, we should choose worthy ones.

Students sometimes ask if something will be on the test. Although the question may be annoying due to its single-minded focus on grades, from another perspective it makes sense. We should grade what matters most, and if something really matters to us, we should find a way to assess it. As Barbara Walvoord and Virginia Anderson put it, "Grade what you teach; teach what you grade."[57] It's useful to think of an assignment not simply as a way to assess how well students have learned what we wanted but also as a powerful impetus to their learning.

If we want students to think about certain things and analyze in certain ways, we should pose tasks that require them to think about those things and analyze in those ways. If we want them to be able to do certain things, we should pose tasks that require them to do them. If we want students to understand certain things, we need to find ways for them to demonstrate that they understand them. The concept is simple, but designing great assignments that actually achieve it is not.

Four principles, described below, help us design effective assignments.

Principle 1:
Assignments should be aligned with our course goals

Assessment (through assignments) leads to learning, but as assessment expert David Boud asks, "What kind of learning?"[58] Assignments that are aligned with our learning goals send the messages we intend. If our goal is for students to recall information, we should design exams that require them to do so (e.g., fill-in-the-blank questions), and if we want students to recognize facts, we might pose matching questions. If we want our students to perform more challenging intellectual tasks—analyzing, comparing, connecting, considering causation or implications, synthesizing, arguing, interpreting, and evaluating—we must design assignments that require those specific ways of thinking. One study suggested that although most historians claim to be teaching historical thinking, their assessments suggest otherwise.[59]

Imagine an introductory course on U.S. history from 1865 to the present for which the instructor hopes that years after the course is over, students will still grasp the concept that people experienced the past in extremely different ways and are convinced of the importance of viewing events from several perspectives. The instructor has to translate that overarching goal into student learning objectives for specific content matter. In her syllabus, she might opt to write one of the following sample SLOs for the unit on Reconstruction.

By the end of the course, students will:

1. Describe the experiences of different groups of Southerners during Reconstruction.
2. Compare and contrast the experiences of different groups of Southerners during Reconstruction.
3. Evaluate the degree to which former slaves and former slave owners achieved their goals during Reconstruction.

Any of these could be an appropriate learning objective. The first is easier, so perhaps is suitable for introductory students at the beginning of a course. Comparing and contrasting (number 2) goes a step further than describing because it involves adding up similarities and differences. Evaluation goes even further and is a higher-order skill. If matched to the level of students, any of these objectives could be fine, assuming that course materials, instruction, and learning activities prepare students for what they will be asked to do in an assignment.

The specific verbs we choose have different implications for the kind of assignment we give to assess student learning. Assuming we have chosen the goal below, the following are some possible assignments we might give at the end of the unit.

Goal: Evaluate the degree to which freed people (former slaves) and former slave owners achieved their goals during Reconstruction.

Assignment A: Write a book review of Kenneth Stampp's classic 1965 work, The Era of Reconstruction, 1865–1877.

Assignment B: Write an essay that speculates on why Republican rule failed and explains the implications of the failure.

Assignment C: Write an essay that answers the question, "By the end of Reconstruction (1877), who achieved more of their goals: former slaves or former slaveholders?"

Of these three options, the third is most directly aligned with the learning goal. To respond to the assigned task, students must understand the goals of former slaves and former slave owners and must understand the experiences of both groups during Reconstruction before analyzing and drawing a conclusion as implied by the verb "evaluate." The other assignments might be valuable, but for assessing different goals. Reviewing Stampp's book (Assignment A) might be a good choice if the main goal of the unit was to evaluate his argument in depth, place his work in context of historiographical debates about Reconstruction, or give students experience in writing reviews like historians. Assignment B would be more appropriate if the goals were comprehending the causes and implications of the end of Reconstruction. Although students writing the Assignment B essay might end up including information about freed people and former slave owners in their discussion of the implications of the end of the era, their experiences would not be the direct focus for that essay prompt.

The simplest way to ensure constructive alignment is to make sure that for each of our goals, we have an assignment that offers evidence as to whether students have met the goal in a one-to-one correspondence:

Goal 1 ↔ Assignment 1

Goal 2 ↔ Assignment 2

Goal 3 ↔ Assignment 3

However, it is also possible to design one assignment that meets multiple goals. In the following example, the assignment below would assess both Goal 1 and Goal 2.

Goal 1: Describe the experiences of different groups of Southerners during Reconstruction.

Goal 2: Analyze primary sources with an awareness of both their value and limitations as evidence.

Assignment: Design a hypothetical museum exhibit that describes the experiences of three different groups of Southerners during Reconstruction. In addition to using information from our lectures and readings of secondary sources, you should appropriately use some of the primary sources we read to illustrate the experiences of each group.

To write text for a museum exhibit that describes people's lives during Reconstruction, students must understand those experiences, so the assignment is aligned with the first goal. The requirement that students select appropriate primary sources for the exhibit will illustrate how well they understand the context in which the sources were created and can be trusted and what information can sensibly be gleaned from them, meaning it also assesses the second goal.

There are other ways students might demonstrate their understanding of primary sources, of course. Turning in an annotated document, developing a list of interpretations one might derive from a source, or answering a question about how to make sense of two or more sources with conflicting accounts all might be assignments that meet that goal.

Sometimes we might want to give students numerous opportunities to demonstrate their understanding of a single goal. For example, one might decide that analyzing primary sources is so important that a portion of every exam is focused on assessing it. (We might increase the difficulty on each one, so that on the early exams, students analyze sources they have already discussed in class, but on later exams they analyze ones they have not seen before.) Or if a main goal of a Western civilization course is understanding events from multiple perspectives, in one unit we might have students write about the perspectives of various stakeholders regarding the Enclosure Acts; in another unit, they describe the perspectives of three different groups of people concerning the birth control movement; and later, we have them teach their fellow students about three different perspectives on membership in the European Union.

There does not have to be a separate assignment for each learning goal that is set, but every goal should be assessed in some way.

Principle 2:
Our assignments should be feasible

Feasibility involves a number of different things. Faculty who teach many students worry about the practical concern of how they will manage to grade work in a timely manner. A later chapter discusses assessment in more detail, including ways to grade writing efficiently. For now, it's good to note two things. First, research suggests that what matters in using writing to promote deep learning is not the quantity but the quality of the assignments.[60] Second, it's wise to design assignments with an eye to how we will evaluate them. That does not mean defaulting to multiple choice or matching questions, despite their ease and efficiency in grading. There are many important criticisms of using multiple choice questions for assessment in the discipline of history. Multiple choice questions ask students to perform tasks that are not realistic (the real world rarely supplies multiple possible answers), and they tend to only assess short-term memory of facts.[61] It is quite difficult to design multiple choice questions that test thinking. Indeed, when researchers asked high school seniors to explain their reasoning for their answers on questions intended to test thinking, almost all the students used strategies other than historical reasoning.[62]

Does that mean that there are no effective, short, easy-to-grade assignments that allow us to evaluate specific history thinking skills? Although more research is needed, there is hope. In introductory courses, David Voelker uses an assessment tool he calls "For and Against," in which students write two brief paragraphs that provide the best evidence for and the best evidence against a historical claim. These claims often involve half-truths (e.g., "the civil rights movement of the 1960s succeeded in creating equality for African Americans") or common misunderstandings ("The coming of the Civil War had nothing to do with slavery"). To perform this task, students must call on their knowledge of the period, draw on multiple perspectives, choose relevant evidence to support a position, and explain how the evidence supports their point. This assignment requires students to evaluate statements as a historian would and furthermore asks them to carry out the kind of task—evaluating a claim and using evidence—that they will regularly encounter in their lives outside the classroom. It has the added benefit of being quick to grade. Voelker reports that after he previews ten or so answers to calibrate his expectations, he can grade most of the responses in about a minute each.[63]

Although designed for precollegiate students, the Stanford History Education Group's History Assessments of Thinking use primary sources and target specific thinking goals, usually by requiring that students justify their answer in three to four sentences.[64] This "Beyond the [Scantron] Bubble" project used a rigorous process of research, development, and testing to ensure that the assessments are valid. Undoubtedly many teachers have designed other short-answer questions that are specifically targeted for the content in their courses and ask students to do more analysis than the generic but pervasive "ID question" that typically simply asks students to describe from memory something that happened. Future SOTL projects should offer additional reliable and valid options.

We need to consider feasibility from more than just our perspective as graders. Our assignments should be set at an appropriate level of difficulty for students. A specific essay question that gives students only two options for a thesis ("Who achieved more of what they wanted during Reconstruction: former slaves or formers slave owners?") is practical for introductory students, who otherwise might give us an "all about Reconstruction data dump."[65] A more open-ended task ("Evaluate whether Reconstruction was successful, taking into consideration the perspectives of all the major groups in the nation") is more suitable for advanced students.

It is not enough to align our assignments with our goals; we also must align them with what we teach on a day-to-day basis. Assignments should be achievable for students who consistently and conscientiously work hard. It is not wise—or fair—to ask students to do tasks that are not aligned with what they have read, done, heard, discussed, or practiced in class. If we do, we can expect negative outcomes. A few students might succeed anyway, because they are very smart or had prior knowledge or experience, but many others will do mediocre work or resent that an assignment came out of the blue.

If I assigned a hypothetical museum exhibit without ever showing students a museum exhibit or helping them understand which kinds of writing and sources are used in such exhibits, that assignment would not be well aligned with my teaching. If I assigned a website project but never worked with students on how to evaluate websites and did not provide any assistance with how to create a website, that would not be a feasible assignment for the majority of students. Assignments may sound good on paper but will fail if we haven't taught students how to develop the types of thinking skills required. I discovered this to my dismay after years of assigning large synthetic essays in my introductory survey courses. I had considered the essays to be well designed, because they were centered on complex, interesting questions that required students to use an enormous amount of information from the readings and lectures and make sense of all that information in new ways.

The case of Karl made me begin questioning my synthesis essay assignment. Karl exhibited all the signs of being an excellent student: he scored 100 percent on pop quizzes because he was always prepared; he was intensely focused during class; he regularly made perceptive comments that showed he had a strong understanding of each day's topic. Because of this, I assumed he would excel on the midterm exam, but instead, his essay didn't synthesize very much and he got a grade in the C range. After returning the midterm essays, we met to discuss his performance. I showed him an "A" essay, and he nodded, because he understood all the arguments and evidence that were in it. Yet on the final essay, his performance was only slightly better. Eventually (after exposure to SOTL), I began to realize what the problem might have been for Karl and others like him: that I never actually taught students how to synthesize or gave them practice doing it (that is, I didn't align my assignment with my instruction). Experts in learning tell us the importance of providing goal-directed practice for novices learning a new skill. If my exams had consisted of a series of short essays, each focused on a week's material, I suspect Karl would have excelled. But synthesizing seven weeks of material and thirty or more primary sources was different from what we had been doing in class. It turns out that synthesis is a very high-level cognitive skill, especially difficult for introductory-level students.[66] Synthesis is well worth doing, and that means it is worth teaching students how to do it. Once I realized the disconnect between my assignment and my teaching, I was able to remedy the problem by doing a better job showing students what it meant to synthesize and designing an in-class exercise that gave them practice doing it (see chapter 3). After students did this exercise just twice, I saw dramatic improvements in the quantity and quality of evidence they used in their synthetic essays. (Sadly, this came too late to benefit Karl!)

Principle 3:
Our assignments should be engaging

An assignment that students find engaging is more likely to motivate them to work hard on it, change them, and stick with them after the course is over.[67] Engaging assignments are especially important in classes where there are nonmajors, students who probably will never take another history course (unless we convince them that what historians do is interesting and meaningful), but engaging assignments pay off in any course.

Asking significant questions is the most important way to design engaging assignments, but research on writing suggests other ways related to shaping the rhetorical context.[68] One option asks students to address a different audience from the one they are used to (their in-structor). In this strategy, we still ask them to write an argument-based essay but change the dynamic by asking them to address their essay to a historical actor who was facing a serious decision, such as:

- British Prime Minister Neville Chamberlain considering what to do about Hitler's threat to invade Czechoslovakia in October 1938;
- A factory worker trying to decide whether to join a strike;
- President Harry Truman trying to decide whether to use the atomic bomb.[69]

With a task like this, students are less likely to ask, "What do you (the professor) want me to say?" and instead must think, "What does Chamberlain/a factory worker/Truman need to know?"

We might instead ask students to address a contemporary audience facing a situation that would benefit from historical understanding:

- You're interviewing for a job with the U.S. State Department and must demonstrate that you understand the history of the Middle East and the perspectives of its peoples and can weigh the costs and benefits of the main strategic approaches that have been tried so far. They want you to make an informed policy recommendation to the United Nations. What would you advise the United Nations to do about the situation in Syria?
- The minor league baseball team in your hometown is named the "Redskins." A group has protested, and now the team is trying to decide if the history of the name was rooted in respect for or ridicule of Native Americans. The local newspaper is soliciting letters to the editor and you have decided to write one.
- You've been hired as a consultant for a U.S. corporation about to enter the Latin American market. In which country would you suggest they locate their business? What cultural knowledge should corporate leaders learn so they will not be viewed as "ugly Americans" or imperialists?

In an advanced course, when we ask students to take a position in a historiographical debate, rather than writing to us, they could address the actual historians involved.

- "Dear Professor Eugene Genovese, I'd like to discuss your famous argument in *The Political Economy of the South* . . ."

Alternatively, we might ask students to address an audience with a particular perspective, such as a skeptical or a less knowledgeable one:

- Your friend is about to go on a date with someone who grew up in Scotland. She knows that Scotland recently had a referendum on independence from the United Kingdom but didn't pay any attention to the news. She would like to be an informed conversationalist, sympathetic to whichever side it turns out her date favored. So she needs a quick primer: Why might a Scot have wanted to stay in the United Kingdom? Why might one have wanted to leave?
- You're going home for Thanksgiving and worry about the radically different ways your relatives talk about immigration. Your conservative aunt says that today's immigrants are very different from those who came to the United States in the old days because they're less skilled and less educated and they resist assimilation, while your uncle says that's a load of bunk. How will you respond when they put you on the spot and say, "So Mr. History Major, who's right?"
- Your eighty-four-year-old neighbor is a white woman who grew up in the South. She asked you what classes you're taking and when you said African American history, she said, "Then maybe you can help me. I really don't understand: What was wrong with calling people 'colored' the way we used to? I don't want to offend anyone, but I'm not sure what language I should use today." What will you tell her?

Even specifying an audience that knows nothing about a topic can be useful, as in the example of a hypothetical museum exhibit ("Imagine visitors from South Korea who know nothing about Reconstruction; what are the most important things they should know about the context, events, and long-term outcomes of the period?") A hypothetical audience works, but if your university or area has access to a few artifacts, a helpful curator, and a small public space, students could create an actual exhibit, which would take engagement to another level.[70] High school or elementary school students can serve as a similar audience with little background knowledge. Brenna Greer assigned the writing of a children's book, which forced students to grapple with the issues of selection and overall message that historians always deal with.[71] I have had success with an assignment with a novice audience for students in an oral history course. After a month of studying the preparation, questions, etiquette, equipment, and ethical issues involved in oral history projects, I asked them to synthesize their knowledge by writing a training manual for someone new to oral history.

Addressing a live audience is especially engaging. It can be powerful experience for our students to actually teach the lesson they have created to local students. The National History Center created resources for a mock congressional briefing program in which students brief real policy makers on the historical background of a contemporary issue, such as the African health crisis or the Russia–Ukraine conflict.[72] In the process called deliberative dialogue, students civilly discuss with members of a community the benefits, disadvantages, and trade-offs of three positions on an important issue.[73] Real audiences in our home communities might include local politicians, police officers, nonprofit agencies, advocacy organizations, or groups of professionals considering civil rights laws, economic policies, environmental regulations, health practices, or treatment of immigrants.

Students conducting historical research might address their work to (or even submit it to) real audiences, such as a regional Phi Alpha Theta conference or the National Conference on Undergraduate Research. We might invite staff, faculty, or students from another class to listen to oral presentations or, like Keith Erekson, assign a research project in response to a community need that culminated in a public poster session.[74] Live audiences add a little pressure for students but also make the project more meaningful, and such assignments demonstrate the relevance of historical knowledge.

Besides using a variety of audiences, examples like policy briefings, exhibits, training manuals, lesson plans, posters, children's books, and presentations show that we can engage students with varied formats. A friend of the court brief is a good format for constitutional history. Letters to the editor or comments on a news blog are good formats for concise argument. In addition to scholarly book reviews, students can analyze popular films for their historic accuracy and submit reviews to the Internet Movie Database (imdb.com), Amazon, or other popular film review sites. There are many great options for digital formats; students may create wikis or websites about events, people, or time periods. Students can build online archives containing and contextualizing documents, images, and maps, and do so in familiar tools like a Pinterest board or a Flickr album, or create digital stories or write and revise Wikipedia entries.[75]

Although digital products look different, many use the same skills required for more traditional written research projects: finding information; evaluating, interpreting, and selecting evidence; making decisions about main points; communicating clearly about the significance of a topic; and ethically using and citing sources. Creating a digital project disrupts the common misconception that history is a finished packet of knowledge to be handed off by professors to students, observed Tona Hangen, and "provides genuinely exciting ways to help students grasp the constructed nature of history."[76] In addition, the ability to create something new using one's knowledge and understanding ranks high in taxonomies of advanced cognitive skills.[77] Although there are important stylistic differences between creating online content and writing a formal argumentative essay, developing skills in this kind of writing and visual representation of ideas benefits students who end up doing public history or many other kinds of work after graduation, increasing their perceptions of the relevance and value of our courses.[78]

As with all our assignments, we need to make sure that digital assignments are feasible for students. To provide the necessary support to do a good job, we ourselves might need to learn new skills or collaborate with technology specialists who can offer instruction and resources (i.e., documentation for software, rules for Wikipedia entries, answers to frequently asked questions, or warnings about typical mistakes). As with any project, we need to allow sufficient time for students to do the separate parts well.

Many of the assignments just described benefit students because they are authentic, meaning they replicate or simulate the ways a person would be asked to use their knowledge or skills in the real world (albeit at an apprentice level). They ask students to be intellectual performers, not spectators. As assessment expert Grant Wiggins said, students should "experience the same 'tests' that face the expert in the field—having to find and clarify problems, conduct research, justify one's opinion in some public setting."[79] Real professionals trained in history conduct research and write scholarly articles like history faculty do, but they do other tasks as well. They create and maintain archives, work in museums and at historic sites, report on the news as journalists, argue about precedent in courts, create documentaries, serve as consultants on movies with historical themes, write historical fiction, testify before Congress, conduct research for governments and policy institutes, teach young people, conduct oral history projects, and take and justify political stands, among other things. One doesn't need an advanced degree to do authentic everyday tasks like evaluating historical claims in the news, contextualizing family photos or documents, or deciding whether a film is hopelessly inaccurate.

Even if an assignment isn't a real-world historical task, it may still be engaging and valuable. An example might be creating a hypothetical edition of a "yellow journalism" newspaper in the 1890s.[80] Steven Volk assigned an "avatar" project in which each student regularly wrote from the perspective of a person who lived through different events in twentieth-century Latin American history. This major shift in rhetorical context profoundly affected students, who grappled with contingency, moral decision making, and "big questions about memory, pain, loss, repression, and history" as one student put it. As another student said, it forced them to "really think about how those people feel, and what is going through their heads, and how they must try to go through every-day life, even when they are confronted with traumatic experiences."[81] The definition of authentic assignments tends to require that students construct their own responses (i.e., write in an open-ended fashion rather than select a response), use knowledge and skills in challenging and complex tasks, require that students "do" the subject, and use judgment.[82]

Principle 4:
Our assignments should be transparent

The Transparency in Learning and Teaching Project (TILT Higher Ed) began in 2009–10 with a group of faculty interested in leveraging scholarship about metacognition. The research showed that students learned better when they understood how instructors had structured their learning experiences and were aware of how they were learning.[83] After starting with scores of faculty from different disciplines, within a few years it involved more than 25,000 students in 160 different courses at more than forty institutions. Faculty participants agreed to make minor changes to a couple of their assignments to improve their transparency and asked their students to take pre- and post- surveys. The instructors aimed to make their assignments as clear as possible in the following three areas:

- The assignment's purpose. Instructors aimed to help students understand why they were being asked to do the assignment. They clarified how it fit into the course goals and what understandings or skills it might help them develop that would be useful in their field, college, work, or life.
- The task(s) being required of them. Instructors specified what the assignment asked students to do, including the intellectual tasks (comparing, evaluating, making an argument, etc.), materials to use, and how to do what was expected. If possible, they recommended steps students should take or pointed out common mistakes to avoid. They tried to craft assignments without any hidden assumptions.
- The criteria that would be used to evaluate the assignment. They described characteristics of the finished product, the main elements of the grading criteria, and how excellent work would differ from adequate work. (Faculty had the freedom to choose different ways to be transparent about the grading criteria; many provided rubrics, engaged students in discussing or applying the grading criteria before they started the assignment, or shared examples of successful work.)

To be transparent on the sample assignment for an essay about Reconstruction, an instructor might create a handout like Example 1.[84]

Careful attention to transparency led to impressive results. Students who received more transparency reported significant gains over students who did not, especially in areas that are important predictors of students' overall academic success. The transparency students reported that as a result of their courses, they had more academic confidence, could learn more effectively on their own, and were better at recognizing when they needed help. They had a greater sense of belonging and a better sense of the skills they were developing. While the transparency students as a group experienced statistically significant gains, the benefits for first-generation, low-income, transfer, and underrepresented students were even greater.[85]

Given the recent data about the distressingly high levels of D, F, and W(ithdraw) grades (and subsequent dropout rates) for less wealthy

Example 1. Transparent Assignment

U.S. History Assignment 1: Evaluating Reconstruction from Multiple Perspectives

Purposes

You're writing this essay for a number of reasons:

- Using information about Reconstruction will deepen your knowledge about the period, especially the hopes, plight, and opportunities of former slaves at the end of the Civil War; the goals and frustrations of former slave owners and the strategies they used to try to regain power; and the challenges the nation faced. This assignment helps you meet the course objective: "Evaluate the degree to which former slaves and slaveholders achieved their goals during Reconstruction."
- Being able to look at events from multiple perspectives is a valuable skill, because we often find ourselves in situations with people (coworkers, family, friends, or those from another culture) who view things differently from one another or us. It's a key component of intercultural competence.
- Developing an argument and gathering evidence to support it is a skill that you'll be using more later in this course and one used in many other disciplines besides history.

Tasks

You'll write a five-page persuasive essay with a thesis that provides a direct answer to the question: *"By the end of Reconstruction (1877), which group had achieved more of its goals: former slaves or former slaveholders?"*

You will need to argue either that former slaveholders achieved more of their goals or that freed people did—one or the other.

You should use examples from the readings and lectures and quotations from our primary sources to serve as the evidence to back up your argument.

To do this task well, you'll need to gather information about:

- planters' goals at the beginning of Reconstruction,
- freed people's goals at the beginning of Reconstruction,
- planters' experiences 1865–1877, and
- freed people's experiences 1865–1877.

Only after you've amassed all that information will you be able to answer the question about which group achieved more of their goals. So start your essay only after doing that process.

Tip 1: You're not being asked to tell the story of everything that happened during Reconstruction. Instead, your job is to write an essay organized around an argument (that uses information about what happened).

Tip 2: Better essays tend to use information from all the readings and all our class days; they don't rely on just one or two.

Grading Criteria

[Assessment is discussed in chapter 4, but to be transparent, one might include a rubric or at least mention the most important components of the criteria, such as in the following statement.]
Your grade will be determined based on the following areas:

- the clarity of the thesis,
- the quality of the evidence used to back it up,
- the effectiveness of showing the perspective of each group, and
- the degree to which you used the materials we've discussed.

In addition, your grade will be lowered if the essay contains numerous errors, is difficult to follow, or doesn't meet the format requirements.

More Details You Need to Know

[Add information about format, length, due date, etc.]
[Add information about the importance of understanding the assignment and asking questions, honor code rules, resources available (office hours, writing center, tutors, citation guides), etc.]

students, students of color, and first-generation students in introductory history courses, transparency seems to be urgently needed.[86] The historians I know want their courses to help level the playing field of higher education, not perpetuate societal inequalities, and transparency offers some hope. Students who are the first in their family to attend college, didn't attend strong high schools, or for other reasons are not already familiar with the unwritten rules of college history courses are logical beneficiaries of transparency. These students are more likely to attend state schools with large lecture courses, less student engagement, and less personal access to their instructors. Therefore it is especially encouraging that another finding of the study was that students in large lectures with transparency felt more valued by instructors than students in much smaller classes where transparency methods were not implemented.[87] Our efforts to ensure that students understand what we are asking them to do, and why, and how their work will be assessed signals to them that we care about their learning.

Instructors also benefited from the transparency project. They reported receiving better quality work, experiencing less resistance from students who viewed assignments as "pointless," and hearing fewer last-minute questions. Because they were clearer in their own minds about their criteria, instructors found grading easier. Inspired by the process, many applied the transparency framework to all their assignments and extended the principles to individual class meetings. As one professor put it, "Incorporating the purpose/task/criteria framework helps me focus on the main goals for each day, which helps students see the purpose of every class session."[88]

Other data confirm the importance of transparent assignments. Research by the National Council of Writing Program Administrators echoes the importance of articulating purpose and expectations. The Wabash National Study on Liberal Arts Education found that instructor clarity (which included clearly explaining course goals and requirements) was associated with meaningful long-term gains for students, including in their critical thinking. Clarity about expectations also improves student motivation.[89]

Some instructors may consider transparency to be "coddling." To be clear, I am a huge advocate of challenge (on principle and because students who aren't challenged are bored). However, I would prefer the challenge come from performing the intellectual task I propose rather than trying to guess what that task is. I want my students to perform significant high-level historical tasks, and I want all those who work hard to have a decent chance of success. I have learned—like many faculty in the Transparency Project—that my assignments aren't always as clear as I think.

For that reason, it is wise to get feedback on drafts of our assignments before students do them. Trading and discussing assignments with another historian enriches us, and it's also helpful to receive feedback from a colleague in a different discipline, who isn't already familiar with historians' typical goals, tasks, and terminology. We can ask former students to give us their impressions. My university's Writing Center offers a service where its student consultants offer feedback on assignments (both faculty and students are anonymous). When we ask others for feedback, we should pose very specific questions related to transparency, such as, "Why would a student want to do this assignment?" "What are the main things you would have to do well to get a good grade on this?" "Where would you start?" "What's the difference between so-so and excellent work on this assignment?" The Transparency in Learning and Teaching website offers many resources, which include a template, questions to ask yourself, and examples.

■

You may recall the advice I got from some busy fellow grad students: get two good textbooks, one for the students to read and one for writing lectures. This advice assumed a seat-of-the-pants approach to each day's class meeting, with the instructor not knowing what the content would be until deciding on it shortly before class started. This approach meant writing the essay and ID questions for a couple exams at the last minute, too, once we knew what we had covered. In effect, both the instructors and the students crammed. Times have changed; although instructors aren't any less busy, we now have research about learning to inform our course design. That research tells us that if we want students to understand and remember significant things after the course is over, it's wise to think carefully about which big ideas might engage them, which historical concepts we want them to grapple with, and which skills we want them to practice—and to decide those *before the course starts*. Doing so gives us a much better sense of what should happen in all our class meetings, so they offer students encounters with challenging intellectual goals, not just exposure to facts. Our discipline offers many wonderful options for student learning objectives, and we can do much more than superficially cover a set of textbook chapters.

What we teach is a crucial decision that we should make very intentionally. The backward design framework tells us it's wise to start by thinking about *the end* of the semester, envisioning how we want students to be different after having taken our course, before articulating clear, specific, worthwhile learning goals. For students, explicit explanation of course goals helps their cognition, performance, and retention. For instructors, staying focused on our goals helps us design major assignments that prompt students to do the intellectual tasks we want them to do and constitute the evidence for how well they have learned. Well-designed assignments—ones that are aligned, practical, engaging, and transparent—are powerful tools for enacting our course goals.

Once we have settled on our goals and major assignments, it is easier to plan what we need to do at the day-to-day level with regard to readings and day-to-day teaching, which is the third stage of backward course design. Before we consider how we teach at the micro level, however, we need to think more about who our students are.

2   Who We Teach

Teaching can be so much fun. I remember one day early in a semester when always-prepared Ashley walked into my 8 a.m. class ten minutes early and started talking with me and another student about an aspect of the reading that struck her. By the time class officially started, other students had begun talking to one another, which created a positive buzz in the room and made me feel optimistic about the day. Soon this dynamic was a norm, and it translated into an enjoyable semester. I remember another time when students got so immersed in an activity that they didn't realize class was over, and they told me the newly designed exercise had really helped them learn.

Teaching can also be demoralizing. I have a depressing memory of a constantly bored and apathetic-looking student, who did the very minimum amount of work necessary. During small group activities, he strayed from the topic and distracted others. I have felt crushed to see a student smiling at a shopping site on her computer screen while the rest of us were having a serious class discussion about the impacts of war. I recall a very bright and enthusiastic student who was so obsessed with every point on graded work that I dreaded interacting with her.

Teaching can also be confusing. Imagine a student sitting in a corner away from others, who never voluntarily participates and whose face rarely shows any expression. Is Aleksandra engaged in the material but just introverted? Is she lacking confidence in her abilities? Is she self-conscious because of her accent, poor grammar, or stutter? Does she dislike me? Is she alienated from the other students in this class? Is she uninterested in this type of history? Unmotivated academically? Unhappy, ill, homesick, or exhausted? It's frustrating when we don't know what's going on in our students' heads.

With good reason, students are one of the most frequent topics of faculty water-cooler conversation. Sometimes we thank our lucky stars for the presence of great ones in our classes, but often we complain about having been stuck with students who we perceive as unmotivated, disengaged, unprepared, lazy, irresponsible, or grade grubbers. In either case, we tend to assume that who our students are and how they behave is entirely out of our control. This chapter argues that although some things are beyond our control, there are actions we can take to influence student cognition, motivation, mindsets, engagement, and perform-ance. Our teaching—and our own experience—will improve if we learn how people learn, how they are challenged by learning history, how motivation works, and how to create inclusive classrooms. All this is part of what I mean by knowing our students.

In graduate school, I imagined that my teaching would simply be concerned with ideas, that my classroom would be a high-minded sphere where disembodied brains had purely intellectual discussions for which I provided the inputs: historical knowledge and a few savvy teaching techniques. Reality proved to be much more complicated. Learning the content of history isn't as straightforward for students as I expected, and teaching is complex partly because it involves whole human beings. What's going on in students' brains matters most, but those brains house emotions as well as ideas and are tempted by com-peting ideas and distractions. The classroom is a social space where complex interactions between the students and me and between the students themselves influence what's happening in positive and nega-tive ways. I now know that what matters isn't just the knowledge I bring and the strategies I use but the impact of those things on my stu-dents. It's embarrassing to admit, but I didn't realize how important it was to understand students—in the aggregate, as learners and learners of history, and as individuals who bring their prior knowledge, experi-ences, and identities to my classroom. It was a paradigm shift to realize that I don't just teach *history*; I teach *students*.[1] Both parts of that phrase—the history and the students—are crucial. For that reason, it benefits me to adopt a model of teaching that focuses on my students' learning.

Prior Knowledge

At its most basic level, learning is a process of physical neurological change: the growing and strengthening of neurological networks. As we take in new experiences and information, our neurons seek out previously existing networks that are relevant. The first time neurons link up in a new way, the connection is fleeting, but the more often we use the connections (i.e., think about recently encountered ideas or information or think in new ways and contexts), the more the linkages strengthen. This creates denser, interwoven networks, fostering what we mean by "comprehension." Neuroscience teaches us that when we encounter something new, our brains interpret it through the lens of our existing knowledge, beliefs, and assumptions, and new knowledge sticks better when it has prior knowledge to stick to.[2]

Our undergraduate students are novices, and novices learn differently from instructors who have spent years immersed in studying in a field.[3] As experts, faculty already have a host of complex neural networks that allow them to learn far more quickly and effectively than novices. When history professors read an article (or hear a lecture, view a source, or watch a documentary), we immediately begin connecting the new material to things we already know, and we can do so because we have a large store of knowledge in our memory that we can access quickly. We aren't stymied by seeing a mass of new facts because we can chunk that information and place new facts, ideas, theories, or concepts into already existing organized structures in our brains; we have the capacity to think about the meanings and significance of what we take in. For example, if we read something new to us about something medieval nuns did to try to influence their society, we can connect that information to many existing mental structures related to the medieval period, religious history, women's history, social history, and power relations, as well as contemporary gender and religious issues and our personal thoughts about them. Novices, on the other hand, have far fewer networks, and what they do have are more sparse and superficial.[4]

Prior knowledge affects everyone's learning; therefore, it influences our history courses. Our students don't enter our classrooms as empty vessels. They may have already taken a history class—or even watched a cartoon—that left them with at least a dim memory of the French Revolution, even if it's just "Off with their heads!" That memory provides a place in their neural networks on which to hook new information. A student may have been fascinated by a documentary about the pyramids, so she remembers some context for the labor force and leadership structures of ancient Egypt. A student's family may have visited a U.S. Civil War site, which spurred independent reading, so he now knows more than some professors about Civil War battles and military strategies. A great-grandparent may have told stories passed down through generations about the Irish potato famine or emigrating from Russia due to pogroms. Even a little prior exposure can help; in studies of reading, those with some prior knowledge about a topic—even if they were weaker readers—comprehended much more than those with no prior knowledge.[5] Learners can also more easily remember new information if they have prior experience or familiarity. In terms of learning, there's no doubt that rich brains get richer.[6]

The catch is that for prior knowledge to be useful to our students, it needs to be accurate. Sam Wineburg's research provides examples of problematic preconceptions. In one case, a strong student in an Advanced Placement U.S. history course was asked to read a series of primary sources about the Battle of Lexington and then choose the picture that best reflected the written evidence. Although he sensibly interpreted the documents, he did not choose the logical picture depicting the battle because the behavior of the militia contradicted his assumptions about how normal (that is, contemporary) soldiers would act in battle. "His existing beliefs shaped the information he encountered so that the new conformed to the shape of the already known," Wineburg concluded. Although the student read the documents, "he learned little from them."[7] In another example, students who were shown an image of pro–Vietnam War demonstrations struggled to make sense of it because they had internalized a simplified narrative of the war as highly unpopular (not realizing that the majority of U.S. citizens supported it for most of its duration). Some of the students invented interpretations clearly contrary to the content of the image to fit their preconceptions. Conversations with the high school students in this study revealed that they had learned a fairly uniform collective memory about the war from having visited the Vietnam War Memorial, seen panhandlers holding "Help a Vet" signs, participated in a school dress-as-a-hippie day, and most commonly, watched Hollywood movies, especially *Forrest Gump*.[8] This "cultural curriculum" likely shapes our students' minds as much as the official school one.

Researchers have pinpointed numerous problematic assumptions that interfere with learning history. Two studies of high school students, one in Sweden and one in the United States, found many students conceptualized history entirely in terms of individual agency—despite the instructor emphasizing the importance of institutional factors.[9] Some students assume that history (especially their own country's history) is primarily a story of progress. When they are introduced to information that contradicts this conception, they may ignore it. For decades, at the beginning of the semester, Lendol Calder has asked students in his introductory U.S. history course to describe the story of American history in 600 words. He found four very common metanarratives, which he and his students labeled the "glory story" (of a largely successful quest for freedom and democracy), the "gory story" (of hypocrisy, white supremacy, sexism, and global domination by any means necessary), the story of "high ideals/mixed results," and the "chaos story" (a chronological listing of events with no themes). Consistent with the advice of neuroscientists, Calder tries to draw these stories and their assumptions out of his students' minds and bring them into the open, where they serve as a starting point to consciously explore (and ultimately make arguments about) the plausibility and significance of the stories we tell about our nation's history.[10]

Students' thinking about reliability may be naive. Some assume that primary sources are automatically more reliable than scholarly articles because their creators "were there" during the period being studied.[11] Questions of reliability are especially tricky in the digital age, when notions of authority have been turned upside down through the ability of anyone to post content online without any expertise or peer review and people automatically turn to websites for information. One study suggested that students rarely considered a website's author or credentials and almost never tried to verify them. Sam Wineburg reported, "In a stupendous misunderstanding of how Google's algorithms work, students equated the placement of a website on Google's list of results with trustworthiness."[12]

In the most fundamental problem, some students will come to our courses with misconceptions about the nature of history itself, assuming that it is simply a collection of objective facts about the past and that their job is to memorize and regurgitate those facts. When they realize their instructors want them to do something quite different, like analyze and think historically, it can be both surprising and difficult. The History Learning Project researchers identified the interpretive nature of history as a basic "intellectual bottleneck" for many students (and others refer to it as a fundamental "threshold concept" of the discipline).[13] Being asked to interpret can be especially troublesome for students in an early stage of intellectual development (such as first-year students). Harvard educational psychologist William Perry called this early stage "duality," because students believe knowledge can be easily divided into right or wrong, and they believe it is to be handed down by authorities, not debated. In the typical next stage of intellectual development, "multiplicity," students recognize that multiple perspectives exist but view knowledge as simply a matter of opinion. Because they believe that all opinions are equally valid, students in this stage are still not motivated or ready to analyze competing claims using disciplinary standards of logic and evidence.[14] These early stages clearly pose a problem for many history courses.

Despite coming to us with problematic assumptions, the good news is that over time students can change. I have seen this in my local context when I asked fifty-seven history majors in a few sections of our senior research seminar to describe in their own words how their understanding of history had changed over their three to four years of study. More than a third of them volunteered some variation of the statement, "I now understand history is not just facts (about names, dates, and a chronology of events)." They reported they had come to see history as an interpretive endeavor and that history is more complex, ambiguous, and contested than they had originally thought. As one student put it, "I realized how much power historians have—the ability to construct the past. We don't just 'know' history—in high school, textbooks seemed so certain. [Now] I see how these historians have an argument, a point of view. . . . History is dynamic and debatable." Their writings showed that these history majors changed from early stage students who saw themselves as receivers of information to actors who do history— who analyzed sources, interrogated what they read, looked at situations from multiple perspectives, conducted research, sought to uncover influences and biases, contextualized events, and made arguments.[15]

What are the implications of the cognitive effect of prior knowledge for instructors? First, we need to figure out what students "know" and whether it's accurate. Options for finding out include a quick assessment at the beginning of the semester, such as an ungraded individual or group quiz, a survey in which students report their understanding of certain topics (with a scale from "totally unfamiliar/clueless" to "I could explain it"), or writing in response to an open-ended prompt. A quick read of informal writings (or even a quick show of hands) can tell us a lot about where our opportunities and challenges lie. We can do the same sort of "brain dump" at the beginning of a new unit of a course or a class period that covers a topic on which we suspect students are bringing either helpful or distorted prior knowledge. This can be done through a ninety-second listing of everything they know on a topic or free writing about the first thoughts that come to mind.[16] Checking in through one of these simple methods means that we activate whatever useful knowledge they have (which is important because it's useless if not activated), giving it a "toehold" to which they can connect the new information they will be encountering. If their knowledge is inaccurate, on the other hand, we can address and correct it. As the authors of *How Learning Works* put it, "In some cases, inaccuracies can be corrected simply by exposing students to accurate information and evidence that conflicts with flawed beliefs and models. However, it is important for instructors to recognize that a single correction or refutation is unlikely to be enough to help students revise deeply held misconceptions."[17]

For serious problematic assumptions held by a significant number of our students, it is wise to explicitly and clearly acknowledge those assumptions and teach in response to them, as Calder did by having students describe their existing metanarratives and then revisit them in light of new topics, readings, and evidence. It's wise to be sensitive to students' difficulties and give them time to discover, reflect on, and make sense of contradictions between the evidence and their prior "knowledge." Asking students to justify their reasoning is always a good practice, and it can be effective for uncovering and remedying this sort of problem. As Ambrose and her coauthors put it, "Guiding students through a process of conceptual change is likely to take time, patience, and creativity."[18]

One might object that it is impossible to figure out and deal with the different prior knowledge that all our individual students bring with them. That's true, so our job is to try to recognize patterns. Asking early in the term allows us to plan a strategy, but we may discover misunderstandings later when a student makes a comment during class. Once I was teaching students how to find scholarly journal articles for a research project when a smart and conscientious student seemed genuinely confused about why the articles she found were considered reliable and permissible to use. After a short conversation, we figured out that because we had accessed the *America: History and Life* database through a library website using an Internet browser, she thought what she was doing was comparable to simply Googling a topic, which she knew was bad practice. Similarly, medievalist Leah Shopkow related a time when she slowly realized why one of her students was drawing very odd conclusions: she thought a monk living in a small room in an abbey was imprisoned because a primary source referred to his "cell."[19] These examples remind us there may be good reasons for our students to be confused. Because faculty are experts who often unintentionally assume prior knowledge, it is wise for us to react to student confusion with curiosity and respect and try to figure out what is behind the misunderstanding (whether with the whole group during class or afterward with individuals). This approach is obviously preferable to dismissing or ignoring the problem.

Problematic assumptions and gaps in background knowledge are difficult for novices to identify on their own, and sometimes we won't realize a pattern of misunderstandings until a significant number of students show it on an exam.[20] We should address it after the exam, but we would prefer to have known it beforehand. Unfortunately, sometimes we don't figure it out until it's too late to correct, and the best we can do is to make a note of it and be proactive the next time we teach the course. In addition, we can try to be aware of and forthcoming with students about the prior knowledge a course requires (whether or not there is a prerequisite) and offer supplementary materials that can provide the necessary background information that might even the playing field a bit for students with less familiarity.

We also can't assume—much as we might like to—that our students know basic things about how to learn. This may include the best strategies for reading history textbooks, scholarly monographs, articles, or primary source documents. It's good to remember that we didn't always know these things either. Given the difficulty many adults have in distinguishing between a sponsored ad and a news article, our students may well need assistance in evaluating the credibility of what they see on websites. (Wineburg suggests that many historians also need help, given their performance in one study.[21]) Students might not know how to write a good thesis or topic sentence, may not know the best strategies for taking notes on a lecture or discussion, or have any idea how or how long to study for an exam. The 2013 Higher Education Research Institute national study of incoming first-year college students revealed that almost 59 percent spent less than six hours a week doing homework as high school seniors. In an earlier and smaller study, only 14 percent of undergraduates said they had ever been taught how to study.[22] Rather than bemoan the poor or uneven preparation of our students, I propose that we figure out what they need to know how to do, prioritize a few learning goals, and commit ourselves to empowering them to learn.

Much has been made of the fact that eighteen- to twenty-two-year-olds are "digital natives" who are different in fundamental ways from earlier generations. It is certainly true that the larger environment for learning has changed radically. The Internet has paved the way for students to learn on their own, connect with others all over the world, collaborate in real time, and create content (not just read it). It's also true that many students are online almost all the time, leaving their smartphones turned on at night and picking them up first thing in the morning. Digital technologies have been "changing how people of all ages learn, play, socialize, exercise judgment, and engage in civic life."[23] However, it's not altogether clear what this means for how students learn (or what this means for us as instructors). Phones and laptops in classrooms do bring the potential for distraction. Many students believe that multitasking doesn't affect them, but the evidence is clear that any distractions from attention impede learning.[24] Students who have grown up in an era when online images are constantly shared and modified (and when laws and norms are in flux) may not have the same concept of intellectual property and plagiarism (and even authorship) that their instructors do.[25] Periodically, news stories bemoan the fact that despite all the potential of information online, students don't know basic facts about history or who their congressional representatives are, don't read as much, write poorly because they are always texting, or are "the dumbest generation" whose brains are neurologically altered by constant interaction with computers.[26]

The impacts of the digital age are more complex than that. Students may be prone to distractions, communicate differently, and read differently online than previous generations (i.e., they browse, scan, and navigate hypertextually to go down whole new pathways). Some studies suggest they may be reading a great deal and may bring certain new skills, too. Their literacy may include images, video, sounds, and symbols as well as text.[27] A Stanford University study of writing in the early 2000s suggested that the students they followed for five years were unusually adept at assessing their audience and shaping their style, tone, language, and technique for that audience. They may have a different understanding of authority than earlier generations or professors (who respect peer review and published paper sources) because on the Web, sources of knowledge making and authority may be less visible, more anonymous, and less concretely institutionalized.[28] However, because they encounter such an overwhelming amount of information online and many competing sources of news, they may be good at reading multiple contexts together and against one another—skills that are useful for students of history—and may be accustomed to triangulating.[29] Michelle Miller, author of *Minds Online*, asserted that there's little peer-reviewed research to support claims that Internet use affects the brain's ability to process information and good reason to doubt that computing causes global physiological changes in the brain. Similarly, the scientists who wrote *How People Learn II* in 2018 observed a dearth of experimental research on the transfer of communication skills and habits between online social and academic media. They concluded that more research is needed about how technology may be influencing the nature of what people need to learn and the psychology of learners.[30]

Thus we should be careful not to assume too much about digital natives. Although students use technology a great deal, they may use it in superficial ways, primarily for communication and entertainment as opposed to learning, and they may not have a very deep understanding of the technology. They may not be very confident about their use of technology or actually want to be connected all the time, and they differ from one another based on individual experiences. Research on the digital divide suggests real differences among students based on geography (rural versus urban) and socioeconomic class, not simply in ownership of the latest tools and access but in digital literacy and the ability to create or modify online content.[31] In such a rapidly changing context (where all the implications of change are not clear), it's especially important to pay attention to our specific students' knowledge and skills. Rather than making assumptions, it's best to find out what they know, what they think, and what they need to know.

Motivation

Motivation is the portal to engagement.

ELIZABETH F. BARKLEY

Why are some of our students so eager, attentive, and ready to learn and accept challenges while others are not? As Elizabeth Barkley suggested, it may be related to motivation.[32]

Motivations are complex. Most of us are very motivated in some contexts but less so in others. Just as we instructors are more excited by teaching some topics and doing certain leisure activities than others, one of our history majors may be hugely excited by Latin American history but not Asian, ancient but not recent, or social history topics but not military ones. A student taking one of our introductory courses to fulfill a general education requirement may be quiet and resentful in our class but talkative and passionate in a course for her major. A student may put almost no time into a writing an essay but spend five hours nonstop immersed in a video game. A variety of factors affect how we feel about a task, including which behaviors will be rewarded and what our goals are. Students in a course may have performance goals, learning goals, or work-avoidant goals.[33] Just like faculty, students may have competing academic, social, economic, and health goals. In the evening, a student might be deciding between studying for class, going to a job, playing an intramural sport, or sleeping. If an activity satisfies more than one goal—intramural sports might satisfy social and health goals—satisfaction is higher than if it satisfies just one. When some of a student's goals align with our instructional goals, "powerful learning situations tend to result."[34]

Psychologists tell us that one of the key factors motivating people's behaviors is the degree to which they value an activity. Students may highly value activities for different reasons, however. One may work hard at a task because he finds it interesting or enjoys it (e.g., he loves doing research in old newspapers), which means it has intrinsic value to him; another values the task for the satisfaction from getting it done and done well, which is known as attainment value; a third values it because it is instrumental or a means to achieving a goal (she thinks the research experience will help her get into law school).[35]

Another crucial factor in motivation is "positive expectancy." Expectancy is the degree to which people expect their actions will bring about a desired outcome. We are more motivated if we believe we can successfully complete a task. Components of expectancy include beliefs about our own abilities and agency, and the ways we attribute success and failure. (Do we think outcomes on a task will be more related to effort, innate ability, or uncontrollable causes?). Some psychologists depict simplified motivation theory with the equation $M = V \times E$, meaning motivation (M) is the product of value (V) and expectancy (E), which act synergistically.[36] As with a mathematical equation, if either one of the factors is zero (i.e., either value or expectancy is missing), it's unlikely a student will feel motivated. If students believe they can do a task but don't value it, they remain unmotivated to do it or do it well. If students value the task but believe they will be unsuccessful at it, they might be passive or hopeless. If they neither value the task nor believe they can succeed, students may be disengaged, apathetic, alienated, resistant, or angry about feeling coerced into doing unpleasant, pointless work that may prove to be embarrassing. Both components are necessary.[37]

Although motivation resides within a student—we cannot make someone want to learn—instructors can have substantial influence on it.[38] This is especially true with regard to value of the work. Strategies to establish value include some things discussed in the previous chapter, such as (1) teaching things that are well worth learning; (2) explaining the purposes for an assignment or activity, including how the knowledge or skills might be useful later in the course or in the world beyond our course; (3) creating authentic assignments (so students see the relevance of the work for the real world); and (4) offering some choices. Offering a choice of topics gives students a greater sense of control and allows them to connect more to their own interests (increasing value).[39] Although it is helpful to show students how the skills they hone in a history course contribute to future careers, we don't simply have to focus on economic utility. In fact, infusing learning with a sense of purpose beyond a "selfish" one, such as the effect that understanding history can have in making the world a better place, can serve as a powerful motivator. In one study where faculty reminded students of this "self-transcendent" power of their learning, students studied difficult review questions twice as long before a final exam.[40]

The value of our topics and the work we ask of students is not always readily apparent. Gerald Graff described what he called "the problem problem," which is that many students don't understand why academics problematize things that don't appear to be serious issues. Faculty seem to overanalyze things (especially texts), and ask students to do things that seem odd, risky, negative, or even arrogant, like make arguments and think critically. He argued that because many of our students do not have the same assumptions as intellectuals, it is best to talk explicitly (and passionately) about why we do the things we do in our discipline.[41] Graff described a situation where students had no idea why the university required a specific course. When students asked why, they felt they were treated like children whose parent responded, "Because I said so."[42] Value and relevance differ in individuals and are affected by one's cultural background.[43] It's a good habit for us to explain why we think specific work is important, but it can also be wise to ask students how *they* imagine ideas, concepts, knowledge, or skills might be relevant in their future personal or professional lives. One semester, I was assigned to teach a course with content I worried students wouldn't connect to or see the relevance of. So I asked them to write two lightly graded "So What?" essays in which they argued for the significance of any two historical topics we had studied. They came up with great and interesting ideas, some of which I wouldn't have thought of. I now realize that without any knowledge of motivation theory, I accidentally used a strategy that activates motivation.

We can do other evidence-based things. Although we can't influence students' individual interests before they enter our classrooms, we can shape what psychologists' call students' "situational interests" once they arrive. Situational interest contains two factors, "catch" and "hold."[44] "Catch" involves capturing student attention (right at the beginning of the semester or a class meeting), which can be done by asking thought-provoking questions, which tap into people's natural curiosity. A compelling story, video clip, or activity may help catch students' intellectual excitement (through the way material is presented or its emotional impact). "Hold" involves sustaining interest. It can be done in a variety of ways: with activities that are enjoyable and varied, with challenge and opportunities to grow, with meaningful content, and with positive student–student and student–teacher interactions. Psychologist Regan Gurung put it bluntly: "Make class time valuable."[45] Some faculty may fear that intentionally trying to activate students' emotions is somehow pandering or manipulation, but a growing body of research underscores the role of emotions in learning. If we don't work toward activating the positive emotions (interest, curiosity, wonder), we risk activating the negative ones (anxiety, frustration, boredom).[46]

Faculty can also increase students' value by showing that they are concerned about their learning. Research suggests "students are acutely aware of whether their professors care about them."[47] Students aren't expecting birthday cards, a shoulder to cry on, easy grades, or inappropriate relationships; these studies indicated students are concerned about whether the instructor is approachable, respectful, and understanding (i.e., acknowledges difficulty and student emotions). Students are very aware if an instructor seems cold, apathetic, uncaring, disparaging, or negative toward students. Increases in instructor–student rapport pay off; they are associated with greater enjoyment of the course, improved attendance and attention, and increased study time. Faculty can affect perceptions of their concern in easy ways: knowing students' names, chatting with students before, after, and outside of class and expressing interest in their lives; and communicating with the entire class about their availability. A prompt response to a student email shows concern, and it's easy to announce sincerely, "I know it's a busy time in the semester, and I hope you're taking care of yourselves."[48]

During class, small behaviors make a difference: maintaining eye contact with everyone, smiling, listening (not interrupting), moving around the room, really inviting questions, and responding to student misunderstandings with empathy or curiosity. These behaviors even make a difference in very large classes where it's difficult to know all the students.[49] In a Gallup survey of 30,000 graduates, the most important factors they pointed to for having a successful college experience were a professor who cared about them as a person, a professor who made them excited to learn, and a mentor who encouraged them to follow their dreams.[50] When students feel valued, in turn they are more likely to value the course work.

Students' success is ultimately up to them, of course, but we want them to see we're on the same team, allies in their learning. We should make it clear that, as Terry Doyle put it, "We want them to be academically and personally successful and that we'd like to help them do that."[51] Having a good relationship with students helps when introducing difficult new material; if students trust that we have their best interests at heart and that we won't put them in an impossible situation, they are more likely to persevere. When we give criticism, our feedback will be accepted if students know we care about them and want them to improve and reach their potential.

Instructors also can influence students' expectancies. We are aiming for students to believe that with effort (and with that effort exerted in the right direction), their work will pay off—they can learn the material and perform at an acceptable level. For motivation, they need to have hope and self-efficacy. To provide hope, we can reassure students that we designed a course that offers chances for them to try out their ideas and practice the necessary skills. Then we should follow through, allocating time in class to provide that practice and offer a chance for students to receive formative feedback before they do heavily graded work. (Practice might be as simple as having them critique a short sample essay or having small groups write a thesis statement with an argument.) As mentioned in the previous chapter, we can design assignments that are transparent about what students need to do, how their work will be evaluated, and what we do to ensure that grading is done fairly (e.g., explain the process we use, share rubrics, and/or grade all student work anonymously to prevent bias). We can "scaffold" assignments (discussed in chapter 3). We can share what we know about effective study skills with the class.[52] We can explain what office hours are for, which issues we are available to help with, and where they can find other resources (such as writing, tutoring, and health centers).

One of our most important levers for building expectancy—and one of our responsibilities, I would argue—is designing assignments that are at the appropriate level for our students. Neuroscientists tell us that when faced with a task or problem, our brains quickly evaluate how much mental work it will take to do it and the likelihood of being successful; if it determines it's too much or too little work, we stop.[53] Humans are naturally curious, but we do need a rationale for our work. That's because our brains encounter a world of other potential things to pay attention to and must prioritize activities. To continue working at a task, we need a sense that we are making progress.[54] This means that faculty should give careful thought to the level at which we set tasks.

Assignments that are challenging but attainable with effort are the history professor's sweet spot. It can be tempting to pose extraordinarily difficult tasks; as I admitted in the last chapter, I used to assign very complex synthetic essays without offering accompanying instruction and support in an introductory level course (thwarting students like Karl). Sometimes, I think, we want to congratulate ourselves for offering tough courses (or hope to wow students or our colleagues by telling them how demanding we are), but this can backfire. In one study in physics, students interpreted the warning that a course had a high failure rate and would require hard work in different ways. Some saw it as a challenge (and all of those happened to be white or Asian males), whereas others heard it as an indication they would likely fail and that the teacher was satisfied for that to happen, which made them less inclined to put effort into the course.[55] Tough becomes demoralizing and unfair if it isn't supported by day-to-day teaching. Well-supported rigor, embodied in tasks that use student knowledge and skills but still stretch them, is a different matter entirely. It is worth striving for.[56]

Nor should we err in the other direction. We shouldn't set tasks that are too easy—such as ones that don't require enough analysis or that simply ask students to give back what they have read or heard in class. If significant learning is our goal, this approach obviously doesn't work. It may be tempting for faculty members, especially those who feel vulnerable, to imagine that students will like the course if almost everyone gets a high grade without much effort. Fortunately, some empirical evidence suggests that high ratings on student evaluation instruments don't go to teachers of easy courses.[57]

It may be difficult for us to find the optimal sweet spot, where students are neither bored because they are not challenged nor frustrated by almost impossible tasks. Especially when teaching a new course, we may need to experiment and be flexible. Above all, it requires knowing our students—checking in with them regularly to see what they're understanding and what they're struggling with. If possible, we can offer an early opportunity for some success, such as a graded assignment that counts for a small percentage of the grade, so it's still possible to pass the course if one does poorly. Expectancies can be higher if the syllabus offers opportunities for drafts, revision, or ways to show that students can identify, learn from, and correct their misunderstandings.[58]

In summary, although we may be used to trying to influence student motivation and behavior solely with extrinsic factors like grades, praise, and punitive policies, we have three other especially powerful levers: value, expectancy, and the supportive nature of the course environment (which will be explored further).[59] We don't need to adopt all the recommended strategies, but motivation experts warn against ignoring any of the three areas altogether. They assert that planning for motivation should be a part of every faculty member's course design. As Regan Gurung put it, "Motivating students may be one of the most important steps an instructor can take to enhance learning."[60]

Naturally, faculty members might wonder, "Why is this my responsibility? Shouldn't students provide their own motivation and just suffer the consequences if they're not mature enough to do so?" We can choose to ignore motivation issues, of course, but we do so at our peril, since motivation is one of the crucial components of learning and is necessary very early in the process.[61] Motivation affects the choices students make about whether they will do tasks (like pay attention or study), the amount of effort they put into a task, and whether they will persist when things get difficult.[62] There's no question that our lives are much easier if all our students enter our classes already motivated, but we must teach the students we have, not the ones we wish we had.[63]

If learning is our goal, why would we not want students to believe that success is possible and support them in strategies that promote learning? If we believe that what we teach is valuable, why wouldn't we do what we can to help students realize its value? Although we may not be able to reach or transform every student, research indicates that it is possible for students to move along the motivation spectrum and become more intrinsically motivated, develop a greater sense of self-efficacy, and adopt a better mindset for learning, and that we can help spur the process. Finally, there's our self-interest to consider: if we want an engaged, hard-working, responsible, persistent group of students who are willing and able to take on the rigorous challenges we pose, why wouldn't we use evidence-based strategies that increase the likelihood of that?[64]

Mindsets

Since we hope to find the sweet spot level of challenge, it behooves us to find out exactly what our students find difficult.[65] Curious about my department's history majors, over the course of a few years, I asked students in five different sections of our capstone seminar, "What's the most challenging thing about studying history? How do you feel about that?" and then categorized their responses. About 40 percent of the things they mentioned fell into the category of research and writing; some of them pointed to the difficulty in conducting an effective search for sources, and many others struggled with the subsequent steps. "Once I have all this information . . . , I often feel overwhelmed," one reported. Others frequently mentioned developing an argument, marshaling the evidence to support it, and writing it in a clear and logical way. These findings echo those of the History Learning Project, which described a category of bottlenecks related to producing arguments, learning how to use library resources for research, and writing historically.[66] A somewhat larger number—about 45 percent of the total number of answers I received—suggested that students found more epistemological or affective aspects of doing history to be most challenging. These aspects included the difficulty of understanding the past due to the passage of time, limitations of sources, or cultural differences; the lack of certainty inherent in interpreting history; or grappling with issues of bias in the sources, the people they were studying, or themselves.[67]

Students felt quite differently from one another about the challenges they faced. About a fourth used negative terms, such as "overwhelming," "scary," "daunting," "frustrating," "annoying," and "discouraging." About three-fourths, however, described their feelings in far more positive ways. Their answers showed that they recognized value in the difficult tasks and the purpose for doing them. "I get why it's like that," one student explained about the need to keep finding more sources. One who struggled with trying to remain unbiased concluded, "I feel it is difficult, but a challenge we must face, and not even just in history but as . . . people." Some found persisting through the difficulties to be interesting, fun, or rewarding. Finally coming across the fact that you need, one wrote, is the "best feeling in the world." These more positive students also tended to believe that they would improve "down the road." Right after describing a task as "FRUSTRATING!!," for example, a student noted, "It's a skill I have to build. I'll get better @ it the more history I 'do.'"[68]

These contrasting feelings illustrate another important thing our students bring with them to our classes: their beliefs about learning. Abundant psychological research has demonstrated the power of mindsets. Some people have a fixed mindset. They believe that they were born with a fixed type and amount of intelligence, which is finite and unchangeable. They believe they are either good at something (such as history, math, soccer, or piano) or not. This makes them skeptical about the possibility of learning and growing. When people with a fixed mindset encounter difficult tasks, if they doubt their ability, they tend to give up easily, avoid challenges, and ignore constructive criticism.[69] When one of our history majors said, "[History] takes a lot of time and good writing skills. I don't like that because I am not a good writer," that student didn't seem to realize writing is a skill at which one can improve. Interestingly, a fixed mindset is an obstacle even if a student does believe he has the relevant type of intelligence—say, he believes he's good at history or writing. A fixed mindset may lead him to think he shouldn't need to work hard at the task (because he's good at it), and if he gets a low grade on a writing assignment, he may attribute it to unfair grading instead of his approach, understanding, or skills. As Saundra McGuire, author of *Teach Students How to Learn*, puts it, "A fixed mindset is kryptonite in any arena."[70]

When students have a growth mindset, on the other hand, they believe that their intelligence is malleable and they can improve it with hard work aimed in the right direction. Like the students who described how they felt about history challenges in positive terms, students with growth mindsets see the value in their efforts to improve and realize that effort paves the path to eventual mastery. They tend to embrace challenges, persist in the face of setbacks, view mistakes as a normal part of the process of learning, and listen to and learn from constructive criticism. The growth view of intelligence is correct in terms of cognitive science. "Scientists are learning that people have more capacity for life-long learning and brain development than they ever thought," noted Carol Dweck, a leading scholar in this field. "Of course, each person has a unique genetic endowment. People may start with different temperament and different aptitudes, but it is clear that experience, training, and personal effort take them the rest of the way."[71] A growth mindset opens up a world of learning.

Fortunately, research suggests that students can change their mindsets and that instructors can make a difference. We can inform students that science has proven that intelligence is expandable and that the specific skills required for doing history are learnable. One isn't born knowing how to interpret primary sources, write an argument, read secondary sources, or conduct research; these are all skills at which one can improve. In case students are skeptical, at the beginning of the semester, we can tell them about others who found something difficult at first but then improved significantly. It's even better if we can find a way for them to hear this from former students. Some do this through a quotation on their syllabus or a first day of class slide, perhaps excerpted from letters they asked past students to write to future ones.[72] I had a constitutional law professor who compared reading Supreme Court opinions to eating mushrooms, asserting that it's strange at first, but you develop a taste for it. (Her metaphor stuck with me as I slogged through the early readings and really did come to enjoy the opinions, if not the mushrooms.) We can also share our own struggles and growth. The research findings have convinced me that from now on, I should tell classes how demoralized I was with the grades and comments I received on the first essays I wrote in college and that I was advised to take a basic writing course to remedy my problems. Faculty who share their own struggles report that students are often surprised that things didn't always come easily to the professors who now seem so competent and confident. Just as we can activate prior knowledge, some research suggests we may be able to cue persistence by asking students to recall other challenges they have overcome.[73]

Faculty can do other things to help foster a growth mindset. When we give positive feedback to students, instead of complimenting them for being smart (which suggests fixed intelligence), we should praise them for the specific things they did well (such as choosing effective evidence or revising effectively) and for the effort they put into doing the appropriate tasks. If they struggle on an assignment, we can make clear that the grade represents their performance on a particular task and their current level of skill and understanding, not their intelligence, potential, or worth. We can help them pinpoint which specific content or skills they struggled with and help them adjust their expectations about the effort and specific strategies required to improve. We can disabuse them when they voice unproductive beliefs (e.g., "I can't write"), alert them to the research about mindsets, and encourage them to focus on their effort, engagement, and learning strategies, such as note-taking, study habits, reading strategies, and writing process. That is, we should advise them to focus on things over which they have control. In terms of course structure, we can design our grading scheme so that it gives students a chance to grow and rewards them for doing so by making assignments later in the semester count more than those earlier. Instead of trying to "weed out" students, we can pose challenging but manageable readings and assignments, model new skills, give students practice and early feedback on how well they're doing it, and help them grow.[74]

Emotions

Students are people who bring into our courses their individual backgrounds, identities, and values. As a result, they may have strong personal and emotional reactions to what we ask them to study. This can be a good thing when it spurs deep reflection. "College was really the first time I studied the Civil War as a self-proclaimed Southerner," one student recalled. "[The course] really forced me to look at the war differently than I had and I really connected with learning more about individual experiences during the war. I remember calling my mom after class one day being really mad about some of the horrors that occurred. It really made me think about how that story has shaped our present day and essentially, my story as well." One student noted approvingly that investigating their grandparents' village during World War II "was emotional," and another concluded, "Research gets personal." Strong feelings result when students identify with victims of oppression due to their own (racial, ethnic, religious, national, or socioeconomic) background or their gender or sexual identity. One student wrote, "I cannot look at the Civil Rights/Women/any liberation movements without interpreting it through my eyes," and reported that it took a concerted effort not to use loaded language "when discussing an event that I feel passionate about. Seeing a photo of someone being lynched, I cannot, with a clear head, write something that isn't opinionated." Of course, any student, regardless of ancestry or identity, may be disturbed by grim events of the past or by having cherished myths shattered. "Wow, America was horrible and unfair and we never learned that part in high school," explained a student who found this to be "heartbreaking and frustrating and angering."[75] Still, these difficult emotions convinced the student that a career in teaching would be very important. Psychologists tell us that emotion can spur both motivation and memory. A study with college history students confirmed that using emotionally provocative images enhanced memory retention not only of the images but also of related historical content.[76] As one scholar puts it, "When educators fail to appreciate the importance of students' emotions, they fail to appreciate a critical force in students' learning."[77]

Occasionally strong emotions can interfere with learning. Faculty in the History Learning Project identified "affective" bottlenecks as one very common obstacle.[78] When some students encountered content that seemed threatening—usually material they thought could imply disrespect for their family ancestry or values—they intellectually withdrew. One instructor noticed that when teaching about the rise of Anglo-Saxonism in the 1870s and 1880s, some students respond, "Hey! You're attacking my heritage," or "This is part of who I am and stop beating up on us."[79] In addition, faculty teaching Latino, African American, Asian, and African history reported that some students from relatively privileged backgrounds had difficulty engaging with course content due to feeling that their families were implicated in events of the past.[80] This is not surprising given the trajectory of identity formation; "resistance" is a common stage students from majority groups may go through when exposed to new perspectives and information about injustice, causing some to push back and others to experience shame or guilt.[81] It can also be troubling to students when course content contradicts narratives of patriotism (such as introducing complexity into the victors' narratives of World War II as a "good war") or deeply held values (that hard work led to equal opportunities for all groups). At the very least, it can be uncomfortable if one's worldview is challenged. Student reactions may include silent disagreement, skeptical mistrust, active hostility, accusing the teacher of bias, or calling the course "worthless."[82]

A handful of faculty at one institution experimented with ways to teach Mexican migration, a topic that sometimes posed affective bottlenecks. They began by surfacing students' preconceptions on a pretest; students drew maps of Mexican migration, frequently depicting what the instructors referred to as a simplistic and inaccurate unidirectional "invasion model." Then the instructors shared more evidence (and a useful metaphor) about the more complex patterns of migration that actually occurred. Finally, they designed an exercise in which they asked students in small groups to examine some of the student-drawn maps and think about the degree to which each was (or was not) supported by the evidence. (They believed having students draw their own conclusions would be more effective than an authority figure simply telling them what was wrong and right, since those with strong misconceptions might simply dismiss the instructor as biased.) Evidence from the end-of-semester test suggested that the new strategy made a difference. Only 43 percent of the students understood the complex and cyclical migration pattern at the beginning of the semester, whereas 76 percent did at the end of the semester. In the second semester of using the new exercises, 97 percent of students drew the more accurate model on the final test. The project's designers concluded, "Putting students' preconceptions on the table—and then directly contrasting them with the accepted historical practice or interpretation—is our working prescription for helping students overcome bottlenecks."[83] Understanding problematic student preconceptions was doubly helpful: first, it helped their instructors design exercises to work through the specific bottleneck; second, it helped students understand that their preconceptions might be based on quick first reactions rather than the more methodical and evidence-based process that historians value.[84]

Occasionally, students might lose control over their emotions and create a "hot moment." A disparaging or sarcastic comment about a whole group of people or a contemporary political view can infuriate other students in the room, who might silently seethe or disengage, possibly just for that day, but maybe for the remainder of the semester.

Things may escalate if other students protest or say that they have been offended, especially if one of the students uses insulting or inflammatory language. Although some instructors welcome this emotion in their class, for many the first instinct is to feel like a deer in the headlights—panicked, frozen, and uncertain what to do next. One might be tempted to ignore the comment and move on, but that response often dissatisfies students, who may feel that silence implies that an instructor agrees with or is unconcerned about an offensive comment or that an instructor prioritizes feelings of harmony over facing an elephant in the room and the fact that some find the climate to be hostile.[85] Some faculty opt for a very different response, which is to explicitly name a racist, sexist, homophobic, or otherwise stereotypical and insulting comment as that, say it is unacceptable, and have that be the end of it. That approach is less than ideal, too, because the student who made the offensive comment doesn't learn why it's not acceptable (hurtful, false, dangerous, etc.), nor does the rest of the class.[86] Unhappily, I can attest to this. A day after the September 11, 2001, terrorist attacks, one of my students angrily referred to Middle Eastern people as "towelheads," and my stunned reaction was a brief angry comment about her attitude that made it clear that I disapproved of it, but also completely shut down any further discussion and learning that day.[87]

It's best to face the situation and try to turn a difficult moment into an educational one. Inclusive classroom experts suggest having a "pedagogical parachute" prepared for when it is necessary to deal with a "hot moment" and that this safety net strategy be connected to our learning goals.[88] For example, if we have a course goal of students learning to clearly articulate their views, we can try to slow things down by pausing and repeating what a student said and asking if that's correct. Sometimes this pause gives the student a chance to realize the problem and backtrack or clarify, which may deescalate matters. If one of our goals is to improve analysis of evidence, we can ask the student how she knows the statement is true. If the goal of the course includes understanding multiple perspectives, another approach would be to turn the focus away from the individual student who made the comment and invite the rest of the class into an analytical discussion: "There are others who think this; why might they think this way?" then after a few answers, saying, "Some strenuously disagree with this view; why might they hold that perspective?" Since simply focusing on two perspectives can be polarizing and oversimplifying, follow up by asking, "Are there other perspectives besides these two?" Depending on the issue, a final step might be to ask all the students to consider what they think (perhaps in unshared free writing) and why, and what kind of evidence they wish they had to feel more certain. Others advise faculty to buy themselves a few moments to think about what to do or say next by asking students to free write in response to the question, "What just happened? How do you think we should handle this? What can we learn from it?" Some experts suggest that asking students to identify how they are feeling actually lessens anxiety and confusion.[89]

If we are simply flummoxed during a heated moment, we can honestly acknowledge it: "I know there are really strong feelings in the room and I'm not sure exactly how to handle this, so I'm going to think more about it after class and come back to it." Then we have time to consider our options carefully (and consult with colleagues, the campus teaching center, or resources about responding to hot moments) in order to plan a response for the beginning of the next class (or a thoughtful email to all the students).[90] That response could be anything from a few calm comments that summarize the different perspectives, new readings that provide additional evidence or perspectives, a very structured discussion, or instruction about how to discuss controversial topics in the future. We can also reach out to the individual students involved to check in on how they are, listen, and encourage them to keep engaging so they continue to learn.

Even though such situations may make us nervous, we should not try to avoid topics that might provoke strong emotional reactions. That's probably not possible, and even if it were, it is not responsible for a historian and not wise for an instructor to do so. In fact, educational researchers define student development as "a response to intellectual, social, or emotional challenges."[91] In studies of difficult dialogues on race, students indicated the importance of having space to express and explore their feelings about race to help them better understand themselves and others.[92] Scholarship on transformative learning suggests that if we want to have a profound effect on our students, we should pose "productive challenges," which "respectfully challenge students' values and assumptions about themselves and the world they live in."[93] Dissonance can be a starting point for growth—if handled in a respectful manner. This can be seen in the writings of my department's history majors. I asked them to respond to the question, "Have you ever studied an idea or topic in history that made you think about who you are or rethink your values? If so, what?" About 83 percent of the students said they had.[94] For example, one student wrote, "Studying the theology behind Germany and the role the church played in legitimating Hitler's regime shook my Christian upbringing to its core," and another said studying the Cold War resulted in "rethink[ing] the way in which I viewed the U.S. and its role in the world." Rather than being upset that had they been asked to think deeply about themselves or their values, these students reported numerous positive results from having done so. It was "extremely helpful in my personal discovery of my own self," one noted. Some said they became better critical thinkers ("question things I hadn't thought to question before"), gained clarification about their personal ethics ("more convinced . . . of my values"), developed a stronger sense of identity ("a better sense of my roots and where I came from"), or felt empowered ("understand I am not stuck in a certain role"). Several offered that they had become better human beings ("more sensitive [about race]"; "more open to new ideas and points of view").[95] "History will do that to us," one student concluded. "It will challenge our ideas and make us think in a new way."[96]

Inclusive Classrooms

> You can't fire the synapses in your students' brains. For the connections to be meaningful and effective, the students have to form them. Your task is to create an environment that facilitates the formation of those connections.
>
> JAMES LANG

How we teach potentially unsettling topics matters a great deal, which is why, as Lang observed, faculty should aim to shape an inclusive environment.[97] By "inclusive classroom," I mean a place where all students feel supported to learn and explore ideas, safe to express their thoughts and views in a civil manner, and respected as individuals and members of groups. In inclusive classrooms, the students view themselves as people who belong in a community of learners capable of thinking about hard things. Creating an inclusive environment does not mean that students always feel comfortable, since we know that discomfort frequently accompanies learning. Experiencing discomfort while feeling supported by the instructor and classmates is quite different from the discomfort that comes from feeling insulted, antagonized, dismissed, disrespected, or shut down due to personality conflicts, disagreements, identity issues, or uncivil behavior. As Shari Saunders and Diana Kardia put it, "Inclusive classrooms are places in which thoughtfulness, mutual respect, and academic excellence are valued and promoted." While faculty in all disciplines can strive for inclusive classrooms, the characteristics of these classrooms work especially well for teaching the content of history. In inclusive classrooms, content is explicitly viewed from multiple perspectives and the experiences of a range of groups are explored, and students understand that individuals' experiences, values, and perspectives influence how they construct knowledge.[98]

Instructors can do many things to foster an inclusive learning climate. We can set a welcoming tone on the first day of class (or even earlier in precourse communications and materials) with what we say and how we behave. Talking with even a few students before class (rather than planting ourselves firmly behind a podium or computer) shows to all the students our interest in who they are, especially if we continue that process with different students throughout the semester. We can acknowledge their individuality by asking them to privately share information about themselves—basic demographics, background, aspirations, interests, and especially what they think may affect them in the course. These might invite confidential disclosures of anxieties about course content and disabilities but also prompt sharing of skills, knowledge, and attitudes. We can make a clear effort to learn and use correctly pronounced names and students' preferred pronouns. Since students may be listening carefully to how we discuss course policies, we can reassure them. We can indicate our awareness of (and willingness to accommodate absences for) all religious holidays—not just Christian ones—and do so in a welcoming way. There's a dramatic difference between saying with annoyance, "If you have a disability, you'd better show me your documentation if you want extra time on exams," and saying, "I'm eager for all students to learn this material. If you need accommodations for a disability, you have a right to have those met, so let's make an appointment to talk soon." Tone is relevant to all students, not just those from specific groups. Research suggests that students in general perceive faculty as more approachable when they give a syllabus with a warmer "inviting" tone (as opposed to a "command" tone, which seems authoritarian and contractual).[99]

Our language can convey respect for our students. We can educate ourselves and use the terminology that groups of people prefer when referring to them (such as "people who use wheelchairs" instead of "wheelchair-bound" people or "LGBTQIA" instead of "homosexual"). When how to be respectful is less clear-cut, we can think carefully about (and be able to explain) why we have chosen to use "African American" as opposed to "black" (or vice versa) or "Latinx" rather than "Hispanic." We can avoid using masculine-gendered nouns or pronouns when we are referring to all people. When we talk about course materials, we can show our awareness that some students in the class may struggle to afford them by saying something like, "I realize this book is expensive, but you will use it a lot, so please find a way to access a copy. The campus bookstore has a limited number of used copies, and it's okay with me if you share one with a classmate, as long as you both get the reading done." We can go further and try to assign less expensive or open source materials. Research on cues suggests that what may seem like a minor or subtle thing to a person from a majority group actually sends a strong message to someone from a less advantaged group, and with some forethought, that message can be one of encouragement that signals they belong.[100]

A sense of belonging is a fundamental human need, and it matters in higher education, too. As one researcher puts it, "One of the most important questions that people ask themselves in deciding to enter, continue, or abandon a pursuit is, 'Do I belong?'"[101] Not having that sense is correlated with negative motivation and performance, whereas having a sense of belonging is correlated with engagement, achievement, and optimal functioning. Some students enter our classrooms assuming that they belong and don't need reassurances, but others, including some from traditionally marginalized or stigmatized groups, may not see many people like themselves on a campus or feel that sense of belonging. Those with high financial need may be working so many hours to help pay family bills or tuition that they have, as student Maybe Lee put it, "very little time to form friendships and have a social life."[102] Socioeconomic differences bombard students, noted one who had difficulty affording her books and a bus ticket home, who watched other students plan European vacations and wear $200 shirts. "College is a lonely place," reported Dane Christie. "I am surrounded by children of upper-middle-class America, and I can relate to none of their life experiences."[103] Ted White agreed, "It's total culture shock to be working class at an Ivy League school."[104] Pressured to pay off loans, working-class students may not even consider history as a major because they don't know what kind of job it could lead to. First-generation students can't ask parents for help on their papers or in choosing a major like many of their classmates do; as one put it, "There's a lot of things in college that professors expect us to know (but I don't)." Students with autism spectrum disorder may struggle with the mental processes related to planning, time management, and multitasking and with social life, which "was very difficult. I was never usually invited, nor did I enjoy attending crowded bars or parties . . . and never really found a niche." It can be worse, as another student explained. "I had to leave the dorms, because I was being teased and taunted all night. I was the joke of the dorm."[105] African American students at predominantly white institutions frequently worry they will be judged negatively by faculty or staff members, witness insulting behavior from other students, or hear assumptions that they aren't smart, are athletes, are poor, or only were accepted because of affirmative action.[106] Students from many marginalized groups lack role models among faculty and staff.

College may be difficult for those who encounter prejudice or constantly hear about disturbing events about people like themselves in the wider world, whether those be shootings of unarmed African Americans, hate crimes against LGBTQIA people, anti-immigrant diatribes, or sexual harassment victims in the Me Too movement ending their silence. Such experiences are painful, but we should remember that individual students are more than simply their group identities and their struggles. Many also bring tenacity, self-discipline, life lessons, and a willingness to work hard. The bottom line is that we can't control what our students experience in other areas of campus or the wider world, but we can affect what they experience in our course.[107]

Great instructors continue to learn, not just about their subject matter and teaching but also about their students. The first step is knowing what we don't know, because it's not difficult to learn about student experiences. There's plentiful research about different groups and abundant first-person accounts available with a few keystrokes in a web browser. Individual students are often eager for someone to listen to their personal stories outside of class time. I had two brothers with a serious chronic disease, so I came to my faculty role with a sense of how hard it can be for such students to make up for frequent absences due to illness and to ask for extensions, but I didn't have any knowledge or experience about what it's like to be an international student, much less the different experience for ones from Ghana and Japan. I can learn, and doing so enriches me.

Because we can unintentionally send a chilling message to some students, it's good to be aware of practices to avoid. We shouldn't put an individual on the spot by asking them to speak for a whole group of people (such as all African Americans, Catholics, men, immigrants, varsity athletes, or fraternity members). Besides putting enormous pressure on a student, such a request implies that everyone from that group is and thinks the same. We should avoid telling jokes about groups of people, interrupting students, and responding to student comments in class with sarcasm, ridicule, or condescension. We should avoid making assumptions about any individual student based on their membership in a group. We should avoid making statements with assumptions about our whole class, too, such as that all students own their own laptop, smartphone, or car; drink and party a lot; have parents who went to college; are Christian or have any religious affiliation; are heterosexual; subscribe to a particular political ideology; can go somewhere on spring break; will marry; or want to have children. We shouldn't prohibit the use of laptops, since some students have a legal right to that accommodation and allowing only those people to use them effectively "outs" their disability.[108] If we make cultural references to popular culture (television shows, music, or advertisements), we should not assume everybody is familiar with them. We should try to make sure that we aren't calling on men or women more often (or overlooking students from any group) and that our responses to student comments are evenhanded and based on the content of the individual contributions. We shouldn't overcompensate; overpraising, especially for mediocre contributions, can send a message of low expectations.[109]

Our words matter. Research suggests that if we sincerely strive to create an inclusive classroom environment where everyone feels they belong, we should tell our students that.[110] We can explicitly say that we know that each person is a complex individual with different components to their identities, that everyone's identities and backgrounds influence them, and that a diversity of experiences, viewpoints, and identities can be quite valuable for learning. (Research shows that it does.[111]) We shouldn't claim to be color-blind or immune to stereotypes, since people from stereotyped groups will rightfully be skeptical.[112] We can say that we hope to live up to our ideals for fairness, inclusion, and respect and that we welcome their input on how to achieve that. Then our actions must back up our words. If they don't, even if we had good intentions, we should apologize sincerely.

The things that faculty say and do constitute the foundation for a good classroom climate, and students are the cocreators of this climate.[113] We can take two important actions very early in the semester to help our students be a positive force. First, we should help them understand what we mean by "good class participation." This matters in any class where there will be discussion or student–student interactions. Students need to know whether speaking in class is an expectation or if they can opt out without penalty, whether asking a question is just as valued as offering a right answer, how much speaking is appropriate (and whether it's possible to contribute too frequently), if they should raise their hand before speaking or can just jump in, and whether offering a personal example is considered valuable anecdotal evidence or a distracting tangent. They should know whether it's permissible to look up a term or view the readings on their laptop during class. In particular, students need to know what's involved in respectful discourse, such as how best to handle disagreements with one another (criticizing the idea rather than the person who voiced it, not using inflammatory words like "idiotic" or "crazy"), not making assumptions about whole groups of people, and accurately portraying another person's position. Instructors can easily find examples of ground rules for class discussion to adapt. Proactively helping students understand civil discourse means that a hot moment is much less likely to occur (and if it does, gives faculty something to call on to reestablish civility).[114]

We cannot assume that students already know what we expect on these matters. Some of them are matters of instructor preference, and students have likely had instructors with different preferences. Students may also make assumptions based on what they see in politics, news media, or online. Learning situations are mediated through culture; when to speak, when to interrupt, and when to disagree and with whom are all affected by one's cultural background.[115] Even matters like making eye contact can be seen as respectful or disrespectful in different cultures. In addition, students are quite different from one another in their personalities; some may be confident and extroverted, comfortable speaking without much thinking time. Others will find participation quite risky and require encouragement; they may fear embarrassment, conflict, or appearing different.[116] Chapter 3 addresses how to facilitate effective discussions in more depth, but for now, the point is that it's good for us and for our students to be transparent about classroom etiquette.

We can establish positive norms in a variety of ways. The syllabus can describe our expectations, and we can explain them on the first day of class. Some instructors have students do a brief exercise to generate more buy-in. For example, individually or in small groups students can list the characteristics of productive or horrible class discussion they have witnessed, which can serve as a jumping-off point for the instructor to convey expectations and show where faculty and students have similar or different perspectives.[117] A bolder option is to have students themselves build the "class rules" or "community agreements," which can create strong feelings of ownership for them. Instructors can also show video examples of positive discussions or model one with a few colleagues. Of course, we can't just mention expectations on the first day and then never return to them; they need to be enforced and reinforced throughout the semester.[118]

The second early imperative is helping students getting to know one another. Meaningful student–student social interactions contribute to learning.[119] Students are more likely to take intellectual risks in the classroom when instructors have taken steps to set up a respectful environment and when they know that expressing their thoughts is a goal supported by the other students. Trust isn't possible without a sense of connectedness, so instructors should get the process started.[120] I like icebreakers that require students to find commonalities, however superficial, and ones that get students to really listen to each other by doing something like having them introduce one another to the class. It helps if we expect students to learn and use their names. Just focusing on getting to know someone can feel awkward, so my preference is to combine early social and instructional goals by giving students an interesting and challenging historical task for which it helps to have multiple people working on it. For example, on the first day of class, Peter Felten asked students to put ten images in chronological order as a way of getting them to think about how to analyze primary sources and what they already know about historic context.[121] Before leaping headlong into a discussion of potentially sensitive subjects, we aim to build a sense of connection and shared sense of purpose that will sustain students through more difficult tasks later in the course.[122]

If we aren't clear about expectations, student–student interactions in classrooms can go badly. While doing group projects, for example, sometimes students opt for an easy division of labor strategy that results in none of them learning the whole content deeply. Sometimes an individual member doesn't know how to contribute effectively or simply doesn't do their fair share of the work. "Social loafing" is an all-too-common, annoying experience, as seen in a Tweet that went viral: "When I die, I want my group project members to lower me into my grave . . . so that they can let me down one more time."[123] Fortunately, there are strategies for forestalling these problems, including creating ways to distinguish individual contributions; setting deadlines that scaffold the work and help prevent procrastination; using tools (e.g., Google docs) that ensure that each member shares their progress with the group and comments on the notes and ideas of others in the group; and requiring a self- and peer evaluation. In addition, I have recently taken twenty minutes before a long-term group project begins to ask students to reflect on what they dislike about group projects and what they like about them, and then quickly create collective expectations for positive behaviors for members of groups, including doing a fair share of the work, doing high quality work, communicating well, being easy to work with, and being reliable. We take time to think about how to talk with the others if there is a disagreement or concern about equitable workload. Since then, more of my groups have worked effectively, probably due to taking students' concerns seriously and empowering them to strategize about them.

Our best efforts to set up a positive and inclusive climate do not guarantee that all students will be able to perform at their full capacity. If we teach a lot of seventeen- to twenty-two-year-olds, we work with people in a life stage where they are still striving to develop their autonomy, manage their emotions, create healthy relationships, find their sense of purpose and competence, and establish their identity. Identity can be a pivotal dimension, involving comfort with one's body and physical appearance, gender and sexual orientation, racial and ethnic heritage, and other factors that make up a sense of self. Without a mature identity, students may feel threatened by alternative points of view and identities.[124] Uncertainty about the future, including what they'll be doing for a living, means young people may be very anxious. Students living on a residential campus may miss home or their former friends. As noted earlier, every student needs a sense of belonging, and this need has heightened importance during late adolescence.[125] Older students may have more stable social networks and more motivation and be less concerned about whether how they look or act is in tune with current trends. Still, they may have significant challenges related to meeting academic standards after a gap in their studies or from balancing competing demands of school, family, or work. Regardless of their age, chances are good that there will be people in our classes who are experiencing difficult things, such as short-term or chronic illness or disability, sexual harassment or rape, divorce or break-up (one's own or that of one's parents), the death or health crisis of a loved one, loss of a job, coming out, poverty or hunger, or the stress of moving or meeting new people. Things that may seem minor to faculty—like a roommate dispute or getting a lower grade than one was accustomed to—can distract from learning. So can something wonderful like falling in love. As psychologist Sarah Rose Cavanagh puts it, "Our students, in essence, are simmering in a giant vat of emotional soup."[126]

Although we can't prevent the impact of what Cavanagh calls "the dizzying emotional complexity and competing priorities of our students' lives," we can recognize them and consider how we want to respond when they affect course work. Some of us are comfortable granting extensions to someone in an especially trying situation. Others hold everyone to the deadlines but express personal concern and tell those students that we understand that a piece of work may not represent all they are capable of but is the best they could do in difficult circumstances. Students seem to appreciate this understanding most of all. For students in emotional crisis, we don't need to assume a role of therapist (for which most of us aren't trained) but can respond as a caring person by listening and checking whether they are familiar with the campus professionals who might be best equipped to help. We can make clear that we think asking for help is a smart strategy, not something to be embarrassed about. Concerned that some students in dire straits won't ask for help, some instructors institute a policy that allows every student to have an extension (twenty-four or forty-eight hours) once during the semester for any reason or to drop their lowest quiz score.

Regardless of the policies we adopt, it's best to try not to make assumptions about why students don't behave the way we want them to. Terry Doyle suggested that rather than assuming students are lazy, rude, or immature, we consider the possibility that they might not know how to behave, don't recognize social cues, or don't understand the effects of their actions.[127] This doesn't mean we don't hold them accountable, of course, especially for academic dishonesty or violations of other important policies. It just means that maybe we should check in before leaping to conclusions about their reasons. When I've asked what students were talking about in a distracting side conversation, I've learned that it's because I said something unclear in a lecture and the whole class was confused. When I once asked a normally attentive student why she was checking her phone, she reported that a friend needed to get to the hospital and she was expecting a text about whether she needed to take him. Repeatedly coming late to class could be due to disinterest or a lack of discipline; on the other hand, it could be a chronic illness or unexpectedly having the responsibility of driving a family member to work or school. I teach at a university that values community, where it's customary for faculty to notice when a student is frequently absent. My first impulse has sometimes been to communicate with the student with a warning or nagging tone, which seems to imply irresponsibility: "Don't you know you're missing a lot of material and in danger of failing?" Recently I began inquiring using a more neutral or concerned tone: "I've noticed you've missed classes recently and I'm concerned. What's up? Are you okay?" Now students tend to tell me the honest reason they're absent and appreciate my approach. Some continue to miss class and end up doing poorly; others rally and turn things around; and with others, the inquiry leads to a meaningful conversation about why things are challenging, whether they can turn things around (and if so, how to direct their efforts), or if it's smarter to drop a course.[128] I've found that I like the role of ally much better than that of nag or fault finder.

Stereotype Threat

Students are affected by their group identities. For decades, social psychologists have uncovered massive and distressing evidence of the phenomenon known as "stereotype threat." Stereotype threat is stress caused by being in a situation in which there exists a negative stereotype about one's identity. As Claude Steele, a pioneer in the field, describes it, "Negative stereotypes about our identities hover in the air around us. When we are in situations to which these stereotypes are relevant, we understand that we could be judged or treated in terms of them. If we are invested in what we're doing, we get worried;

we try to disprove the stereotype or avoid confirming it. We present ourselves in counter-stereotypical ways. We avoid situations where we have to contend with this pressure. It's not all-determining, but it persistently, often beneath our awareness, organizes our actions and choices, our lives."[129]

Stereotype threat has negative consequences. People influenced by stereotype threat simply do not perform as well as they do in other contexts. They underperform on all sorts of tasks, including mental ones (such as on verbal, mathematical, analytical, IQ, and memory tests) and physical ones (like putting a golf ball, driving, shooting free throws, and reaction time). Magnetic resonance imaging shows neuroscientists the exact part of the brain that fires when a person is under the stress of stereotype threat. Their heart rate and blood pressure rise. The threat affects a person's thinking: while worrying about confirming the stereotype, the mind races, raising self-doubt and constant monitoring about what's happening. Trying to deal with or suppress threatening thoughts takes up mental capacity, distracting someone from the task they're supposed to be working on, which hurts performance and general functioning, and which, in a vicious cycle, further intensifies one's vigilance for threat and the attention diverted to those concerns. Frequent exposure to stereotype threat can affect long-term health. The stress of constantly feeling like they have to prove themselves may influence students' decisions about what classes to take, what discipline to major in, and whether to remain in college altogether.[130]

Stereotype threat also may lead to unwise academic strategies. In one study of math students, some African American students adopted an approach that was intensely independent, private, and hard-working, and when they struggled, they doubled the number of practice problems they did instead of studying with others or seeking help. Researchers called this strategy "over-efforting." Those students also got discouraged, worried whether their problems reflected their own or their group's inability, and wondered if they really belonged at college. By working in such a solitary fashion, they were not aware that other students also experienced anxieties and difficulties. In contrast, the white and Asian students in the study had more effective study strategies. They more frequently worked in groups, which helped them focus more on concepts and less on arithmetic, and gave them a chance to correct misunderstandings quickly. They were also more willing to seek help and drop a course if advised to.[131] Seeking help when struggling may seem like an obviously wise strategy to instructors, but it's not always an easy or straightforward process for students. Students may come from a culture that prizes the ability to figure things out on one's own, where needing help is seen as a weakness. Even if they do decide to ask for assistance, they may not know the best place to go for it; they may opt for informal choices like friends or family as opposed to the instructor or a university learning or writing center.[132]

Because there are stereotypes about almost every group, no one is entirely immune to this phenomenon. But not everyone is affected in all situations; the phenomenon is contextual. For example, white male sprinters did worse on certain athletic tasks only when the tasks were framed as tests of "natural ability," which they were stereotyped as lacking; when researchers intentionally tried to trigger stereotype threat, African Americans underperformed on the GRE, aware of the stereotype that African Americans don't do well on standardized tests; and college women performed worse than men on tests that measured mathematical ability, an area which some believe women are inferior.[133] How is this relevant for historians? Steele described the example of a white student who was hyperaware that he was one of only two white students in the class of forty-five taking an African American history course. In an interview with Steele, the student explained that throughout the semester, he was trying to prove himself as a good person; he was trying to avoid being perceived by others as the stereotype of an insensitive or racist white person. As a result, he was very careful in his comments, worried about whether he really understood things correctly, felt tense and less confident than usual, and felt as though he was multitasking. At the same time, he observed African American students who were thriving—unselfconscious, involved, and smart— in a class where they were in the majority. The setting, Steele noted, affected his performance.[134] We can imagine a similar fear of being seen as prejudiced for a man in a women's history course, a heterosexual in an LGBTQIA history class, a Latina in an Asian history course, and so on. Being the only one of a few of a certain type of student (perhaps a woman in a military history course, a conservative in a Marxist history course, or the only African American in a course on a predominantly white campus) is not the same as being stereotyped, but it also heightens one's anxieties.[135] Unfortunately, these threats based on identity exist in our culture, prior to anything an individual faculty member may have done or said.

The good news is that instructors can do "quite feasible things" to reduce stereotype threat.[136] One way is through the feedback we give on assignments. Psychologists tested three different types of feedback to African American students, a group whose members frequently did not trust the comments they received from their professors: one type was fairly neutral, simply focusing on weaknesses and strategies for improvement; another prefaced suggestions with assuring and positive statements; and a third indicated that instructors had used high standards in judging the work and conveyed the belief that the student was capable of meeting those standards. It turned out that the last approach (referring to high standards and expressing confidence in the ability to meet them) increased the students' motivation and receptiveness to feedback. The same type of feedback also helped women in lab sciences improve their work.[137] Researchers have also tested various ways of putting white students more at ease before having a conversation with an African American about a controversial race-related topic. One might expect that it would be effective to tell participants that there would be no recriminations or judgment about anything they said in the conversation or saying that differences in perspective were valued and appreciated. However, neither of these proved as effective as saying that tension is natural in those sorts of conversations and that the students should treat the conversation as a learning experience. Those who heard these two phrases literally placed their chairs closer to their conversation partners. The researchers found that framing the difficult conversations as learning experiences was better at lessening tension. This approach suggested that it is natural for everyone to make mistakes; and when mistakes were made, they weren't viewed as immutable signs of prejudice.[138]

Researchers recommend a few other ways to reduce stereotype threat. First, we need to be attentive to the cues we send, especially about belonging and fairness. Cues are the messages we communicate about inclusion, which can include our words and tone, course content and authors, messages about availability, and things in the physical surroundings like images, classroom setup, sounds, and the accessibility of the space. We can teach students that worries about belonging in college are normal and transient.[139] We can put students into diverse groups when working on tasks.[140] Fostering intergroup conversations among students from different backgrounds can help those from minority groups realize that other (nonminority) students encounter some similar difficulties related to the material and the stresses of college life and that their identity is not the sole cause of negative experiences.[141] We can be transparent in sharing with the whole class strategies that we know to be effective for learning history and improving one's writing. As mentioned in chapter 1, we can be transparent about expectations for assignments and how they will be graded and reassure students of fairness by grading them anonymously. Before an exam, we can try to activate their identities as smart college students (rather than their gender, race, or ethnicity).

■

Clearly, there's much about teaching that we cannot control, including who our students are and what they bring with them. Our students are unique individuals influenced by their identities related to race and ethnicity, gender, socioeconomic class, sexual orientation, religious affiliation, and so forth. Many components affect their learning, including their background, experiences, attitudes, values, interests, health, living situation, academic skills, previous schooling, mindsets, and prior knowledge.[142] Some students come with advantages for learning, some with challenges, and many have some of both. We cannot control how the world and the academic world are not level playing fields. However, we can set up classrooms that reflect our values and pay attention to the research about how to give all our students a good chance of success.[143] We can be transparent about expectations and strategies for success, promote a growth mindset, provide opportunities for growth, connect with student values, seek an optimal level of challenge, foster an inclusive classroom environment, help students know they belong, and communicate our desire to be a supportive instructor who is concerned about student learning. We can take heart from the fact that strategies shown to mitigate stereotype threat, belonging uncertainty, or a fixed mindset help more than just those from traditionally disadvantaged groups; they are effective teaching strategies that can help all students.

Over the past few decades, there has been a movement in higher education toward being "student-centered." Although many faculty have embraced the new perspective, others have worried that it connoted students (and their parents) as consumers, to whom faculty should give whatever they want, such as easy work, entertaining classrooms, and high grades. Some have feared that shifting the focus to the students could create a slippery slope in which highly educated professors could be overruled by entitled "customers." That skewing of the notion of student-centeredness couldn't be further from what I'm proposing, which is that faculty adopt a "learning-centered" model.

In a learning-centered model, students' learning is our ultimate goal.[144] This model assumes that learning depends on what each student does (not just what the instructor does) and that students will perform differently from each other based on differences in comprehension, effort, and skills. It assumes that academic challenges are necessary and, if handled astutely, may lead to positive growth and even transformation. It also assumes that there are many ways we experts in history can design and implement courses to increase the odds of student novices learning history. In addition to listening to the scholarship about good practices, we must pay attention to our students.

In his book, subtitled *How the Mind Works and What It Means for the Classroom*, cognitive scientist Daniel Willingham concluded that knowing students is one of the most important things an instructor can do. He recognized that this sounds like little more than common sense: "Your grandmother could have told you it was a good idea. Can cognitive science do no better than that?"[145] In fact, Willingham asserted, cognitive science contributes by explaining why it's important to know our students. Understanding how the brain works helps explain why prior knowledge gives learners an important neural advantage, which is why we should try to activate it; and why incorrect prior knowledge and assumptions are so problematic and thus why it's wise to start the semester by figuring out what students know (and assume) about our specific content and the discipline of history. Similarly, knowing who our students are and what they value helps spur motivation. Understanding students' emotions and the impact of their identities, especially what excites them and upsets them, helps us avoid resistance or disengagement and instead turns difficult content into material that catalyzes the deepest thinking and change.

While psychology and educational research tell us we should know our students, it is also okay to justify it based on common sense. Students are the reason we have jobs; their learning is our purpose. Trying to teach them certainly can be difficult and frustrating, but success—and making connections with them—brings great satisfaction. Knowing what confuses and challenges our students is a precondition to helping them learn. As the designers of the History Learning Project discovered,

we don't have to simply accept (or complain about) student misunderstandings. Instead, we can dig in exactly where those bottlenecks are.
They concluded, "By reframing this problem [of student misunder-
standing], not as a misfortune to be endured, but rather as an opportunity to gain knowledge about our students and how we teach them,
new strategies for teaching evolved quite naturally."[146] With that encouragement, we turn toward consideration of specific, day-to-day
teaching strategies.

3   How We Teach

Once we have thought carefully about the content that we most value and the people we will be teaching, it's time to consider our methods—how we prompt students to think about and use our content during and outside of class. There are many different teaching strategies available to us. We should choose ours intentionally—opting for ones that achieve our goals—in a way that is informed by evidence. This chapter describes some teaching techniques that work well in history courses, sharing evidence about how best to use them. Before doing so, I offer six principles that should inform instruction regardless of the particular strategies we adopt.

First, we should hone our skills in asking questions that target the specific types of historical thinking we want to promote. Second, we should incorporate active learning. Third, we should give students opportunities to practice historical ways of thinking and communicating in a low-stakes context accompanied by formative feedback. Fourth, we should hold students accountable for doing the work we assign, especially the readings. Fifth, we should align our day-to-day class meetings with our main learning goals and assessments. Using backward design leads to sensible decisions about readings, schedules, and teaching activities. Finally, we should pay special attention to beginnings and endings, making sure we get off to a good start and provide the closure that promotes understanding and retention. These principles lay the foundation for intentional, inclusive, and effective teaching.

Principles to Guide Teaching

Ask Effective Questions

Questions are the entry point to the discovery of knowledge, the key to intellectual growth.

ROLAND CHRISTENSEN

Questions promote thinking before they are answered. It is in the interstices between the question and the answer that minds turn.

MARYELLEN WEIMER

Whatever the specific history content we're teaching, we need to stimulate students' thinking. As Roland Christensen and Maryellen Weimer point out, one of the best ways to do that is by asking questions.[1] Asking questions is a fundamental skill for history instructors. It's powerful because it works across a variety of teaching methods—in discussions, lectures, and small group activities—and at any moment in the instructional process. Outside of class, good questions guide students to ponder the readings. During class, they evoke curiosity, prompt analysis, and help students articulate their ideas. They function at the beginning of a unit to prime students for learning, in the middle to assess how well things are going, and at the end (on exams, papers, and projects) to consolidate it.

Throwing out just any old question isn't effective, however. Some questions are problematic, including ones that are:

- *Confusing*—Examples are run-on questions or asking too many things at once.
- *Closed*—Closed questions (in contrast to open-ended ones) have a single factual right answer, such as a yes or no question, which usually doesn't lead anywhere.
- *Boring or too easy*—These questions don't have sufficient interest, complexity, or ambiguity, such as "Was Stalin cruel?"
- *Too difficult*—Examples include ones that are not rooted in any course material, so students have nothing to base an answer on, which may lead to silence or bad guesses.
- *Leading*—Leading questions are comments disguised as questions, such as, "Don't you think the author meant . . . ?" or "That was a great article, wasn't it?" Because students can tell what the instructor thinks, they have little incentive to answer.
- *Impatient*—If we don't allow enough time for students to think about a question, or if we answer it ourselves almost immediately, we aren't asking real questions. There's little reason for students to respond if they know the instructor will supply the answer.[2]

Good questions are clear, interesting, pitched to an appropriate level of challenge, and purposeful. To prompt higher-level thinking, we ask open-ended interpretive questions. Although sometimes we need to check that students understand the basic concepts and facts, better questions require students to use information, rather than simply repeat it. One research study found that the most effective questions had four characteristics: they were divergent, higher level, straightforward, and structured. Divergent questions encourage more than one answer. Higher-level ones require intellectual skills such as analysis, evaluation, or synthesis. Straightforward ones are clearly expressed. For the most important questions, clarity might involve expressing them both orally and on a slide or the board. This practice helps students with disabilities and all students who want to understand before they respond. Structured questions are not completely wide open, but provide some focus or direction. An example might be, "What are some similarities and differences between X and Y?"[3]

Different types of questions serve different purposes. To choose the best questions, we need to know exactly what we want. At the beginning of class, for example, are we hoping to provoke curiosity or elicit students' prior knowledge? In the middle of class, what kind of historical analysis do we want students to do? Do we want them to compare people or time periods? Do we want them to consider causation, context, motivation, or the effects or implications of events? Are we hoping to get them to see issues from different perspectives? Are we hoping to get them to evaluate other people's arguments, or do we want them to build their own? In table 2 I have synthesized the suggestions

---

Table 2. Types of Questions

Interpretation	What do you think the author/source meant by the quote, "..."
	Who do you think was the audience for this source?
	What was the purpose of this source?
	What assumptions does the author make?
	To what degree do you trust this source?
	What are the limitations of this source?
	What can we conclude from this source? What remains unknown?

(Continued on next page)

Perspective-taking	From whose perspective are we hearing? How might X have felt or responded? What about Y? What alternative arguments might be made?
Evaluation	Would you characterize the X period as effective or ineffective? Which leader's actions proved shrewdest? What adjective would you use to describe the outcomes of . . . (the New Deal)? Which historian's argument is most persuasive? Do you agree with Smith's argument that ". . ."?
Warm-up/ remembering	What image/moment/quotation most stands out from the reading/document/lecture? How would you finish this sentence? (Mao Zedong . . .)
Prior knowledge	Which of the following do you think was true of . . . (Columbus)? What do you know about . . . ?

Prediction	[After instructor relates a short story], what do you think
	    happened next? How do you think this story ended?
	Given what you know so far, how would you expect . . . (Eva
	    Perón to govern)?
	Which do you think would have . . . (Costa Rica or Nicaragua)?

Comprehension of information	What were the main points of . . . ? How would you explain . . . in your own words? What was . . . (the Monroe Doctrine)?
Application of a concept	Which of the people we read about most embodied the concept of . . . (noblesse oblige)? Which of these people was . . . ("conservative" or "radical")? Which of these examples constitutes . . . (plagiarism)? Which of these sources is "scholarly"?
Causation or motives	Why did . . . ? Why else? Why then? Why do you think [an alternative] didn't happen? Was it inevitable that . . . ?

Context	Why isn't it surprising that this happened at this time?
	Why might it be surprising that this happened when it did?
Effects, implications, significance	How did this affect . . . ? How else?
	Why did this matter to people at the time?
	Which effects were short-term and which long-term?
	So what? Why should we care? Does this have any contemporary significance?
	What lessons do you draw from this?
Reasoning	What is the author's argument?
	Why does he or she think that?
	What evidence or examples does the author use?
	Do you find that persuasive?
	Why do you think that? How do you know? Do you have evidence or an example of that?
Prioritization	Which quotation best captures . . . ?
	Which causative factor would you say was most important?
	Which effects were most significant?
Relationships/ comparison	Does this event/period/person/source/reading remind you of anything else we've studied?
	How was this similar to . . . ?
	How was this different from . . . ?
Generalizations/ synthesis	How do we add this up? From all these sources, what are the conclusions we can draw?
	Now that you've studied . . . , what advice would you give (a world leader, activist, voter) considering . . . ?
Personal reflection	How did you react to/feel about this topic/reading?
	What is your personal takeaway?
	How does this material connect to anything you've experienced, thought about, heard about in the news or in another class?

(Continued on next page)

(Continued from previous page)

Metacognition	What have we just learned?
	Why did we learn it (that is, how does it fit into the course/unit goals)?
	How confident are you of your grasp of the material?
	Can you put that in your own words?
	What still seems unclear to you? How might you become more clear?
	What does this make you wonder about?
	How would you find out . . . ? How would you approach the task of . . . ?
	How does this connect to other things you know?
	Can you imagine another time when you might use this knowledge or skill?

and categories of a number of different discussion experts with specific questions that prompt different types of historical thinking.[4]

Incorporate Active Learning

The one who does the work is the one who does the learning. If students are to learn, then it must be their brains that do the work. We must be the designers and facilitators of that work.

TERRY DOYLE

As Terry Doyle pointed out, our job is to spur students' thinking with the intellectual activities we ask them to do.[5] We commonly ask students to write, for example. Writing comes in many forms and may be graded or ungraded, formal (such as in essays or projects) or informal (in list making, note taking, freewriting, outlining, thesis writing, commenting on a discussion board, or tweeting). Although specific writing tasks vary in difficulty and cognitive requirements, in all cases writing is an action, something that engages a student's brain. We also frequently ask students to communicate orally—in whole class discussions, one-on-one or small group conversations, or formal presentations. There are good reasons to do this, because the act of trying to articulate one's ideas helps a person learn.[6] The second part of this chapter describes some of the intellectual activities historians can usefully ask students to do.

The topic of active learning inspires strong feelings, partly because it is often contrasted with lectures.[7] In one acrimonious exchange about the relative merits of the two methods, historian Molly Worthen argued that listening to a lecture is a valuable "exercise in mindfulness and attention building, a mental workout that counteracts the junk food of nonstop social media." She characterized active learning as a "craze," and "the latest development in a long tradition of complaining about boring professors, flavored with a dash of that other great American pastime, populist resentment of experts."[8] Energetic rebuttals ensued. Medievalist Josh Eyler criticized Worthen's article as "snarky, condescending, [and] elitist," and flawed because it relied on "disproven notions of teaching."[9]

Students weighed in, too. Undergraduates from the University of Illinois said that Worthen didn't understand that at a large university, students hear "lecture after lecture after lecture. For three to four hours of our day, we sit in cavernous rooms—with up to 800 strangers—where the professor doesn't know our name, let alone ask us to speak." Too often the lecture was "just a monotone recitation of the PowerPoint presentation, or a regurgitation of the textbook," giving them little incentive to attend class. Although some instructors inspired and engaged them, those professors were "too few and far between." Even students who wanted to ask questions sometimes found it "intimidating to approach the stage, especially if the professor has a 'you should probably just know this by now' attitude." They concluded that "Condemning or celebrating the lecture isn't, in the end, as useful as understanding what we need. So please ask us."[10]

Unfortunately, such polarized debates tend to dichotomize teaching strategies and shed little light on the more important question: when and how should we use which methods?[11] It is useful to think of instructional strategies on a continuum, each with different levels of student activity and engagement, different kinds of learning, and different depths of learning. For example, lecturing, when done at appropriate times and effectively, can stimulate thinking and incorporate active learning. Indeed, research exists about the most effective ways to lecture (described later). Lectures that are "continuous exposition by the teacher" for the whole class period, however, tend to result in less student learning, poor retention, surface learning, and student passivity and inattention.[12] Of course, if ill-conceived or poorly implemented, active learning strategies may be unproductive, too.[13] However, effective incorporation of well-chosen active learning techniques can increase students' engagement, deepen their thinking, and lead to more lasting learning.

"Active learning" is an umbrella term referring to a variety of different types of learning, including cooperative, collaborative, discovery, experiential, problem-based, and inquiry-based, some of which involve students working with other students. Although these methods differ somewhat, they have certain things in common. As Elizabeth Barkley puts it, "Active learning means the mind is actively engaged . . . that students are dynamic participants in their learning and that they are reflecting on and monitoring both the processes and the results of their learning."[14] The core components, then, are that students do tasks that promote learning, are engaged in the activities (not "checked out"), and think about what they're doing and understanding.

Why incorporate active learning strategies? Constructionist learning theory posits that students must interact with content—that professors cannot simply transmit understanding to students. Brain research supports this theory. As we saw in chapter 2, learning is a process in which the learner builds her mind by adding to and changing her existing neural networks. Each individual has to make an idea, concept, or skill her own.[15] In his book subtitled *Putting the Research on Learning into Practice*, Terry Doyle summarized fifteen years of cognitive research about attention, understanding, and how the brain processes and stores information in long-term memory. Doyle concluded that research tells us, "The one who does the work is the one who does the learning."[16] Unfortunately, in some conventional-style lectures, the instructor is working hard, but the students aren't.

Research studies on active learning methods support the cognitive science. Designing research studies to compare the benefits of different instructional methods is tricky, because there are many variables to control. Despite the challenges, one careful assessment of the research on active learning concluded that the empirical support for its improving student learning is "extensive" and "compelling."[17] Another meta-analysis examined 225 different studies comparing traditional lecturing and active learning in STEM classes and found that student performance on exams improved in active learning sections.[18] Studies in other disciplines and on specific types of active learning, such as discussions and cooperative learning, suggest that active learning methods are more effective at engaging students in higher-level and conceptual learning; long-term retention of what's been learned; critical thinking; exploration of ambiguous or controversial materials; examination of attitudes; and encouraging nonsurface approaches to learning. In addition to greater achievement, active learning often brings other benefits, such as building relationships, self-esteem, and positive attitudes toward the university.[19] Not surprisingly, then, national surveys of teaching faculty show that over the past twenty-five years, faculty across disciplines have been consistently diversifying their teaching approaches and strategies to engage students and promote critical thinking skills.[20]

This research matters for teaching history because many of our goals involve critical thinking, interpreting ambiguous sources, cultivating judgment, and understanding the construction of knowledge. We can see this by reviewing some of the AHA Tuning Project's learning outcomes for history majors:

- Explain and justify multiple causes of complex events and phenomena using conflicting sources.
- Describe past events from multiple perspectives.
- Identify, summarize, appraise, and synthesize other scholars' historical arguments.
- Collect, sift, organize, question, synthesize, and interpret complex material.
- Generate substantive, open-ended questions about the past and develop research strategies to answer them.
- Apply historical knowledge and historical thinking to contemporary issues.[21]

The verbs in these outcomes represent complex intellectual tasks that students of history should be able to do—not simply watch their instructors or authors do. History SOTL confirms that, for most students, observing a professor weave a sophisticated argument is not sufficient to teach them how to do it themselves. "Students will need to learn this by doing it," concluded Leah Shopkow. "If we want students to understand how arguments are created, they need practice creating arguments. If we want them to determine whether a particular use of evidence is appropriate or inappropriate, they need to practice finding and using evidence and getting feedback on how to do it better. In other words, they have to practice being historians, at least in a scaffolded way."[22]

Offer Practice and Feedback

As we've seen, historical thinking does not come naturally for many students—there are many bottlenecks where novices get stuck. As instructors, then, we should consider "*how* students make the leap from being exposed to material to actually learning something worthwhile."[23] We help students make that leap, according to history SOTL researchers and cognitive scientists, by asking them to practice the various mental skills that we want them to learn. Thinking occurs in the part of our brains called working memory, which has a limited capacity. The only way to become better at thinking—more fluent and more efficient—is to make an intellectual process "automatic," because automatic processes don't require space in our working memory. Thus we should unpack the various intellectual skills students need to master and use a multistep process for teaching them: first, we instruct and/or model, then we give students opportunities to practice (and coach them in that practice), and subsequently we fade out of the picture and let students do it on their own.[24]

We must not overlook the first step. If we don't explicitly instruct students how to do historical skills, those who are most likely to succeed will be those who have already been exposed to our disciplinary ways. This privileges some students and penalizes others based on their background. If we want to provide a level playing field, we should take a little time for explicit instruction. I believe this transparent instruction and practice is an ethical obligation. Of course it's tempting to speed past it because we don't want to "waste" class time or because we assume that students already know how to do something. Unfortunately, our assumptions can be wrong, and sometimes we don't realize when we're making assumptions. "No matter how organized and animated my lectures, most students simply could not perform well on the midterms and final essay exams," Charles Bonwell recalled. "I then realized that I had never explicitly taught students to do this [thinking]. Assigned them papers, yes; tested them, yes; taught them how to be successful at the task, no. And yet, like most other instructors, I despaired of my students' inability to 'think critically' when addressing what I perceived as straightforward questions. . . . Finally I decided that I needed to help students develop those critical thinking skills."[25]

"Work on the hard parts" is good advice for those performing sports, music, or historical thinking, but simply repeating a process doesn't improve performance unless there is "conscious effort invested in understanding the task better."[26] Practice should be deliberate, focused on specific goals, and facilitated by instructors who provide targeted feedback.[27] Practice is especially beneficial when done on low-stakes (ungraded or lightly graded) work while students are first trying out new ways of thinking or working with new material.[28] Low-stakes tasks lower students' anxiety (and increase motivation) because making a mistake doesn't have serious ramifications.[29] We are familiar with the value of targeted feedback when it comes to learning a new physical skill (like a weight-lifting technique) or a foreign language. We know it's much better for someone to inform us if we are doing it wrong—and to be told when we're just starting out rather than spending a lot of time practicing it incorrectly. Psychologists note that "illusions of fluency" represent a fundamental obstacle for learners and that in general, both instructors and students underestimate the amount of practice students need.[30]

Our feedback on a small bit of practice is known as "formative" assessment, which is quite different from a formal grade (known as "summative" assessment). In general, formative feedback happens during learning rather than at the end of a unit. Instead of judging a performance, formative feedback aims to inform instruction and learning. Rather than quantitative feedback, formative feedback tends to be qualitative.[31] This feedback is most useful when it's specific, not vague. For foreign language instruction, for example, it might be "Remember how we pronounce a *j* in Spanish." For weight lifting it might be, "Do you see the position of your elbow? That's exactly right." For a history essay outline it might be, "Have you considered any examples from the sixteenth century?" or "It's great that you're including evidence from lots of primary sources." Besides benefiting students, providing opportunities for practice helps instructors, who learn how well students understand the material in time to help them improve if they don't. Ultimately, it results in better quality learning.

Some instructors might balk when they imagine the time required to provide formative feedback. Before jumping to conclusions, it's important to realize that there are many alternatives to writing comments on every student's work. These will be described in the next chapter and include giving group feedback and showing examples of excellent and weak work.

In a course where students need to learn how to interpret primary sources, a teacher could apply the process of instruct, offer opportunities for practice, give feedback, and fade in the following steps:

1. During the first class meeting, the instructor demonstrates how to analyze a source. "First I try to figure out what kind of source it is and think about the context when it was created. In this case, we have some hints. . . . Then I concentrate on what the main messages are. In this case. . . . Then I go back and think about who created this and for what purpose. . . ."

2. Immediately afterward, the class breaks into smaller groups to analyze a different source. After they have worked on it, the instructor facilitates discussion of their reasoning, asks for alternative interpretations, and gives positive reinforcement for sensible interpretations.

3. At the end of class, the instructor reviews the approach historians use (i.e., summarizing the various steps to take or questions to ask in a heuristic).

4. For homework, students interpret some new primary sources, practicing the process just modeled.

5. During the next class period, the instructor facilitates discussion of those sources so students receive feedback about what they successfully figured out themselves, and they correct, add to, or otherwise annotate their notes.

6. The instructor posts an example of a well-annotated source on a learning management system, so students can consult it when needed.

7. The instructor keeps assigning primary sources and integrating them into class discussions and increases the challenge by making the sources progressively more complex.

8. On the next exam, students analyze one source they've already read (to give credit for work already done) and one that is new (to assess their understanding of the process and ability to transfer the knowledge to a new situation).

Skills that are especially difficult can be improved through scaffolding. The metaphor of scaffolding alludes to adding structure and support (as a painter might use in reaching high places). In teaching, scaffolding means relieving some of the "cognitive load" of a complex intellectual task so that a particular aspect is isolated and practiced. Eventually, after students develop greater facility with that task, instructors remove some of the supports. In a research seminar, for example, instructors frequently isolate different skills and tasks, such as finding

appropriate scholarly sources, writing a historiographical section, crafting a thesis, creating an outline, and writing topic sentences; they work
on these steps one at a time, before putting all the component parts together.[32] When teaching students to find the argument in a scholarly
article, an instructor might scaffold by having students practice reading
the first and last few paragraphs of numerous articles (rather than having
them read the whole articles) until they're good at finding the thesis.
When they're learning to do Chicago-style citations, we might have
students find the errors in some examples we provide before having
them create their own citations.

Hold Students Accountable

Although we should adopt methods that support students, we also need to challenge them. Without an appropriate level
of challenge, students will be bored or not learn anything significant.
One crucial component of challenge is holding students accountable
for the work they are supposed to do. Too often, evidence suggests,
students don't do the readings we assign—or they only do a fraction of
them, or they read them superficially.[33] As a result, they are unprepared
to deepen their learning during class. If a substantial number of the students aren't prepared, we can't have high-quality, sustained, and engaging discussions; we can't ask students to connect what they read to previous materials or to new content on which we're going to lecture. Other
common ways that students may not assume responsibility include
mentally checking out during lectures, allowing other students to do all
the talking in discussions, or "freeloading" during group work.[34] Too
often, we allow or even enable these phenomena through our actions
(like lecturing on the reading), lack of actions, expectations, or course
incentive structure. Unfortunately, bad behaviors exhibited in the beginning of the semester only tend to get worse.

When I propose that faculty hold students accountable, I don't mean
by nagging. Instead, I propose that we design the course so that students
understand what they are expected to do, get them doing it right away,
make it worthwhile for them to do it, and have consequences if they
don't. "Social norms aren't etched in stone," observed Jay Howard, who
studied student behavior during discussions. "We can help change
them."[35] Ensuring accountability will eliminate most of the typical problems, get students into the habit of engaging with the readings and class
activities, and make us much happier with what happens during class.

How can we get students to do the reading? Obviously we would like to simply appeal to their intrinsic motivation. As we know, however, all of us have things competing for our time and attention, and students make choices about their priorities. Research suggests that students make decisions about whether to do the reading based on whether they will have to hand in some kind of homework, will be tested on the reading, or will have to speak publicly about it.[36] If the readings are important, allocating a portion of the final grade to class preparation/reading only makes sense. "Reward what you value," advise the authors of *How Learning Works*.[37] Students might demonstrate to us that they have done the reading in a number of ways.

One option is giving quizzes, either regularly scheduled or unannounced. The benefit of pop quizzes is that because students don't know when they will occur, they get in the habit of preparing every day. Whichever format, frequency helps—and it's important to start giving quizzes very early in the semester. If they are pop quizzes, they should only cover major points or key aspects of the reading, not details, because questions geared at the factual level reinforce surface rather than deep approaches to reading.[38] It's better to ask one or two open-ended short-answer questions that a student can't answer without having completed and understood the reading. If we want to ask questions that require higher-level analysis, or if we want students to take notes on details or specific evidence in the readings, it's useful to provide reading questions in advance or allow students to consult their notes during the quizzes. Whether we administer these quizzes at the beginning of class or before class (on a learning management system), we should make them easy to grade (see next chapter). The bonus that comes from having students do some kind of writing at the beginning of class means that the material moves to the front of their minds and they are primed for doing something with it during class.

Instead of a quiz, we can require students to bring with them some evidence that they have thought about the readings. That evidence might be notes, an outline or summary, answers to specific questions, a couple great quotations or pieces of evidence, questions they have, or annotated primary sources. Students might be required to have this work with them (i.e., to be their "ticket in the door") or post them to a learning management system before the beginning of class. Alternatively, we can collect these notes on unannounced occasions (or do spot checks that they have them). One benefit of requiring students to bring their work to class is that they have it available during discussions. On the other hand, if students submit their work online before class, we can peek at a sample to find out "just in time" whether there were aspects of the reading that students struggled with or really want to discuss so that we can address them during class.[39]

Instructors can also encourage accountability by "cold calling" on random students to talk about the reading. If we like this option, at the beginning of the semester we should warn students that we'll be doing it, so they understand the potential for discomfort or embarrassment if they don't prepare. (We should also think carefully about how we respond when students say, "I don't know," so that their embarrassment doesn't turn into humiliation or resentment.) Another option is assigning a task that requires students to use the content from the reading.

The bottom line is that there should be consequences for not doing the reading and a clear payoff for having done it. How much of the course grade should preparation count for? It's up to us. One study suggests 5 percent is too low.[40] I've often used around 15–20 percent, because I want to reward consistent effort in the foundational daily work of the course and exact a penalty for those who don't put in the effort. For me, allocating a substantial part of the grade to reading is worthwhile, because I've chosen the readings carefully, really want the students to engage with them, and my plan for what happens during class depends on them being prepared. Simply put, students learn more deeply and perform better on the bigger assessments (exams, essays, etc.) when they read well. Students realize this and often appreciate being "forced" to do the work.[41]

We have another lever for spurring high-quality preparation for class: the readings that we assign. It's wise to choose really good readings—interesting, meaningful, and accessible ones—for the beginning of the semester, and make sure that students use them during class. This helps reinforce that it's worth the time and effort to complete them.[42] (Save the drier, more theoretical works for after students realize there's a good reason for reading them.) It's also useful for faculty to "sell" the readings a bit by letting students know why we've assigned a specific selection, how it fits into the course, and how it will help them succeed. As we consider how much reading to assign, it's good to remember our quest to find that sweet spot of challenge. Assigning more reading may make us feel like we're rigorous, but it isn't always wisest. Ideally, we assign material that's clearly relevant to our purpose (maybe that's only some of a book, instead of all of it) and an amount that our students (not PhD candidates) can and will do well.

Because we are experts, we don't always realize how long it takes novices to read the same material we read. It's hard to predict how long it will take students to read something, because that depends on many factors: students' abilities, the purpose for reading (are they supposed to just grasp the big ideas, understand the meaning of everything, or deeply engage with the material?), and the difficulty of the text (including the number of new concepts and terms). As we get to know our students, we can ask them how long it takes to prepare for class and decide if that's reasonable. Alternatively, we can try a course workload estimator.[43]

To improve the odds that all students have a chance to succeed, we should also give some instruction in how to read the kinds of material we assign. Students don't automatically approach texts the way we do. (For example, they often highlight passages but don't really interrogate meaning or interact with the content in margins with stars, question marks, or comments.) Norms for historical writing are different from those in other disciplines, and even within history, scholarly articles are very different from textbooks or monographs.[44] Scholars like Saundra McGuire have described general strategies for effective reading that boost comprehension, including previewing the big picture of the selection and its component parts, thinking about the purpose of the assignment, crafting questions about it, reading actively, and stopping regularly to paraphrase.[45] Peter Filene created a handout describing strategies for reading historical monographs efficiently (not word-for-word) while honing in on their argument. (I was his teaching assistant and wished someone had shared those strategies with me before I got to graduate school.) Discussing the handout only took a few minutes, and research confirms it is well worth the investment.[46] If we know that students will be using websites to learn about historical periods or events, we should teach them how to evaluate the credibility of claims they see.[47] The same advice goes for studying; many students think rereading material is an effective strategy, when in fact asking questions about it, explaining concepts aloud, writing summaries, and testing oneself are better strategies, especially when spaced out rather than crammed the night before. A little bit of explicit instruction goes a long way toward empowering students to become independent, effective, active readers who understand what they have read.[48]

Stage 3 of Backward Design: Align Teaching and
Learning Activities with Goals and Assessments

Which readings should I assign? What questions should I ask? What should I have students actively doing? On which tasks should I give students practice and feedback?

We answer all those questions by first consulting our fundamental goals. As we know from chapter 1, articulating what we most want students to learn is the first step of backward course design. After that, we decide how students will show us that they have learned—what kind of big assignments, exams, projects, or other materials will serve as evidence. Once we've decided on those assessments, we have a better idea about which teaching and learning activities will enable students to perform well on them. By knowing at the beginning of the semester how we are going to assess students, we know exactly which ideas, concepts, and skills need special attention throughout the semester. Those are the things for which we need to provide instruction, practice, scaffolding, and feedback. For a well-integrated course, what we do at the day-to-day level is aligned with our goals and our assessments.

Dee Fink advises instructors working on alignment to use a three-column graphic organizer to list and connect their goals, assessments, and main teaching and learning activities.[49] The alignment diagram in example 2 does so for a course on Nazi Germany.

In example 2, the instructor has five main goals (seen in the left column). Some of them are content goals related to understanding different aspects of German social and political history. Some are related to understanding historical concepts (causation is complex, people experienced the past differently depending on identity and luck), and some are historical skills (interpreting sources, evaluating and making arguments). The fifth one is both intellectual (requires understanding the long-term consequences of Nazism) and affective (awareness of and personal reflection on the continuing relevance). There is some overlap in these goals. Students aren't studying causation in a vacuum; they are studying it in relation to the rise of Nazism and by exploring why different groups of people had different experiences. Students learn to analyze primary sources not simply as a useful skill but in order to understand the experiences of people in the period before and during Nazi rule. In this case, then, the content goals merge with the historical thinking goals.

Example 2. Course Alignment Diagram

Goals/Objectives	Assessments/ Evidence	Teaching/ Learning Activities
What do you expect your students to know, be able to do, or value at the end of the course?	*How will you and your students know how well they are learning this?*	*How will students learn to do and/or practice this?*
Find and interpret primary sources	Pop quizzes to check reading of sources An annotated source done at the beginning and end of semester to show growth Poster project—groups investigate experiences of a specific group, using and annotating primary sources	Demonstration of how to interpret sources (second day of class) Practice interpreting sources in small groups in class with formative feedback Mini-workshop (with reference librarian): finding sources Discussion: being a good group member Mini-workshop: creating a good poster
Explain the rise of the Nazi Party and understand causation as complex, multifactorial, and contingent	Pop quizzes to check reading Essay exam 1—Rank the four most important factors contributing to rise of Nazism and describe historians' challenges in explaining causation	Discussion of A, B, C readings Lectures on context (for material not in readings) Mini-workshop: writing a good essay
Describe how Nazism affected different groups of people differently and why	Essay exam 2—compare and contrast the experiences of three different groups and explain the reasons behind them Poster project	Discussion of X, Y, Z readings Jigsaw where students teach one another about different groups Mini-workshop: creating a good poster

(Continued on next page)

Evaluate and make good historical arguments	Exam 1 Exam 2	Exercise outlining three different historians' arguments and discussion of effectiveness Mini-workshop: writing a good essay Evidence-building exercise
Demonstrate and reflect on the continuing relevance of Nazism today	Find two contemporary news articles Two personal reflections	Mini-workshop (with reference librarian): finding sources Periodic discussion of contemporary news articles—who is affected and how

The middle column lists different ways that students' learning will be assessed—that is, the evidence with which they show they're achieving the goals in the first column. Each goal should be assessed in some way (even if only for a small percentage of the final grade). In chapter 1, we noted that the most straightforward way to ensure alignment between our goals and assessments is to have a 1:1 correspondence, as indicated below.

Goal 1 ↔ Exam 1

Goal 2 ↔ Exam 2

Goal 3 ↔ Exam 3

Sometimes, however, a single assignment can assess multiple goals. In this example, an essay exam asking students to create an argument about the causes of the rise of Nazism assesses both understanding of the rise of Nazism and the complexity of causation and the ability to make an argument. Because making arguments is an important skill for students of history, this instructor has opted to give another argument-based essay exam later on the topic of how and why Germans had different experiences during the Nazi regime. Repeating the format gives students a chance to improve their ability to build good arguments. A poster project is another kind of assessment in this course, and it also gives students a chance to show they have met two different goals. For the project, they must find and analyze relevant primary sources and describe the impact of Nazism on a group of people.

The middle column shows that in addition to the two essay exams, the students will have regular pop quizzes that ensure that they're doing the readings (including primary sources). In addition to doing so in the poster session, they will demonstrate their improved ability to interpret primary sources in an end-of-semester annotation of a source that they first interpreted at the beginning of the semester. In addition, for evidence of achieving the final goal—related to the contemporary societal and personal significance of Nazi Germany—the students will find news articles and write some informal reflections.

The third column lists some of the main teaching/learning methods and activities that will be used to help prepare students to perform well on the assessments. This instructor will regularly have students discuss the readings that were intentionally chosen because they help them meet the "end point" of course goals. Readings will provide students with the information and evidence they will need to answer the essay questions with depth and complexity for various groups (e.g., civilians, soldiers, Jews, homosexuals, communists, resisters, and youth). For the goal of evaluating different historians' arguments about the factors that contributed to Nazism, this instructor plans an in-class exercise systematically comparing and contrasting three arguments. In addition, there will be evidence-building exercises to practice building effective arguments for the essay exams. Because finding primary sources is a requirement for the poster session and students will need to find contemporary news articles, there will be a session facilitated by a reference librarian giving them tips how to do so. When the poster project is first assigned, the instructor will spend part of the class period having students discuss the behaviors of a good group member and do a mini-workshop on the elements of a good academic poster. Earlier in the semester, students will receive demonstrations on how to analyze primary sources and how to prepare an argument for an essay exam, two other skills necessary to do well on the assessments.

Although some assessments evaluate multiple goals, and some goals are assessed in multiple ways, the most important concept reinforced by the alignment diagram is that every goal (in the first column) is assessed (second column) and students are equipped (through instruction and activities in the third column) for every type of assessment. Using a three-column diagram like this helps us see the big picture of our course. It helps us ensure that we are being systematic, that our daily activities have a purpose aligned with our goals and assessments. This alignment substantially increases the odds that students will learn exactly what we want them to learn. It makes us *intentional* teachers.

Seeing the big picture for the whole semester in this way also helps us plan an effective semester calendar. It's helpful to view the semester as a series of smaller multiweek units, each ending with an assessment (exam, large assignment, project, etc.). If we know what's involved in the exam or project that comes at the end of a unit, we can work backward from when the assessment is due. For example, for the group project that results in a poster, once the instructor considers what knowledge or skills the students will need (such as how to be a good group member, how to make a poster, and how to find primary sources), he can decide how much time students will need to learn and do those things. That helps him decide when he will hand out the assignment and when he will share the necessary information and teach the skills necessary to complete it. (Sometimes when we begin this backward planning process, we realize we may need to scale back on our goals.)

When planning a unit, we should coordinate what students do outside of class with what they do inside of class. Students are capable of learning some things on their own (through reading, writing, finding sources, watching video, etc.) outside of class, and during class we shouldn't simply reiterate what they were supposed to learn. Instead, we should build on whatever they did outside of class. Students should use what they already learned by discussing, comparing, connecting, evaluating, or making arguments about it. If students are confused about the work they did on their own, we can help clarify it, but primarily we should focus on helping them deepen their understanding of the material. During class, we can also add new information (through lecture on material not in the reading, sharing alternative viewpoints, or by introducing different primary sources, etc.) and/or prepare students for their next readings or tasks. Table 3 adapts Dee Fink's way of representing a good relationship between activities inside and outside of class.[50]

It's wise to use backward design for each class meeting, too. That entails deciding on a few learning goals and a few teaching and learning activities intended to accomplish those goals. Then if one of those activities takes longer than anticipated, we quickly assess what we can delete from the plan while still accomplishing the main goals. For

Table 3. Relationship between Inside and Outside of Class Activities

	Inside of Class	Outside of Class
Day 1	Instructor sets up topic A	
Between class meetings		Students read on topic A
Day 2	Discuss, use, or build on material on topic A Set up topic B	
Between class meetings		Students read on topic B
Day 3	Discuss, use, or build on material on topic B Set up topic C	
Between class meetings		Students read on topic C
Day 4	Discuss, use, or build on material on topic C	

example, if a lecture goes too long, we don't need to speak at breakneck speed, cramming twenty minutes of material into five minutes or postponing material to the next class meeting. Instead, we can eliminate some material (i.e., an interesting story or extra evidence) and still accomplish the purpose for the lecture. Or let's say we planned to have students discuss the autobiography of a writer persecuted during Mao's Cultural Revolution to illustrate the state's sponsorship of propaganda art and its persecution of artists. If the first part of the discussion on Mao's early life takes longer than expected, rather than asking every prepared question, we can skip some interesting but nonessential ones and make sure that the next questions focus on the most important goals (Mao's thoughts about propaganda art and experiences of perse-cution). Similarly, we may plan to have students in small groups make lists of similarities and differences between the Great Awakening and the Second Great Awakening and then have each group trade its list with another group. If part of class took longer than expected, we can eliminate the last step where the groups trade lists. Or if we're running way behind schedule, the whole class can build the lists together (which goes faster), rather than breaking them into small groups.

In these examples, the instructor successfully adjusted the plan and still met the learning goals thanks to backward design, which kept the big picture goals in mind. True, it also requires some flexibility and quick thinking, but those are much easier with good forethought. Usually there are multiple ways to achieve a learning goal, and those methods differ in how much student engagement, independent thinking, depth, or time they involve. As we're planning a class meeting, it's wise to consider which parts are essential and which are interesting or useful but not es-sential. Identifying these in advance ensures that the class meeting will meet our goals while protecting the overall plan for the semester.

We enhance our planning of an individual class meeting by asking ourselves certain questions:

- Which of my goals can students accomplish on their own or by working with others (with good questions from me)?
- Which goals are better suited for me to accomplish through lecture or demonstration?
- Which goals are harder—and thus require some practice and feedback?
- Have I offered some variety in methods?

Similarly, when we plan a whole unit of the course in advance, we should ask ourselves important questions about a multiweek period:

- Do I regularly offer some key methods (e.g., document analysis, discussion, small group tasks, interactive lecturing) so that students get used to how I expect them to work?
- Do I occasionally change things up so that things don't get stale?
- Is there enough active learning?
- Am I providing enough opportunities to check how well students are understanding?

A unit plan helps me think through these questions and avoid my worst tendencies. Every semester, I want to achieve too many goals. Or I get bogged down in the details of a particular topic or book and "lose the forest." Sometimes I plan too much for individual class meetings. Setting up a unit plan forces me to focus on the bigger picture. To create one, I allocate a small space (usually one side of one page) and map out the multiweek unit. (I often have three or four units in a semester, each ending with an exam or project.) On the page, I list each day's topic and three or four learning goals for the day. Then I look for the specific readings that students will read, meaning that before the class period begins, they will have achieved or partially achieved one or two of the goals. I think about how I'll get the students to use the material in class and how I'll assess or build on their understanding. The number of methods I use depends on the length of my class period. I use more if one method is a couple minutes of writing at the beginning or end of class or if it's a long class period, for which it is especially important to switch gears frequently with active learning strategies. Example 3 shows a unit plan for the first few weeks of my introductory level course on race, gender, and sports in the United States, which meets for 100 minutes twice a week. (It's a short unit because I wanted to give an early exam that asks students to synthesize a manageable amount of material.)

The plan is not perfect—I'm continually adapting it—but laying it out in this way helps me check whether my methods are varied and consistent with my goals, whether the readings align with my goals, and whether I'm teaching and giving feedback on the skills and ways of thinking I most value. Without clarity of purpose from the backward design process, I would have great difficulty designing a coherent course and conveying its organization to the students. According to the multi-institutional Wabash Study of liberal arts education, clear and organized classroom instruction is one of the critical factors influencing students' cognitive growth.[51]

Attend to Beginnings and Endings

Get off to a good start

As the saying goes, we only get one chance to make a first impression, so we should make the most of it. The first few days of the semester lay the groundwork for everything we hope to accomplish. We want students to understand what the course is about—and ideally, value the

Example 3. Unit Plan

Aug 30, First Day of Class	Sept 1, Early 20th c.—Sports and Manliness

Goals:
 • Introduce big questions of course:
     o Sports as liberating or oppressive?
     o Did sports reflect historic context?
 • Begin to build community
 • Convey course expectations.
 	
 Methods in class:
 • Students fill out info sheets; begin learning names
 • Large group list making: how sports are good for people and not good
 • Context exercise matching sports photos w/ other U.S. occurrences)— small groups, then give answers and debrief exercise
 • Short lecture on class expectations
	Goals:
	 • Concept: Gender as socially constructed
	 • Association of sports and manliness in late nineteenth century
	 • Learn approach to primary sources
	
	 Reading/preparation:
	 • Riess, "Sport and Redefinition of American Masculinity, 1840–1900"
	 • Analyze documents WWilson and TRoosevelt on football
	
	 Methods in class:
	 • Interactive lecture on gender
	 • Discuss article
	 • Practice analyzing two sources— small group then large
	 • Minute paper assessment technique

Sept 6, Early 20th c. African Americans— Sports in Context of the Nadir	**Sept 8, Early 20th c. African Americans— Boxer Jack Johnson**
Goals: • Race as socially constructed • Context of nadir and different strategies African Americans used • Sports as opportunity or oppressive late nineteenth cent.? • Not all African Americans had same experiences • Practice method primary sources Reading/preparation: • "Strange Career of Wm Henry Lewis" • Annotate three docs re baseball and Chicago sports Methods in class: • Lecture on nadir (lynching, race baiting, disenfranchisement) • Discuss Lewis reading— opportunities? Discrim? • Small groups teach class on different documents	Goals: • Jack Johnson as challenge to white supremacy • His successes; his struggles • Contrast to separate strategy Reading/preparation: • Gerald Gems chapter on Johnson • Write sample short answer question Methods in class: • Quiz • Discuss article • Show ten minutes of documentary on Johnson • Analyze comments of black leaders criticizing Johnson in documents • Introduce short answer question format for exam; critique example

(Continued on next page)

(Continued from previous page)

Sept 13, Early 20th c. Women—Basketball	Sept 15, Early 20th c. Women—Didrikson
Goals: • Understand Victorian and New Woman—early twentieth-century context of changes but limitations • Assumptions re women's nature and abilities • Significance of bball as team sport—fun, exciting but limitations and modifications • Observe class differences in sports Reading/preparation: • Grundy, College Ladies on the Court Methods in class: • Quiz • Lecture on context • Discuss reading • Analyze docs by Berenson and Sargent re gender	Goals: • Popularity and enjoyment but limitations (Babe D) • Socioeconomic class differences • Synthesizing/exam prep Reading/preparation: • Babe, chapters 4+5 of autobiog • 1932 "The World-Beating Viking Girl of Texas" Methods in class: • Source analysis: video of Gertrude Ederle • Discuss Babe readings (diff sources); • Compare track versus bball • Small group synthesizing exercise (pre-exam): In the early 20th cent., did sports reflect what was going on in American society?
Sept 20, Exam • Short answer question re social construction of race or gender • Document analyses • Synthetic essay on sports as reflecting historic context or on whether sports was more of an arena of opportunity or oppression	

content and feel motivated to engage with it. We want students to understand our expectations for the work they'll be doing, how they should behave in class, and course policies. We need to assess their prior knowledge and instruct them in how to use key methods. Rather than conveying our expectations in an intimidating manner, we should aim for a balanced tone of challenge and support. We must begin setting up an inclusive classroom with a good vibe, a place where students feel respected as individuals and members of identity groups and ready to learn. That means, in part, sending welcoming cues to those who are hoping to hear them, getting to know the students and starting to build rapport with them. We also need to begin the process of students getting to know one another. Research suggests that students form their impressions of the instructor and the course very quickly. (It might be almost instantaneous, but certainly during the first couple of weeks.[52]) At the very least, on the first day of class we want students to be reassured that their instructor is a competent, fair, and caring person who wants each of them to learn—and has designed the course to support that goal.

Yikes! That's a lot to accomplish during the first couple of class periods. Obviously we shouldn't waste the first class meeting by handing out the syllabus and then letting students leave. We should also resist the temptation to lecture at students for the first class period about every one of our expectations, all the methods they'll use, why we chose each reading, the whole semester schedule, the value of our course, and our CV. We want to be transparent, but not long-winded. Surely we don't want to say we'll be using active learning techniques and then disprove it by lecturing the whole period.

Fiction writers are encouraged to show, not tell, and that's good advice for faculty on the first day of class. The first class is a great opportunity to model the methods we will use during the semester and engage students with our content. Instead of simply telling them about the ideas they will be discussing, get them discussing one of them right away. Begin building the class climate by having students introduce themselves to others in a small group before discussing. Instead of simply telling them about the types of analysis we will use in the future, have them start analyzing a rich primary source. Instead of explaining why we value the course content, show them an overview of the topics and ask them to tell us about their value. Instead of telling them we care about who they are, show them by getting there fifteen minutes before class starts and chatting with any early arrivals. Then have all the students fill out a confidential personal information form where they share some of who they are with us; tell us what they want to be called and their preferred gender pronouns; report their useful background knowledge, skills, experiences, or attitudes; and share their concerns about the course.

Asking students to do something meaningful within the first half hour sends important messages. First, it tells students they are expected to be active in this course, which typically motivates them. Second, it begins orienting them to specific historical ideas. In a course on the 1960s, Peter Felten asked students in small groups to put ten primary sources in chronological order. None of the groups put them in the correct order, but that didn't matter; simply grappling with the sources disrupted their often inaccurate, *Forrest Gump*-informed assumptions about the era, and had them concluding, "It's more complicated than I thought."[53] I've adapted Felten's exercise for my sports history course by asking students to match photographs of athletes with an iconic image illustrating political or social history from the same period. My purpose is to get students thinking about context, because one of the main questions of the course asks to what degree sports mirrored other trends in U.S. history. Other instructors ask students in a small group to take an engaging (ungraded) quiz, which activates (and informs us about) their prior knowledge and spurs curiosity. This approach usually reassures students, too, because it shows them that other students don't know much more than they do. (If we like, we can give the same quiz at the end of the semester to show students how much they learned.) Others jump right into the first topic by asking them to make sense of primary sources conveying diametrically opposed accounts of the same event.[54]

Ideally, we also prompt students to interact with the material in the syllabus. We should find a better way than two common problematic strategies: monotonously repeating aloud everything in it or saying nothing at all and assuming that the students will understand all the details on their own. I've known instructors who put questions about the syllabus on the first quiz. Therese Huston recommends a first-day syllabus review exercise in which she puts students in small groups to answer the following questions (with one person taking notes) on a sheet she has distributed:

- Look at the course objectives. What other classes have you had that will be helpful?
- Look at the course calendar. Which topics interest you most? The least?
- Identify two or three things in the syllabus that concern you. What strategies could you use to address these concerns?
- Identify two or three things in the syllabus that you're glad to see.
- When do you plan to submit your first work for a grade? What do you think it will cover?
- List three questions you have about the course that aren't answered in the syllabus.

After debriefing the exercise, Huston collects the answer sheets and later responds to questions that were not raised during class. She finds the exercise provides valuable information about her students, contributes to their agency (by having them consider strategies and to see their past experiences as relevant), and builds rapport and good energy. Of course, faculty can craft their own questions, including aspects of the syllabus they worry students won't notice.[55] For example, asking, "What specific advice would you give a student who wants to succeed in this course?" synthesizes various parts of the syllabus and builds expectancy (for motivation). Asking, "How do you expect the content of this class might be relevant to you now or in the future?" builds value.

We should pay special attention to the beginning of our individual class meetings, too. Given what we know about attention, cognition, motivation, and memory, we shouldn't waste the beginning of class time with tedium like taking attendance.[56] Instead, our first goal should be to catch students' attention and direct it toward the goals for the class period. ("The question of the day is, 'Was the civil rights movement successful?'") Students also need to know how the day's class material fits into the bigger picture of the previous class and/or the course unit—that is, how it's relevant. They need to understand the organization of the class meeting, which we can convey through a posted outline, oral explanation, or (ideally) both ways. This transparency makes an enormous difference in metacognition, which is especially important for novices in a discipline, "who initially need lots of help seeing the framework or organization of the material to be learned."[57]

Student interest can be sparked in many ways, such as displaying a powerful or ambiguous quotation, showing a provocative photograph, playing a short video clip (or song) that sparks emotions or heightens one's senses, telling a quick evocative story that connects to the big ideas of the day, or asking an important question. If we ask a question, students can quickly free write on it ("Based on what you know right now, do you think the movement was successful?"). Then at the end of class, students return to their writing and see if their thinking has changed. Such questions evoke prior knowledge. Alternatively, we may help students find a personal connection to the material. ("Today we'll be examining political activism during the French Revolution, so I'm going to ask you to think a little about yourself: can you imagine participating in a protest? If yes, for what kind of action and for what kind of cause? If not, why not?" Or before a lecture about socialist critiques of capitalism, "Do you think people are basically cooperative or competitive?")

Asking students to predict something inspires curiosity.[58] Before a lecture on the Puritans, Stephanie Cole asked students which of five statements reflected Puritan life (some of which included common misconceptions such as disapproval of sex, condemnation of alcohol, or wearing all-black clothing). Students recorded their answers on a classroom response system (using "clickers" or an online app), which gave Cole instant results. When she saw that many students chose incorrect answers, she "pointed out that the vast majority of the students surely need the day's lecture because they have much to learn about Puritan life, a suggestion that is usually met with a bit of good-humored agreement."[59] Such questions immediately engage students (because they are expected to answer and have to think to do so), but are valuable for more than that. Prediction and connection questions set in motion brain activity seeking prior knowledge that might help answer the question; by activating the knowledge, the mind is prepared to put the new material into a more richly connected neural network, which increases the ability to understand it and retrieve it later.[60]

Finish well

Endings matter, too. The end of the semester offers a unique opportunity for closure. Often we ask students to consolidate and articulate what they have learned on a final exam or project that is a summative assessment, which is important, because if we don't ask them to pull things together, it's unlikely they'll do so on their own. Researchers who study metacognition and experiential learning assert that intentional reflections matter. They have found that when students' reflection on their experiences is weak, their learning may be "haphazard, accidental and superficial."[61] Indeed, some go so far as to say, "People don't learn from experience; they learn from reflecting on their experience."[62]

I believe it's also useful to give students a chance to reflect in a more personal (nongraded) way about what they want to take away from the course. In this more individual process (perhaps done before or during the last day of class), students mull over what has been most important to them about what they've learned, what they want to remember, and why. Because they are integrating course work into their personal experiences, values, and future expectations, their answers will probably differ dramatically from one another. Instructors can guide such reflections with questions such as:

- What are the most important ideas you learned this semester?
- What did you learn about yourself, about others, or about the world around you?
- What skills did you improve?
- Why do any of these ideas, lessons, or skills matter to you? (Can you imagine using any of these in the future?)[63]

The end of the semester also offers instructors a chance to celebrate students' achievements and thank them for their efforts and contributions to class.

We also should pay attention to the end of each class meeting. If we aren't careful, we simply run out of time and students walk out the door while our voices trail off ineffectually. We would never end an article or formal presentation that way, and we shouldn't do it in a class meeting. Closure can be powerful for reinforcing key points and highlighting their significance. For students prone to getting lost in the details, a good closing brings them back to the big picture. Summarizing and connecting learning confirms and enhances it. Although it's tempting to cram in a few more points to a lecture, students' learning is more important than our delivery.[64] Before they rush off to their next class, job, or other activities, students need to take a few minutes to consolidate what they learned. Making sense of how the material fits together and assigning it value increases the probability that it will be retained.[65]

Wrapping up may be especially important after active learning. "I have walked away from far too many . . . discussions, even lively and interesting ones, wondering whether anyone learned anything," James Lang observed. However engaging a learning exercise may have been, if students didn't understand how it connected to learning goals, they might characterize it as "busy work."[66] In addition, sometimes students get caught up in a discussion or activity but forget to capture their insights in their notes. Unfortunately, that probably means that a week later they have no memory of what seemed interesting and important at the time. (Indeed, they may have forgotten 38 percent of the material within minutes after class.[67])

In the interest of time, instructors can efficiently summarize the connections between and implications of the lectures and learning activities. This helps students improve their notes. At times, though, it's useful for students themselves to do the closure. For example, after giving them a minute or two to review their notes, we can call on a

117

couple of students to recapitulate the main points of the class period, correcting or clarifying if necessary, asking for additional points from others, or confirming and thanking if they do a good job. An alternative is to ask students to *not* look at their notes and think of the main points (which is called "free recall"). Trying to remember the main points without checking their notes helps students retain more.[68] A quick, well-designed quiz question can accomplish the same goal.

Many instructors occasionally ask students to write a *minute paper*.[69] In this technique, students write for a minute or two at the end of class on a question, such as, "What was the most important thing you learned during this class session?" After class, the teacher quickly reads the essays and looks for trends in understanding or confusion. As with all formative assessments, it's important to provide group feedback on minute papers by taking a couple of minutes to address them at the beginning of the next class period or by posting a few comments on a class site. Other questions work well for minute papers. To ascertain which issues students aren't clear on, we ask "For you, what's the muddiest (least clear) point of today's class?" or "What important questions remain unanswered?"[70] Any question linked to the day's content is effective (e.g., "Which of the three arguments was most persuasive to you?" or "Which image stood out and why?" or "How does the material we studied today connect to the reading from a couple of classes ago?"). If we started class with a question or prediction, we can circle back to it, asking, "How would you answer this question now? Has your thinking changed at all?"

A minute paper does more than test and enhance students' recall. To select the most important thing they learned, students have to do some evaluation of what they recall (which is a higher-order skill than simple recall). Similarly, to craft a question, answer a specific question, or make connections, they must assess their understanding, which helps build metacognition. In addition, the simple act of writing elucidates learning. As Pam Kiser described, "What had perhaps been a dim awareness becomes clarified into a coherent statement through the written word. Having constructed this statement, students more clearly 'possess' the knowledge, having greater command over it as a tangible, concrete, lasting entity which can be retrieved and used as needed."[71] A minute paper helps students make the material their own while providing instructors with a simple way to get feedback on students' understanding with minimal investment of time and energy.

Specific Teaching Strategies

Those six principles guide how we teach in general, but it's also important to know what research tells us about how to use specific teaching techniques.

Interactive Lecture

Lectures have been around since medieval times, but by the nineteenth century, some were already questioning their instructional value.[72] Many of us fondly remember brilliant lecturers who piqued our interest in a topic, told compelling stories, persuaded us with impressive arguments, and modeled the intellect of a historian. On the other hand, many spoofs of academia feature dull, long-winded professors oblivious to their snoozing students.

It's hard to deliver a really good lecture that engages students, makes them think, and leads to significant and lasting learning. The attention of an average adult flags after fifteen or twenty minutes. As our minds wander, the quality of our note taking diminishes, even after the first five or so minutes, and then it takes another plunge after ten or fifteen minutes. Poor note taking correlates with poor understanding. Nor do people remember much from lectures. We retain information fairly well at the beginning of a lecture, miss a lot in the middle, and then have another good spurt at the end. Even immediately after hearing a lecture, students tend to recall only 62 percent of the material, and this percentage falls dramatically with the passage of time. The problem is not simply that humans are easily distracted; our retention deteriorates because our brains need time to process information.[73] They can only take in so much at a time.

Lectures pose other problems. In a traditional lecture, information flows in one direction, and many students become passive. Some hardworking students don't know how to learn from a lecture and try to transcribe everything rather than think about what they hear. In addition, lecturers frequently present only one point of view, which is unfortunate because consideration of multiple perspectives stimulates critical thinking. After completing a lecture, many instructors have no idea whether the students have understood what they conveyed. They may save time for questions but don't tend to receive many from passive students who haven't been thinking very hard or who know their fellow students want the class to be over rather than extended by questions. Even if a few students ask questions, instructors don't know whether most of the students understood the content.

Despite its limitations, it's not necessary to banish the lecture method. It's better to know the best circumstances for lecture and how to lecture well. Good lectures are an efficient and effective method for conveying information. However, we shouldn't lecture on the content of the readings. (If we do, students will have no incentive to do the readings.) Lectures can profitably augment the readings—perhaps by extending them, contradicting them, or otherwise using them—but they should not summarize them. As we consider whether to lecture, we should opt only to do so on topics that are not available in other course materials. Besides transmitting information, lectures can be helpful for explicitly modeling something, such as a type of argument, analysis, interpretation, or skill we will be asking students to perform. Lectures can also work well for piquing curiosity. A short lecture at the end of a class meeting can prime students for the next reading or topic. In addition, the lecture format is well suited for storytelling (on a topic we might ask students to connect to the reading); historians are fortunate that a short narrative is such a powerful tool. Good stories, according to one cognitive scientist, include four components: causality, conflict, complications, and interesting characters.[74] Before we decide to lecture, we should determine that the topic is aligned with our goals for the class meeting. Unless we want students to forget a big chunk of the lecture, we should limit lecture length to twenty minutes or so at a time.[75]

We know some ways to make lectures effective. Even short ones should have a clear beginning, middle, and end. The introduction should capture students' attention and direct it to the big ideas or questions. Whether we or the students provide it, the end of the lecture provides closure. Because the body usually contains a lot of content, it's helpful to provide oral and/or visual signposts about what we're doing:

- "The second historian's interpretation . . ." (reminds them that I'm on number two of the three I promised).
- "What kind of evidence do I have for that? Well, one example of that is . . . . Another piece of evidence is . . ." (models argumentation).
- "If you remember nothing else from this lecture, I hope you'll remember . . ." (this is a key point, underline it in your notes!)[76]

If using slides, we should avoid packing them with too much text. It's difficult to read and listen at the same time. Presenting an image or a short phrase and then offering a verbal explanation works better. When presenting a lot of information, it's especially important that we lecture at a reasonable pace. In one study, the same lecture was delivered at three different speeds and the students who performed best on later tests were the ones who experienced the slowest rate. This probably occurred because of the time the brain requires to process information. Students whose instructors were expressive and enthusiastic (those who varied the volume and tone of their voices, moved, gestured, and varied their facial expressions) performed better, too. Finally, students may ask for the instructor's slides or lecture notes; while a case can be made either way, some research suggests that it's better for us to teach students how to take notes and provide a skeletal outline rather than all the details.[77]

The single best way to enrich our lectures is to build in pauses and interactions. Interactive lecturers intentionally pause at the end of a fifteen- or twenty-minute segment. During that pause, they ask students to actively do something that involves thinking.[78] At the beginning of the semester or when dealing with difficult material, students may benefit from a comprehension check during that pause. In this scenario, after giving students a minute to review their notes, the instructor calls on a random student (not a volunteer) to quickly summarize a few main points. (To avoid embarrassment, some instructors allow students the option of asking a question about a confusing point.) Or we can ask students to write a single sentence summary. An alternative is to have students pair up and quickly exchange notes to see if their partner heard something different. Allocating another minute provides the chance to ask the other student a question and improve one's notes.[79] This technique, like other interactive lecture strategies, works in a class of any size.

Alternatively, interactive lecturers pose a direct question that assesses students' understanding. For example, after explaining the concept of Southern honor, including the role of dueling among social equals as a means of maintaining one's reputation, Stephanie Cole designed a postlecture multiple-choice question. "I ask them to imagine themselves as a planter who must decide how to respond when hearing that his overseer had insulted the virtue of the elite man's wife or daughters. If their first impulse is to pick the 'challenge him to a duel' option over 'thrash him with a cane,' I know I need to spend a bit more time emphasizing the importance of social status in the Old South."[80] This quick assessment paid off for Cole. Rather than hearing from only one or two volunteers after her lecture, using a *classroom response system* gave her an immediate sense of how the whole class understood the concept. While "clickers" or free phone/laptop apps instantaneously tabulate students' responses, instructors can also use the low-tech method of having students indicate their answers by raising their hands.[81]

Asking a specific question that tests understanding of a concept works much better than asking the bland prompt, "Does anyone have any questions?" When David Voelker suspected that many of his students had inaccurate prior knowledge about the rebellious American colonists' demand of "no taxation without representation," he crafted an in-class multiple-choice question about what the colonists meant by the phrase. When 60 percent of the students chose the wrong answer, the subsequent conversation helped him understand their reasoning. Then he explained and showed evidence for the correct one, which most students still understood later in the course.[82] His pause-and-ask-a-question method clearly resulted in important benefits for the students, who got immediate feedback. Cognitive science tells us that the testing made it more likely that the concept moved into long-term memory.[83]

A well-crafted open-ended question also works well. During the pause, we might ask students to characterize, evaluate, or react to what they just heard. They might finish a sentence starter ("Slave owners maintained control by . . .") or supply an adjective to characterize a person, event, or phenomenon.[84] Prediction questions fit well in a pause before another segment of lecture. Asking students to connect what they have just heard to previous sources or events strengthens understanding of both the new and older material.

Because students need time to think before developing a good answer to a difficult or open-ended question, many instructors use the strategy known as *think/pair/share*. In this format, instructors ask students first to think for a minute or two and write an individual answer. Then they pair with a student sitting nearby and discuss both their answers (giving equal time to each student). Finally, the instructor asks some of the students to share their answers publicly before the whole class.[85]

Discussions

Many historians consider the seminar, where a small group of students has thought-provoking conversations, to be an ideal way to teach, and evidence confirms that style of discussion offers many benefits. Discussion frequently increases students' engagement, interest in, and perceptions of a course. Students do the reading more carefully when they know they will be asked talk about it. Most importantly, discussion promotes deeper learning and better critical thinking skills. That's because discussion prompts students to think about and interact with the material rather than just recall it. Trying to articulate one's thinking aloud helps clarify ideas and improves communication skills. Even if some students do not speak a great deal, discussions can hone their listening skills and develop the ability to consider alternative perspectives.[86] Because discussions in a history class often center on interpretation and evidence, they help students recognize and test their assumptions and arguments and increase their tolerance for complexity and ambiguity. Interchange improves intellectual agility. Proponents of discussion also believe that giving students practice in respectful discussion "helps students learn the processes and habits of democratic discourse."[87] As sociologist Jay Howard put it, "At a time when . . . many Americans seem to have lost the ability to engage in reasoned, respectful debate and dialogue, encouraging the development of skills and dispositions necessary for civil discourse is particularly important."[88] Finally, discussion provides instructors with plentiful evidence about how students are thinking and sends the message that student voices are appreciated.

Discussions aren't perfect for achieving all of our goals, however. Because they require interchange and aim for students' own discovery of ideas, discussions don't cover material as efficiently as a lecture. They require time. Nor do they always go as we hope. When we invite students' voices, we sometimes hear comments that are poorly supported, tangential, confused, anecdotal, or even offensive—in addition to the ones that are thoughtful, productive, curious, and brilliant. It's much harder for an instructor to feel in control of a discussion, especially compared with a lecture.[89] Many instructors live in fear of a common problem: that no one talks, and the awkward silence feels like it goes on forever. Sometimes only a few students participate, a

Before the Semester	First Week of the Semester	Day Before the Discussion	Day of the Discussion

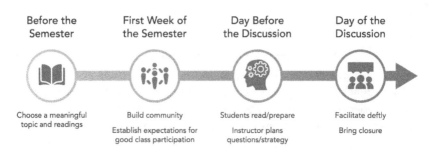

| Choose a meaningful topic and readings | Build community | Students read/prepare | Facilitate deftly |
| | Establish expectations for good class participation | Instructor plans questions/strategy | Bring closure |

Figure 2. Components and timing of good discussions

phenomenon Jay Howard calls "consolidation of responsibility" where the majority of students allows a handful of others to do most of the work.[90] Other common problems include the instructor talking too much (perhaps because they are afraid of the silence), the discussion getting repetitive or going nowhere, or the students only speaking to the instructor, not to one another.

Although it's impossible to guarantee a good discussion, problems usually can be avoided or remedied. Typically, problems result from insufficient attention to one of the six components of a good discussion: students' understanding of expectations, meaningful topics, student preparation, instructor planning, instructor facilitation, and closure.[91]

As figure 2 illustrates, most of the groundwork for a good discussion takes place before it ever begins. We must lay a good foundation so that students understand what "good discussion" looks like and what traits (e.g., attention, a willingness to listen, and mutual concern) a good participant exhibits. There should be some guidelines or ground rules. Students should build trust with one another and know how to disagree in a respectful way.[92] Second, the instructor must choose good topics and readings. If the material isn't sufficiently interesting, meaningful, and complex, students have no incentive to talk. Third, students need to have prepared, usually by reading, before the discussion starts, so they will be capable of informed conversation rather than simply shooting the breeze.

Instructors need to prepare well for the discussion, too. We should have clear goals for what students will learn from it (and we should share these goals with the students). Though there will be times during the discussion when we pose some spontaneously generated questions, we should design the main questions in advance, so they are clear, open-ended, and effective. We should design questions with a sense of what we want students to grapple with, yet realize that the discussion may well go in different directions, given student interests and responses. The opening question, of course, is especially important, and we must save time at the end for students to reflect on and consolidate their learning.

Effective facilitation of the discussion requires careful listening and quick thinking. It also requires clarity about our role as instructors—because ultimately what matters is not what we're saying but what students are learning—and attentiveness to the dynamics of the discussion. (Do students look confused? bored? angry?) Facilitation requires flexibility—while not losing sight of the goals. It also requires patience and willpower. After we ask a question, we can't panic during the silence. We need to wait. (One study suggested instructors only waited an average of one second before calling on someone.[93]) Silence may result from having asked an unclear or ineffective question, but it may simply indicate that students are thinking. Thinking is good, and we don't want to discourage it! If I quickly jump in and revise my question because I can't stand the silence—or worse, start answering the question myself—I'm undermining the process. It's better to wait longer.[94] If my question is effective, and the students are prepared, someone will jump in eventually. If my question isn't clear, and I've built rapport with the students, someone will ask for clarification. Research suggests that instructors often perceive themselves as pausing and inviting students in more frequently than they actually do.[95]

If the dreaded extended silence happens regularly, it's helpful to explore why students are not participating. There may be dynamics in the classroom that we are not aware of (see chapter 4 for ways to ascertain them). Individuals may be quiet for a variety of reasons (related to previous experiences; a minority cultural background, identity, or opinions; worries about a disability or an accent, etc.). Even if we have created a welcoming environment for all students, individuals may hold back because they are introverted or not confident about spontaneously expressing their ideas in front of many people. Students are more hesitant to speak when they perceive the class to be large.[96]

One strategy, then, is to minimize the risk of speaking publicly. Some instructors allow students to participate in an online discussion board instead of orally during class; this gives them more time to think about what to say. (However, because being online may encourage people to shed some of their normal social inhibitions, we need to help students understand online discussion etiquette.[97] For instructors who want live, face-to-face discussion, there are two useful strategies. First, we can give students time to gather their thoughts by posing a question and asking them to write for a minute or two before calling on anyone. The other is to have students discuss with a single partner or a handful of students in a small group, which also lessens fears of embarrassment.[98] The great thing about having students discuss in small groups is that it increases the probability that *every* student in class will participate. Students from traditionally marginalized groups participate more in small groups than in large ones, and generally students perceive that they learn more in small groups.[99] The method works in a class of any size, even in a lecture hall, where a pair of students can turn around and talk to a pair in the row behind them. After the small group members talk, instructors can ask a representative from some of the groups to report their thoughts to the larger group.

Once discussion begins, facilitation involves using process questions that keep the discussion going and productive. When the class isn't sure what a student's comment means, we ask clarification questions ("I'm not sure I followed; could you say that again?" or "Do you mean X or Y?"). If we are concerned that discussion isn't flowing, or that the students aren't addressing one another, we ask connection questions ("Kyle, how does that fit with what Lakesha said?" or "Who wants to respond to that idea/comment?"). When we want to focus on argumentation, or if a student makes a shaky assertion, we ask evidence or reasoning questions ("Can you show us the quotation that made you conclude that?" or "Can you give an example of that?" "Will you explain how you came to think that?"). To push students' thinking further, we ask challenge questions ("If I were to play devil's advocate, I might say . . . , and how would you respond to that?" or "But earlier someone said . . ." or "Are you sure?"). When we're concerned the comments are too superficial, we ask extension questions ("Can you say more about that?" "How can we dig deeper?").[100]

Response involves "instant artistry," Roland Christensen observed, making it one of the most challenging skills required of discussion leaders.[101] We can encourage student participation through positive reinforcement, with comments such as, "Very helpful" or "Great start." If we aren't careful, though, we'll create the expectation that we are going to respond to each comment, which will lead to a series of one-to-one interchanges between the teacher and a student instead of a group discussion. Sometimes, a silent nod and smile works better while we wait for other students to jump in. It's especially tricky to respond to students who make inaccurate or tangential comments. If we respond in a way that some interpret as harsh or embarrassing, it can effectively shut down further discussion, possibly for a long time.[102] The same is true for responses perceived as aggressive.[103] I don't enjoy telling students that they're wrong, but if I'm dealing with important factual errors or flawed assumptions, I cannot let an incorrect assertion stand, because the other students may assume it's correct. To prevent that from occurring, I first ask if anyone wants to respond to the comment. If no one offers a correction, I say something like, "I can see how you might think that, but . . ." or "That's a common misconception . . ." When someone moves us too far off-topic, Jay Howard suggests saying, "Intriguing idea, but off on a tangent; if you want to explore more, let's talk after class."[104] I like to direct us back with, "Okay, but I don't think we've really answered the original question yet."

It's not surprising for a few students to begin to dominate the conversation. They may do so because they are quick thinking and enthusiastic, eager for approval, extroverted, competitive, arrogant, ideological, or unaware that their behavior is stifling or annoying others. We're not powerless in this situation, and it's helpful to act before it becomes an entrenched pattern. Sometimes a reminder about the expectations or ground rules may help, but sometimes we need to do more. Explicitly inviting in the quieter students by saying, "I'd like to hear from some students who haven't spoken yet today," may make a difference. After allowing some thinking time, we can call on specific individuals who are shy but have good ideas. When I find the class falling into the pattern where a handful of students speak a lot, I announce a practice that gives everyone more time to formulate an answer and usually results in new volunteers: "Today I'm not going to call on anyone until at least five hands are raised." Others occasionally use an exercise (a *circle of voices*) in which each student speaks (uninterrupted) before opening the floor to everyone. In a large class, this is done in small groups.[105] Others ask the class to suggest a limit to the number of times an individual student might speak, causing the frequent speakers to slow down and decide whether to talk.[106]

Students can learn how to become better discussants. Stephen Brookfield and Stephen Preskill describe two strategies for helping them do so.[107] In one exercise, each student is randomly assigned one "conversational move" they should make during the discussion. They receive an instruction such as:

- Ask a question that encourages someone to elaborate on something they've said.
- Make a comment that underscores the link between two people's contributions.
- Make a comment indicating that you found another person's ideas interesting or useful (and why).
- Disagree with someone in a respectful and constructive way.
- Create space for someone who has not yet spoken.
- Make a summary observation that takes into account several people's contributions and touches on a recurring theme in the discussion.

Alternatively, they assign students a "role." Roles include devil's advocate (who introduces an alternative view when consensus is emerging), active listener (who paraphrases), evidence assessor (who listens for unsupported assertions), umpire (who listens for any potentially judgmental comments), speculator (who introduces new ideas or lines of inquiry), or underscorer (who describes the relevance and accuracy of someone's comments). In the beginning, students may find these conversational moves or roles amusing or artificial but using them heightens their awareness of the consequences of their actions. Some instructors find that asking students to evaluate their own class participation in response to specified criteria positively influences the dynamics. (See chapter 4 for a class participation rubric.) If an individual student continues to display problematic behaviors even after we've tried numerous strategies, we should initiate a private conversation with them.

As suggested earlier, at the end of the discussion, we should save some time for closure, so students reflect on and note what they've learned.

Deliberative Dialogue

I've found deliberative dialogue to be an especially valuable type of discussion for helping students consider multiple perspectives and understand different arguments. In this structured format, after agreeing to ground rules, students discuss three different position statements. They do so deliberately (systematically, at a slower pace), giving equal time to the pros and cons of each position. In contrast to a debate, where the emphasis is on winning, the emphasis in a dialogue is on understanding. Considering at least three perspectives means that students don't fall into two polarized positions. Although deliberative dialogue has usually focused on present-day issues, the Kettering Foundation has created some issue guides on historical subjects. The guides provide background information and spell out three perspectives; the foundation also shares sample ground rules and tips for facilitators.[108] Any instructor can adapt the model for their own course content and materials (including either primary sources or secondary sources to help understand historiography). For example, after a unit on the 1960s, I facilitated a dialogue about three positions:

- The 1960s was a period of dangerous disorder.
- The 1960s was a great period in which the United States truly and effectively enacted its principles.
- The 1960s was disappointing because the nation did not go far enough to address its problems.

These dialogues have good outcomes. In addition to deepening their understanding of an issue, students usually realize that issues are complex, and as a result of open-minded listening, they don't vilify the people they disagree with. Indeed, some evidence suggests that practicing deliberative dialogue positively affects how students think about democracy and decision making. The AACU's National Task Force on Civic Learning and Democratic Engagement called this method one of a few "powerful pedagogies that promote civic learning."[109]

Small Group Collaborative Activities

Small collaborative groups provide an excellent venue for students to practice historical thinking and writing. Putting students in small groups (of three to six) effectively makes our classroom smaller, giving all students, including introverted ones, a chance to participate.[110] They allow us to incorporate active learning techniques associated with positive learning outcomes.[111] Small group work is ideal for lower-stakes tasks, on which we give students formative feedback. Working in groups engages students in one aspect of metacognition, accurately judging their learning, because as they work, they get feedback from each other.[112] If a student is struggling to understand something, sometimes hearing it explained by a peer can help. The students who do the explaining often deepen their understanding of concepts—or sometimes realize that they don't understand something as well as they thought. (Teaching students to ask each other, "How do you know that?" makes the work even more powerful.[113]) As long as we are available to guide students while they are working and structure tasks to minimize "social loafing," students find doing work with others to be enjoyable and motivating.[114]

Still, small group collaborative work can go awry without proper planning and execution.[115] Some students may be reluctant to do it because they don't understand the point of the activities, think the instructor should be doing all the work, or have had bad experiences with peers who don't contribute a fair share. As with all our teaching strategies, then, it's important that we lay the foundation for collaborative work. We should explain why we're using the method, emphasizing evidence that putting more minds together leads to better answers, that collaborative work helps most students learn better, and that it's a skill that employers value.[116] It's also important that we design good tasks for groups—ones that are intellectually challenging, are meaningful, and benefit from multiple minds. Finally, students need to know what is expected of them while working in groups. It's worth it to spend a little time at the beginning of the semester having students discuss which behaviors are helpful and which are annoying and thus create a set of ground rules. Airing the typical unproductive behaviors lets the "slackers" (noncontributors), the "distractors" (those luring the group off task), and the "dominators" (those who push their will on others) know that their peers and the instructor disapprove of those negative behaviors.[117]

Good execution involves thinking through some issues. First, informed by the research on transparency, we should prepare a clear explanation of the task and its purpose. To avoid confusion and wasted time, it's best to explain the instructions aloud and have a written version (on a slide, small slip of paper, or online). We also need to consider the makeup of groups. If it's a quick task and we don't care about the precise number in a group, allowing students to form their own groups with people sitting near them works fine. But it's important to mix it up sometimes for building community and hearing diverse voices.[118]

Many kinds of students benefit from positive, goal-oriented interactions with people who are different from themselves.[119] Arbitrary methods (such as counting off or asking people to move to groups based on the month of their birth) add interest to the otherwise tedious task of assigning people to groups. It may sound silly to encourage instructors to think through a detail like how groups will be organized, but a miscalculation can be confusing for the students and discombobulating for the instructor. (I speak from experience; one time I forgot that having students count off by fours meant there would be four large groups, not that there would be four students in each group!) It's good to think through timing, too. The first time we do a task, we might not accurately anticipate how much time it will take and may need to be flexible so the groups can finish. In general, it's good to allow just enough time that the students feel a little hurried rather than so much time that they dawdle. (Because we don't want some groups to finish quickly and become bored, we might have an additional task ready for them.)

Accountability matters in group tasks. If the instructor roams around the room, his physical proximity (asking questions or making suggestions) keeps students on task. So does offering some small incentives for participation. Sometimes we might collect and grade the group's work or give a quiz on the material.[120] We can also ask students to evaluate their participation. Grades aren't the only kind of incentive, though. Motivation results from seeing that one has learned or knowing that one will be asked to use the results of group work on a later exam. Enjoyment is another incentive, as is public or private acknowledgment of a job well done.

So that we can provide formative feedback, it's helpful to publicly debrief the group work. Asking one group to report its ideas is a good practice. Many instructors randomly select one person from the group to report—so that each person is invested in the group's work. After the report, the teacher can comment on the group's report, or if there's time, ask the rest of the class to respond. Groups who reached the same conclusions might raise their hands, and instructors can invite those groups who reached different conclusions to share them. (It becomes repetitive and boring if we ask all the groups to report.) Alternatively, having groups exchange and comment on one another's work ensures that each group is reporting and receiving feedback. Groups either get confirmation that others had some of the same ideas or realize their work did not have as much depth or complexity. Finally, asking each group to type their answers into a shared document (e.g., Google Doc)—or write them on the board—means that everyone sees the range of answers.[121]

The beauty of the small group collaborative method is that it accommodates many types of intellectual processes, including brainstorming, drawing conclusions, explication of texts, question raising, and writing.[122] Many of the next strategies I describe work well when done in small groups.

List Making

Creating a list is a flexible method for prompting learning, adaptable to many kinds of historical thinking. It's efficient because making a list requires focused thinking but does not take as long as writing out complete sentences. History instructors can ask students to make lists of:

- Similarities between two events, people, periods, or texts (comparisons)
- Differences between two events, people, periods, or texts (contrasts)
- Contributing factors to or causes of an event or situation (causation)
- Consequences of an event (short- or long-term implications)
- Problems faced by a historical actor or group (perspective taking)
- Actions or strategies a person or group used and/or responses by others to those actions (perspective taking)
- Events, in order (chronology and context)
- Adjectives to describe a situation (interpretation)
- Lessons students derived from an event or reading (interpretation)
- Truth statements—for example, "It is true about politics in the 1950s that . . ." (drawing conclusions).[123]

Synthesizing

Many students understand individual portions of course content but struggle to make connections or see themes across time. Others struggle with the use of evidence. A synthesis exercise gives groups practice in assembling lots of evidence for a specific theme or argument. I first used this exercise in an LGBTQIA history course, where one goal was for students to understand the various factors that impacted LGBTQIA Americans in the colonial era, mid-nineteenth century, and twentieth century. Factors suggested by our sources included laws, religion, science and medicine, political and social organizing, popular culture, and a person's race, ethnicity, region, and socioeconomic class. I assigned each group a different factor and told them to find as many specific examples as they could of that factor influencing people in our primary sources, secondary sources, or lectures. The students stood or sat near a portion of the whiteboard where I asked them to list their examples (in a phrase or quotation). Most groups came up with a couple of examples quickly and then got stuck. That's when being with a group helped; each member person flipped through their notes, and occasionally I would hear a tentative suggestion ("What about . . . ? Remember that article . . . ?").

The point of asking groups to write their answers on the board (or on a huge sheet of paper hung on the wall, or in a Google Doc) is making them visible to all. Each group has a different colored marker, so it's clear whose ideas are whose. Once each group has a handful of answers up on the board, I call time, and each group moves clockwise to the spot where another group wrote its evidence about a different factor. The new group reads what the previous group has written and puts a check mark next to examples that seem sensible and a question mark next to ones that are confusing or inaccurate. Then the new group must add a new example to the previous group's list. When I call time again, each group moves clockwise to repeat the process. The more students move, the harder it is to come up with examples, because the more obvious ones have already been listed. This makes the students dig further. (If a group is stuck, I provide a hint: "Can you think of any examples from the mid-twentieth century?" or "Remember the X text; could you find something from that?") The process of moving clockwise continues until the groups are back where they started. Now their spot on the board contains more information and has feedback (check marks and question marks) from other groups about their work. I facilitate a whole-class discussion, asking if anyone wants to ask a question of another group. ("Why did you have a problem with this example?" one group might ask, and then the original group might offer a defense of it or agree it's not a good one.)

The last step is asking the groups to look carefully at all the examples and then make an argument about them. For example, in the LGBTQIA history course, I asked, "Overall, would you say this factor had a positive or negative influence on LGBTQIA people?" Most groups did a fine job of adding up the evidence, making generalizations that took into account complexity (e.g., "Until the late twentieth century, the law tended to have a negative effect." "Although medical ideas were helpful in terms of X and Y, they were harmful in terms of A and B.") By the end of the exercise, students have a long list of relevant examples in support of an idea (in fact, they often ask if they can take a photo of the material on the board). More importantly, they realize how much evidence should be examined before making an assertion. My impression was that after I began using this exercise, students used about twice as much evidence in their essays.[124]

Writing

Writing a whole essay takes time, but we can isolate parts of the process and have students help one another practice separate skills, such as:

- Crafting a thesis (after a lecture, readings, unit, or synthesis exercise)
- Making an outline (in response to a prompt)
- Writing a paragraph with a good topic sentence and supporting evidence
- Arranging citations in proper format
- Critiquing a peer's (or a sample) essay, thesis statement, or paragraph. (Students should only critique one another's work when there are clear criteria that have been discussed. A worksheet with specific questions can facilitate the process.)

Document Analysis

When students analyze primary sources in groups, they often discover more complexity than they found when reading on their own. We prompt analysis with questions, such as:

- What are the main messages?
- What are the most significant quotations, and why?
- Which interpretations do you feel sure of or less certain about?
- To what degree do you find this source reliable? What are your reasons for trust or skepticism?
- Where do two or three documents agree and disagree?

- How do these documents relate to (confirm/contradict) our secondary sources (or a lecture)?
- What kind of an argument might this source serve as evidence for?

We can give all the small groups the same sources and then do some debriefing with the whole class, or if we have more time, give groups some different sources, which they might teach to the larger group.

Perspective Taking through Creative Tasks

Occasionally instructors change up the usual methods by asking groups to use the content creatively, such as by writing an imaginary conversation between two historical actors. Students choose the setting (e.g., Phyllis Schlafly and Gloria Steinem meet outside a women's clinic or at the wedding of their children), then write a page or so of dialogue. The only rule is that the dialogue should accurately convey the perspectives of the people (garnered from sources they have read). They get bonus points for incorporating actual quotations from primary sources. I say "bonus points," but in my course, this exercise is simply in-class active learning. I save time for each group to do a quick performance of their dialogue (some ham it up) and then ask the class to vote on which did the best job. Writing a dialogue is challenging because it requires integrating ideas, understanding multiple perspectives, drawing reasonable inferences, and thinking creatively, so it takes time.[125] It's well suited for checking whether students understand the gist of ideological differences, such as those of Confucius and Lao Tzu, Ida B. Wells and Marcus Garvey, Vladimir Lenin and Joseph Stalin.

Other creative tasks similarly blend intellectual work and fun. Some instructors ask student groups to characterize a period or event in a small format—haiku or a tweet—to hone in on its essence.[126] Maria Metzler won a learning innovation award for her "Bring a Goddess to a Party" activity in which students investigated an ancient female deity or demon—thinking about her appearance, interests, and personality traits, among other things—and then introduced her to their classmates. Metzler said the act of "befriending" personalities from the past helped students see them as more real and remember their distinctiveness.[127]

Graphic Organizers

Sometimes it's helpful for students to convey ideas, concepts, information, or events in a visual manner. Visual representations

Example 4. Matrix Graphic Organizer

	European Colonizing Nation (+Date)	Resources Colonizers Wanted	Slavery Established? (When? Who?)	Method of Independence (+Date)	Contemporary Racial Categories
Mexico					
Haiti					
Cuba					
U.S. South					
Brazil					
Jamaica					
Suriname					

may help show relationships and patterns or help students see or re-member the big picture.[128]

Timelines convey both chronology and the relative amount of time between events. For an in-class activity, it only takes a few minutes for students to plot a timeline on a piece of paper or the board. If we have more time or want to create a larger assignment, digital tools create visually appealing interactive timelines that convey complexity using spatial arrangements, categories, and color schemes and include many types of information, including text, images, multimedia, hyperlinks, and geospatial data.[129] For example, students in a course on Love and Marriage created a timeline on the history of marriage from 1500 to 2014 that included events and materials color-coded by whether they fit in legal, religious, or literary and artistic categories.[130] Students might also depict spatial relationships and events using mapping tools. In a course on San Francisco history, students mapped their findings on topics such as the number and location of banks before and after the stock market crash or the location of gay bars over the course of the twentieth century.[131]

Sometimes it's helpful for students to create their own mind map of the relationships among ideas or information. Free online tools facilitate the process of drawing arrows between ideas (and turning a graphic organizer into an outline). Alternatively, filling in an empty matrix may help students categorize information, such as in example 4, where students in an Atlantic World course compare and contrast European colonization in the New World.[132]

In her Historian's Workshop course, Catherine Denial asked students (who had been discussing the limitations of timelines to capture permeating ideologies, uncertainty, and multiple perspectives) to come up with a timeline replacement. Using their knowledge, creativity, and experiences, students designed honeycombs, event pyramids, scraps of fabric, and models of molecular structure.[133]

Peer Instruction: Jigsaw

When students teach one another, it develops interdependence and leadership. It also deepens their understanding of the material, because a person needs more than surface knowledge to be able to teach something.[134] A "jigsaw" is a distinctive peer instruction technique that requires advance planning and takes a whole class period. It involves four steps:

1. Divide students into four groups (numbered 1, 2, 3, 4), each with its own content to learn and eventually teach. For example, one might assign each group a different person's experience during the Holocaust or four different documents about the rise of segregated private academies after the *Brown v. Board of Education* Supreme Court decision.[135] Give each group readings to be completed before class meets.

2. In the beginning of the class period, all the 1s sit together, 2s together, and so on, and discuss their specific content, deciding what is most important for the other students to learn and how they'll teach it. The instructor checks in with each group to make sure they're on track.

3. Within each group, assign each student one of four new designations (A, B, C, D). Students then move to sit with those in their lettered group so that each of the original groups has a representative in the new group. The experts from groups 1, 2, 3, and 4 then teach their topic to the students in their new (A, B, C, D) group. The instructor keeps time, giving each topic the same amount.

4. After each topic has been taught, debrief the exercise with the whole class, helping add things up, with questions such as, "Now that you've heard about the experiences of four different people, what conclusions can we draw? Which experiences were shared, and which unique? How do you explain the differences? Which sources were most useful?"

Other types of peer instruction include oral presentations, small groups reporting their analyses, peer review of writing, and pairs of students explaining their answers to questions to each other.[136]

Experiential Learning

Multi-institution research identifies certain "high-impact practices." Many of these work well for learning history, including undergraduate research, internships, global learning (including study abroad and domestic travel courses), community-based or service learning, collaborative projects, writing-intensive courses, and capstone projects.[137] These practices tend to share some common characteristics—they require considerable time and effort (on an authentic task), contact with people different from themselves, substantive discussions, meaningful feedback, and careful reflection. Many involve experiential learning. Study abroad or study elsewhere in the United States may offer a powerful immersive experience. Community-based projects—such as an oral history project for a local group, an institutional history for a nonprofit organization, service learning on a topic related to the course, or an exhibit for a school or historic site—move students to interact with people outside their campuses and bring history to life. Using a high-impact practice requires a good deal of advance preparation by the instructor—with oral history, for example, instructors arrange community partners and train students in expectations, ethics, and methods—but the payoff can be enormous.

Immersive *games* or *simulations*—such as the elaborate, weeks-long, student-run Reacting to the Past pedagogy—also intensely engage students as they assume roles and find (unscripted) ways to express ideas persuasively.[138] Our students may already be playing video games set in historical periods (such as ancient Egypt or Rome, Victorian London, medieval Italy, or almost any war).[139] Games have very enthusiastic proponents, largely due to their power to engage users cognitively and affectively in a sustained manner. Video games may ask students to identify with a particular type of historical actor (e.g., a Vietnam veteran in the Deep South in 1968) or grapple with a historical problem (e.g., smallpox, military strategy, food shortages in communist-era Poland). The most effective games have characteristics that improve motivation or learning: interesting characters and settings and a sense of mission; choices; challenge (allowing failure, multiple tries, and increasing levels of difficulty based on complexity); and feedback (they let students know where they stand).[140] The power of gaming is still being explored, and there's little empirical evidence so far for claims that games improve cognition.[141] However, it's possible that games are already affecting some of our students' prior knowledge, and it's possible to imagine ways to use a "serious game" to advance a course goal by asking students to evaluate the historical accuracy or epistemological limitations of a specific game on a relevant topic.

Instructors who don't want to dive into very involved experiential practices may find smaller, less time-intensive ways to incorporate valuable aspects of them. Someone who doesn't want to dedicate three weeks to a Reacting to the Past simulation may try a one-day role play. Some short in-class games (like Jeopardy!) tend to focus on lower-level tasks (such as remembering facts), but creative instructors might invent a one-day game that uses competition and teamwork for higher-level tasks. To understand power, context, and agency, I have had students read about a labor conflict, assigned them to groups representing workers and management and asked those groups to take turns deciding the most effective strategies and when to use them, awarding points for the best historically feasible choices. It's always one of the most engaging class meetings. Many students can't afford a study-away course, but instructors may be able to arrange a field trip to a cemetery, dam, factory, battlefield, or museum that conveys a sense of context. Perhaps not every student can conduct an extensive (recorded and transcribed) individual oral history interview, but they can ask questions of a guest speaker or have a brief conversation with an elderly friend or relative. Perhaps students can't do a full research project, but they can visit a local archive and interpret some primary sources there.

A note on technology: Education writers refer to the "affordances" of new technologies, meaning the benefits they offer to support teaching. Various online technologies offer ways to collaborate and communicate; practice skills; make choices; interact with content; quickly assess student understanding; give and receive feedback; find information; express ideas with images, sound, and text; organize ideas and concepts; and present material in multimodal ways to capture and hold students' attention, which is a necessary precursor for memory and comprehension. However, even the strongest advocates of technology warn that digital tools should not be adopted mindlessly, simply because they are new and shiny. We should be selective, using technology (like any instructional strategy) when it expands our repertoire of techniques to elicit the attention, specific efforts, and engagement that are necessary for learning—that is, when it helps us achieve our goals.[142]

■

We should choose our teaching strategies intentionally, informed by an understanding of the strengths and weaknesses of various possibilities, and we should implement them using evidence about how to do them well. Whether we decide on interactive lectures, discussions, small-group tasks, or other strategies, it's useful to hone our skills in asking questions. Questions aid students' reading and preparation for class, direct specific kinds of analysis during class, and prompt reflection on and consolidation of learning.

We should choose teaching techniques based on our specific goals. Because alignment between goals, assessments, and day-to-day teaching strategies increases clarity, organization, and learning, it's beneficial to use backward design for our unit and individual class planning. Such planning ensures that we're teaching the material that we're going to assess, which means that we're being fair, giving all students a fair chance to learn the material. Having a firm sense of our goals helps us be transparent with students about the purposes of each class meeting.

Good planning means we coordinate what students do inside and outside of class, and that during class, we build on readings that we hold students accountable for doing. Good instructional design means that we pay special attention to the beginnings and endings of the semester and individual class periods and notice whether we're offering variety in our methods. We should incorporate active learning where possible, not simply because it engages students but because they need to practice the ways that historians discover, analyze, and communicate. Active learning also shows us how well students understand the material and can perform the work, so we can offer formative feedback for them to make adjustments.

As we mature as instructors, we experiment with new methods and add more strategies to our repertoire. Earlier in our careers, it's a good idea to pick a few flexible methods and become adept at using them. That's because—as we know—becoming proficient at something involves deliberate practice, ideally accompanied by formative feedback. Mastery is impossible without some kind of assessment of how we're doing—so we know what to try to improve.[143] Assessment, then, is the topic we turn to next.

4   How We Assess

Who among us has not read a student paper less closely
than we should have, and hence awarded a strong student
a lesser grade than deserved? Or, perhaps worse yet,
assigned an indolent student a better grade than she has
earned, and thus provided misinformation to that student
rather than responsible guidance?

EMMA J. LAPSANSKY-WERNER

When it's time to grade papers, I suddenly go into house-
cleaning frenzies. I start preparing next semester's courses.
I finally get around to reading the most obscure and boring
articles on my research reading list. I actually clear out my
email inbox. . . . I would rather lick the bottom of a New
York subway car than grade papers.

KATHERINE PICKERING ANTONOVA

WHAT HAVE I DONE WITH MY LIFE? ALL THE HOURS I
SPENT WRITING THINGS YOU WON'T READ!

KEVIN GANNON,
after learning many of his students
didn't read his comments

Every historian I know hates grading students' work.
Partly that's because the process—especially writing
comments—takes so long. We despondently count how many remain in
the stack before we "escape from grading jail."[1] It's not just the tedium.
As Emma Lapsansky-Werner pointed out, many of us aren't confident
that we're doing a good job. We wonder whether there is a significant
difference between a C+ and a B− and whether we used the same
standards on the first student's essay that we used on the twentieth or

fortieth.[2] Grading may disappoint us because it reveals that students didn't learn as much as we had hoped. As Katherine Antonova put it, it's worse when "you spend hours and hours . . . so that your evaluation and feedback will, hopefully, help the students to do better next time . . . [o]nly to hand back the papers and watch the students glance at the letter grade and then stuff the paper away, or even straight into the trash can."[3] Some dislike grading because of the emotions it can provoke in students—getting upset, losing confidence, fuming, taking the grade personally, or protesting, which leads to conversations we dread. Most of us view summative assessment (grading) as an unpleasant obligation.

This is unfortunate, because assessment should be a productive and transparent process that we do intentionally and effectively. Grading effectively means using carefully considered discipline-based standards that distinguish between important levels of students' work, applying our criteria fairly and consistently, clearly communicating those criteria and providing useful feedback, and grading in a fairly efficient manner (so that the process doesn't kill us). We can learn how to do a competent job from assessment experts. We should start by thinking about assessment in a helpful way—as another strategy to promote student learning. As Ken Bain said, "Testing and grading are not incidental acts that come at the end of teaching but powerful aspects of education that have an enormous influence on the entire enterprise of helping and encouraging students to learn."[4]

Sometimes we are the ones being assessed. Other people evaluate the quality of our teaching in ways that have significant professional implications. We can approach this assessment in ways that maximize its benefits and communicate intelligently about our effectiveness as instructors. We should also assess our own work, because without some kind of assessment, decisions about whether to keep or alter course methods and materials would be based on nothing but intuition. Taking a scholarly, evidence-based approach to assessment pays off in our growth as educators, positive evaluations from others, and better learning by our students.

Assessment of Students' Learning

Formative Assessment

Before discussing summative assessment of major assignments, it's important to review some basics. The assignments we give students should be meaningful ones that we have intentionally designed to meet our specific course goals, so that doing the assessment helps cement students' learning. The purpose of feedback is to help students learn—and we should provide students with feedback on frequent, low-stakes work throughout the semester before we ask them to do more high-stakes graded work. Some instructors might panic when reading that sentence, believing it's impossible to find time to give more feedback, but before freaking out, consider that formative feedback doesn't need to be written, formal, long, or individual.

Group feedback can be efficient and effective. When students perform a task during class (e.g., listing differences between World Wars I and II), the instructor can circulate around the room, noticing some common difficulties, and announcing patterns he's noticing. Or he can show the class an excellent example of work, pointing out (or having students figure out with his guidance) its positive characteristics. No work needs to be collected to give this kind of feedback. To minimize the number of pieces of work to be assessed (and simultaneously encourage students to learn collaboratively), an instructor can collect group products rather than individual ones. If the instructor collects individual work on an ungraded in-class task, she can read a sample of it (not all of it!) and at the beginning of the next class make a few comments about patterns she observed. Instructors who don't want to use class time for this purpose can annotate strong and average (anonymous) examples of work and post them. Although students might not recognize it as such unless we call it feedback, even responses to questions given during interactive lecturing constitute formative feedback.

Feedback can be concise, especially on short low-stakes work (such as a list, a sample thesis, or a response to readings). A check mark for adequate work communicates the feedback, "You're on the right track," or a minus mark means, "There's something you're missing here." Some instructors are more creative, such as Katherine Jewell, who used emojis to indicate the quality of students' historical thinking on a low-stakes blog post assignment. A snail represented "just starting to move around," while a house cat indicated "gaining comfort," and a tiger symbolized mastery.[5] If we must assign a grade to small assignments, we should only use as many grade levels as are needed; the fewer we use, the faster we can grade.[6]

We can structure low-stakes assignments in ways that make the grade fairly obvious. I designed a format for daily note taking on the readings that rewarded students with more credit for doing higher-level intellectual work. They received a C if they did a short summary, a B if they also analyzed the quality of the argument and evidence, or an A if they summarized, analyzed, and connected the reading to previous readings or class topics. After I had given feedback on their early attempts, the notes were easy for me to grade; I simply had to decide if a student succeeded at the level she or he had attempted (yes or no). I was thrilled at how many students regularly chose to do the most advanced level of work, which improved the quality of class discussions. They were pleased because they had more choice and control over the grade they earned.

In some circumstances, students can provide feedback to one another. For a complex formal assignment, it's a good idea to require a draft, thereby ensuring that the students don't do everything at the last minute and actually make revisions. Receiving feedback at the draft stage is far more helpful than on a final draft when it's no longer possible to get a better grade, so students are more motivated to be attentive to suggestions. Many writing experts build in an initial step of getting peer feedback before instructors comment on the drafts.[7]

Some instructors worry that peer review might result in low-quality feedback, which is possible if students don't have a clear understanding of the standards used in historical writing or if they are afraid of saying something negative to a peer.[8] Therefore it's important to teach students how to be a helpful reviewer. My first efforts using peer feedback were mediocre. I created a peer evaluation worksheet with questions such as, "Is there a good thesis?" or "Is there appropriate evidence for the argument?" which sounded sensible, but actually allowed a weak or lazy peer evaluator to simply mark "Yes," even when that was not the case. My second attempt worked better, because, as writing experts recommend, my reviewer worksheet asked neutral, open-ended, and more descriptive questions. The revised question, "What is the thesis?" required that the reviewer read carefully enough to write down the thesis. If she struggled to find it, even that feedback would be helpful to the author. Similarly, instead of asking peer reviewers to answer, "Is the paper well organized?," it's better to ask them to jot down the basic outline of the paper. This process forces peer evaluators to read carefully and share very specific information with the author about the paper's organization, including places they got lost. Peer reviewers might also be asked to mark a place or two where the evidence seems especially effective and others where the evidence could be stronger.[9] In addition to helping the author of the paper, peer review benefits the reviewer, who by using it, becomes more familiar with criteria for good work.

Students might also evaluate their own work as part of the formative assessment process, after which we give them feedback on how well they did. After all, it wastes energy to write a lengthy comment only to have a student respond, "Yes, I knew that aspect needed work." One way to implement self-assessment is to ask students to turn in assignments accompanied by a note that finishes the sentence, "If I had more time, I would have improved this paper by_____." If the student has correctly gauged one of his weaknesses, the instructor can start her comments with "Yes, you should work on that," and then add other comments as necessary.[10] In the same vein, one might ask which aspects of their work students perceive as strong.

Self-evaluation can raise awareness of any aspect of student work. For example, at mid-semester (or earlier) one might ask students to assess the quality of their own class participation on a form like the one found in example 5.

Students circle the boxes that best describe their participation in each of the three areas. One benefit of such a form is that to rate themselves, they must read the criteria, which reinforces their understanding of what "good quality class participation" looks like.

Others ask students to consider their class participation frequently, with a form like the following.[11]

Name_____   Date _____

In the small-group work today, I was a:

_____ a. Well-prepared leader

_____ b. Positive contributor

_____ c. Bump on a log

_____ d. Distractor

Please explain your answer. If you answered a or b, provide an example of a specific positive contribution you made.

Whatever form students use, instructors may provide feedback with a quick response, such as "Yes, I agree"; "Keep up the good work"; "Your

Example 5. Class Partricipation Rubric

	Excellent	Strong	Okay	Weak
Large-group contributions	Contributes regularly (voluntarily) and very intelligently, using readings, raising smart questions, synthesizing, or answering questions; doesn't dominate; improves the learning of others	Volunteers to contribute fairly regularly and does so in a sensible, clear, and knowledgeable manner	Is prepared but rarely volunteers; speaks sensibly in the large group when called on; or speaks frequently but responses are sometimes confusing, inaccurate, or tangential	Rarely participates; or answers in an unproductive (confusing, inaccurate, repetitive, disrespectful, or tangential) manner; or volunteers when not prepared; or doesn't realize when speaking too much
Small-group contributions	Contributes to and sometimes leads small group very capably (though doesn't dominate); deepens or provides insights; makes the group significantly better because of the quality of preparation and manner of contributing	Actively, positively, and intelligently contributes to the discussions or tasks; well-prepared; shares the load	Cooperates in and contributes to the group task, though less frequently, consistently, productively, or confidently than others	Passive and not very involved; or distracts the group or gets group off on tangents; or can't participate because is unprepared; or is inattentive
Effective use of class time	Really focuses and thinks hard all class long, from walking into the room through the conclusion; takes notes carefully, actively, and with an inquisitive mindset, trying to understand both the big picture and the details	Concentrates throughout the class period and makes a consistent effort to be open to learning; has notes on the readings accessible and ready to consult; takes notes regularly, carefully, and intelligently	Is usually attentive but gets distracted occasionally; a bit passive about learning; doesn't take notes as thoroughly as could; isn't fully "present" all the time	Mind wanders frequently; allows self to be distracted; checks phone or uses computer to look at non-class-related sites or distracts other students with behavior, attitude, or computer; may give off vibe that uninterested

notes suggest you're well prepared, so I hope you'll try to stretch your-self a bit more in large group"; or, if a student's self-assessment is un-realistic, "Your perception doesn't match mine; I think we should talk."

In all these cases, formative feedback is intended to provide students with a better sense of how well their performance meets the standards for quality historical work. Feedback on lower-stakes but critically important day-to-day work—thinking about and taking notes on the readings, interpreting sources in class, working on analytical exercises in small groups, participating in discussions—improve students' ability to perform well on high-stakes assignments.

Summative Assessment

The AHA concurs with assessment experts that the best way to assess students' understanding of the higher-order concepts and skills of historical thinking is to pose summative assessments in which students present their analysis and interpretation rather than using "objective" tests (such as multiple-choice questions).[12] Rather than memorizing and parroting back information, we want our students to demonstrate that they are adept at skills like extracting meaning from sources, weighing and synthesizing information from various sources, building arguments, considering multiple perspectives, and pondering significant questions about the causes and implications of events. Although innovators in history assessment are trying to develop short-answer questions that reliably measure student understanding of historical thinking skills, for the moment, synthetic, argument-based essays appear to be one of the better methods for doing so. When students prepare for essay exams, they focus on concepts, issues, and inter-relationships, which is an effective approach for learning the content more deeply.[13]

Still, in-class essays aren't perfect. Their hurried nature prevents some students from performing at their best. In addition, some studies show unreliability in grading; not only do different instructors award different grades on the same essays, but the same instructor might award a different grade at a different time. Essays are harder to grade because the kinds of open-ended prompts and performance tasks needed to assess understanding do not have a single, correct answer. Fortu-nately, instructors can lessen the impact of time pressure, by teaching students how to write effective essays, revealing potential questions in advance, or allowing the use of some materials during an exam.[14] They can address the problems of reliability by implementing the following recommendations from writing and assessment experts.

Recommendation 1:
Think through the criteria while designing the assignment

In integrated course design, our assessments are aligned with our goals and what we teach each day. The ideal time to decide on the grading criteria is while we are designing the course and deciding on the major assignments/exams and which specific materials (readings, lectures, films, discussions) and information the students will need. It's quite depressing to face a huge pile of essays and realize that I'm going to have to read a lot of them before I truly know what constitutes great, decent, and unacceptable work—and worse, that to be fair I should go back and reread the essays I read before I had a firm grasp on this. Even if before the semester I can't anticipate every way students' work will differ in quality, I can decide which components matter most to me and will serve as the main criteria. There are scores of different elements that one could look for in student work, but in practice, we can't look for all of them.[15]

We can assess a handful of elements, though. Will those elements include the quality of the analysis of a specific reading? The degree to which students have synthesized multiple readings and lectures? Clarity of the thesis? Sophistication of the argument? Use of evidence? Appreciation of multiple perspectives? Creativity? The number of sources? Quality of the research? Error-free writing? Length? Depth? Compliance with the format? Assessment experts advise us to focus on a small number of significant elements rather than ones that are simply easy to recognize.[16] For example, while it's easy to see the number of works listed in the bibliography, that number may not reflect how well a student actually used ideas from multiple sources. We should consider the context for the assignment. For an in-class essay written under time pressure, many instructors choose to ignore stylistic and spelling issues that they wouldn't dismiss in a formal paper written outside of class. As shorthand, we express the primary elements of our criteria as nouns—such as thesis, evidence, organization, and research.

Most writing and assessment experts advise us to go further in spelling out our criteria, describing what we mean by different levels of student work on each element in a rubric. That is, we describe the characteristics of poor, good, better, and best work. (We can call the different levels of students work by various names: the letter grades A, B, C, D, and F; or terms like "exemplary, proficient, acceptable, and unacceptable"; "sophisticated, competent, not yet competent"; "advanced, intermediate high, intermediate, novice"; or "distinguished, average, developing, beginning."[17]) In general, for the interpretive questions historians ask, student understanding exists on a continuum (from in-depth, complex, and sophisticated to naive, basic, or superficial).[18] With some experience in carefully observing student work, we can articulate the characteristics that distinguish differences in quality.

For example, I've noticed that my students' argumentative essays show differences in the quality of the argument. Weaker students write a thesis that isn't very clear or write a narrative of events rather than crafting a thesis to defend. Meanwhile, excellent work has a clear argument that is complex, perhaps deftly acknowledging counterarguments or considering multiple perspectives or changes over time. There are also significant differences related to the use of evidence. An excellent essay has a lot of evidence and others have less, but the difference is more profound than that. Weaker essays use examples that don't quite support their point. Proficient essays use appropriate evidence but it primarily echoes examples discussed in class; excellent essays include ones that the author found independently, showing a deeper understanding of the sources. Finally, some essays show that their authors consistently did all the work and understood how all the ideas in the readings, class discussions, and lectures fit together, whereas weaker essays have obvious omissions (e.g., no reference to a whole book, topic, or an important lecture). I call the criterion for this phenomenon "scope of coverage."

The rubric in example 6 (known as a "full" or "analytic" rubric) reflects these observations. The three components of the criteria are listed in the left column, and the levels of quality move from left to right from highest to lowest. Each box contains a descriptor of the quality for a component at each level. A student's work might be rated as exemplary in some components and problematic in others.

In a similar vein, Joel Sipress created the rubric in example 7 for an out-of-class argumentative essay, which creates a clear and straightforward grading scheme.[19]

Why use a rubric? There are numerous benefits for instructors. First, creating a good one requires that we understand the distinctions between levels of student work, which is a significant accomplishment.

Example 6. Essay Rubric A

	Exemplary	Proficient	Developing	Problematic
Thesis	Clear, consistent, and complex	Clear and consistently argued	A little unclear or inconsistent in spots	Absent (or tells a narrative instead of making an argument)
Evidence	Abundant and extremely well chosen	A good amount that supports the arguments	Not very much or occasionally doesn't support the argument well	Very little
Scope of coverage	Comprehensive— skillfully uses both primary and secondary sources and materials from virtually all the readings, lectures, and video	Strong—uses most of the relevant materials and clearly under- stands how they were relevant	Somewhat limited—relies on materials from some class meetings but not all, or primary sources but not secondary, or lectures but not readings	Very limited— relies on a very small selection of the relevant materials (or uses inappropriate ones)

Having a firm grasp on these distinctions reduces uncertainty about our grades. Good, full rubrics improve the reliability and fairness of our grading. Instructors are more consistent when they systematically check each component on the rubric. I am less likely to be wowed by an essay that is beautifully written but contains little evidence or under- appreciate an essay that has a basic thesis but impressively uses a lot of evidence, and my weighting scheme will tell me what grade these different essays should receive. Instructors are less susceptible to the inconsistency that can result from fatigue or distractions and are less likely to subtly change their standards after hearing the same argu- ments over and over.[20] For large classes where teaching assistants share the grading, the use of a rubric helps ensure inter-rater reliability. Last but not least, as I become more conscious of my standards, I become more capable of teaching students how to meet them.[21]

Example 7. Essay Rubric B

Your essays will be graded on three criteria.

The thesis: Do you have a clear and effective thesis? Is it clearly stated? (Unless you have a good reason not to, the thesis should be stated in the introduction.)

Organization: Does the essay provide a well-organized argument in support of the thesis? Is the point of each paragraph clear? Is the relationship between each paragraph and the thesis clear?

Evidence: Does the body of the essay provide sufficient evidence to support each assertion?

Grading

An **A paper** is strong in all three areas.

A **B paper** has a clear and effective thesis but is weak in either evidence or organization.

A **C paper** (a) lacks a clear and effective thesis; (b) is weak in both evidence and organization; or (c) has a serious weakness in any one of the three areas.

Other Policies

1. Any essay based entirely on material from class lecture/discussion (i.e., without evidence from the course readings or outside research) will receive a grade no higher than D. Internet sources cannot be used, except with the permission of the instructor.

2. No paper that lacks proper citation will be accepted. (See "Plagiarism and Proper Citation" handout.)

3. Any paper that fails to meet the minimum length requirement will receive no grade higher than D.

A rubric can improve grading efficiency. The instructor simply circles the description of a student's work on each level of the criteria (and adds up the totals), meaning he doesn't have to write repetitive comments to justify the grade. The levels on the rubric make clear (visually and in words) where the student's work fits on the continuum of quality. If we have time to give more feedback, we can write individualized comments on a couple of key matters.

Descriptive rubrics help students understand the criteria. It may take time for them to understand why their work is located where it is on the continuum, but with practice (in class and seeing examples of different work), rubrics may help them learn to recognize various components of quality work and their own strengths and weaknesses. These are crucial steps in being able to monitor their progress as they work (a metacognitive skill known as self-regulating). Thus rubrics not only assess learning but promote learning.[22] Rubrics can also increase students' trust in the grading process. Some disappointed students believe faculty grade arbitrarily. The rubric demonstrates our criteria—thereby discouraging complaints about grades.[23] If individual students do want to discuss their grades, the rubric serves as a helpful starting place.

Rubrics can be created for any kind of assignment. Although the criteria will often include common historical concerns related to the quality of analysis, use of sources, accuracy, and context, different types of assignments often include distinct criteria.

If assessing the strategy that a student used while conducting research, for example, one of the elements of the criteria might be the quality of the searching for articles in scholarly databases.

Exemplary	Proficient	Acceptable	Unacceptable
Intelligently experimented with lots of sensible keyword combinations and carefully noted which worked well in different databases, resulting in a large number of good articles.	Experimented with various keywords and combinations and found some useful ones; found numerous and appropriate articles for the topic.	Tried more than one keyword search; overlooked some good possible keywords, however; list of articles is short or may include irrelevant articles.	Didn't try many keyword combinations or didn't carefully keep track of which ones were used; list of articles is very short or includes many irrelevant articles.

For a poster session, criteria might include the content, organization, visual appeal, and students' interactions with visitors to the poster. For this last element, the rubric might describe levels of quality in the following way.

Excellent	Strong	Adequate
Attentive, informative and engaging; behaved professionally and answered questions very knowledgeably, and stimulated great discussion of the topic and its implications.	Attentive, informative, and welcoming; behaved professionally and answered questions effectively.	Willing to answer questions but passive or awkward in engaging viewers; answered most questions correctly, but occasionally struggled; or less professional in some way (e.g., got off-topic or looked unenthusiastic).

For an oral examination, in addition to overall understanding, evidence, and implications, one unique element of the criteria might be how capably a student offered answers without prompting.[24]

Exemplary	Competent	Weak
Didn't need to be prompted at all.	Needed minimal prompting (required one or two probing questions).	Needed a lot of prompting.

John Rosinbum created an assignment that asked students to analyze the "virality" of a nineteenth-century poem, short story, recipe, or news article. His grading criteria included a component for how capably students visually conveyed spread of the text.[25] He described the different levels of quality in the following way.

7 points (maximum score)	5 points	3 points (or less)
The visualization effectively demonstrates the geographical AND temporal range of the article's reprinting.	The visualization demonstrates the geographical OR the temporal range of the article's reprinting.	The visualization fails to demonstrate the geographical AND the temporal range of the article's reprinting.

Example 8 shows a full/analytic rubric for an assignment that asked students to conduct research about an event and then create a website about it. In this rubric, the presumption is that each component counts

Example 8. Website Rubric

	Excellent	Strong	Adequate	Weak
Background information	Excellent in accuracy, relevance, and quantity; provides very helpful historic context for the event	Accurate and clear; event is placed in relevant historic context	Accurate but viewer could benefit from a little more, better, or clearer historic context	Background information and context are not effectively communicated; may contain errors, overlook important information, or be unclear
Narrative	Very informative, clear, accurate, interesting, and concise; excellent choices of information to include; links to other sites help a reader who wants to dig deeper	Clear, informative and accurate; reader gets useful and necessary information without being over-whelmed by too many details; good links show how to learn more	Mainly clear and accurate but some choices might have been better (perhaps there is a bit too much or too little, or it's not 100% clear or accurate, or includes few links to other sites)	Narrative has inaccuracies, overlooks important information, includes few links, or is unclear, poorly written, or too short
Significance	Very effectively and powerfully conveys the significance of the event on an individual and its more general impact; helps make the viewer understand and care	Effectively conveys the significance and impact of the event generally and on an individual, with evidence	Conveys some of the event's significance but doesn't help the viewer gain perspective as well as it might; or it pays attention to either the personal or general societal impact but not both	Struggles to show the personal and societal significance of the event with evidence, clarity, or historical perspective

(Continued on next page)

	Excellent	Strong	Adequate	Weak
Research	Used many reliable secondary sources; featured excellent primary sources; images used with permission and all sources are correctly cited	Used a solid number of reliable secondary sources (beyond encyclopedia and Internet); featured relevant primary sources; images used with permission and all sources are correctly cited	Would have benefited from more or better sources; there may be some problems with citations or incorporating relevant primary sources; images used with permission	Relies on only a few sources or unreliable ones; struggles to paraphrase, quote, or properly and ethically communicate the sources of information; citations may have problems; there may be some images used without permission or proper attribution
Functionality	Webpage works perfectly; it adheres to all the instructions in terms of font, links, photos, spacing, headings, etc.; looks great, too!	Webpage works very well; there may be a minor error or two, but it generally adheres to the instructions in terms of font, links, photos, spacing, headings, etc.; it looks professional	Webpage mostly works correctly, but a few things weren't entirely consistent with the directions in terms of font, links, photos, spacing, headings, etc., detracting a bit from its professionalism	Webpage has some noticeable problems with the functioning and/or look in terms of font, links, photos, spacing, headings, etc., which suggest insufficient proofreading or lack of adherence to the directions and which detract from the user's experience

equally. After marking the appropriate description for each element, the instructor would simply average the five scores to determine the final grade. Alternatively, instructors may opt to weigh some elements more than others and create a percentage or point scheme that leads to a quickly calculated numerical grade.

Whether I create a detailed analytic rubric or simply decide my main criteria in advance, this anticipatory thinking means I can accomplish the next research-based recommendation.

Recommendation 2:
Share the criteria with students at the time
we assign the work

As noted in chapter 1, the Transparency in Learning and Teaching Project demonstrated that we level the playing field for all our students when we explicitly communicate the criteria before they do the work.[26] To be clear, sharing criteria is not giving students the answers. Saying that I will be looking for students to use evidence effectively does not relieve them from the process of figuring out which evidence backs up their arguments. As proponents of learner-centered assessment put it, "The task they face is still formidable—to produce work with these qualities."[27] Even if we are transparent about our standards, not all students will perform at the same level.[28] Being transparent about our criteria removes the hidden advantages that some students have from receiving better preparation before coming to our course. If we believe in our standards, there is no point in keeping them private; sharing them is simply good, inclusive teaching. As Leah Shopkow put it, expecting students to be able to intuit the rules of our discipline's academic game "seems rather more like hazing than teaching."[29]

Because it can be difficult to know all the characteristics of the different levels of student work on a newly designed assignment, we can at least share a list of the main criteria. For an argument-based essay, that might mean saying we will assess the quality of the:

- thesis
- evidence
- historical accuracy/context
- use of available materials
- organization and writing.

Simply listing the main criteria is vaguer than a fuller descriptive analytic rubric.[30] However, when an assignment is brand new, this vagueness gives the instructor the flexibility to figure out what realistically constitutes the various levels of quality once work is turned in. (I might create an experimental full rubric but not share it with students until after I have tested it with student work and refined it.[31]) When I need to provide such vague criteria, I should spend some time in class discussing what each criterion means. I could tell students that by "evidence," I mean both the number of sources and how well those sources back up the argument. Even better, I could get students to interact with the criteria in some way—perhaps first asking them what "good evidence" involves or if quantity or quality is more important. Or I might ask them which of three thesis statements is better, or which of three pieces of evidence best support a specific argument. The Transparency Project also encourages faculty to warn students of common pitfalls. I might say, "Don't simply narrate a chronology of what happened; you really do need a thesis that has an argument," or "Don't simply rely on the lectures. I want you to use evidence from the readings, too." Time spent helping students understand an assignment is better spent than time grading.[32]

Recommendation 3:
Grade with an eye toward fairness

When the pile of assignments arrives, a couple of practices help ensure fairness from the outset.

A. First, quickly read a handful to see if the rubric and grading criteria are realistic (or whether we need to make minor tweaks).

When developing my grading criteria, I sometimes don't know how much evidence will be "a lot," so I need to skim some to get a sense. Sometimes it turns out that almost no student comprehended a specific idea, so I shouldn't penalize everyone for its lack, but reward the few who did get it.[33]

B. Read all essays anonymously (without knowing who wrote each one).

Finding a way to guarantee anonymity (e.g., students using an ID number) may add a few minutes of work at the end of the grading process, but it prevents us being influenced by identity-based biases. In addition, research suggests that knowing the author has done strong work in the past (or is someone you like) can create a "halo effect" that influences you to interpret the work more generously than you might for another student.[34] When pondering a B versus B+, I used to notice thoughts creeping into my mind about the students most likely to be very disappointed or complain, but grading anonymously has freed me from those thoughts and improved my confidence about my consistency. It affects how students perceive the fairness of their grades, too.

C. If students have written more than one essay, grade all the essays on the same topic before moving on to grading a different essay topic.

This practice ensures that we keep the criteria for one specific task in the front of our minds. It also helps avoid the halo effect that a student who did well on one essay will do well on the next, which is not necessarily true. In addition, it's a good idea to shuffle the papers before starting to grade a new essay topic, in case we tend to be tougher or easier on the first or last ones we grade.[35]

D. Don't try to grade all the papers in one sitting; give yourself breaks.

Although it's good to return assignments promptly, being rested increases our ability to read each one independently and apply the criteria consistently. It probably improves our mood, too.[36]

E. Read with the purpose of understanding a student's meaning and how well they have met the criteria.

Writing instructors observe that novice graders tend to read with the purpose of finding fault, stopping frequently (even midsentence) to point out problems, and get distracted by surface details. Ronald Lunsford described the novice grader as a "marker-of-errors hovering over the text, looking for some trigger to set off an alarm and cause him to attack a passage in the paper." In contrast, more experienced assessors read in large units of text, aiming to understand a student's meaning and the major strengths and weaknesses of the work, giving primary attention to content and organization.[37] More effective assessors "sit back in their chairs to take in the whole of a student's paper before deciding on a strategy for teaching some important principles," and then carefully construct their comments.[38] For an instructor like me who has difficulty stopping myself from writing on the essay before reading it all, it may be wise to take the pen out of my hand while reading. Focusing on the big picture—the main criteria—means I can first decide on the grade and then decide how to craft useful comments.

Recommendation 4:
Comment strategically

Our ending and marginal comments constitute an important opportunity to teach. Research on writing suggests effective ways to write comments.

A. Focus on the highest-priority issues.

For example, if the assignment is a research paper but there are almost no sources, there's no point in spending ten minutes commenting on one badly written paragraph; similarly, if the assignment is an argument-based essay and there's no thesis, that's the place to start.[39] It's wise to focus on just a few substantive issues.

B. Avoid writing too many comments.

Providing a massive quantity of comments might actually backfire. Research suggests that when faced by too many markings all over the text, many of which seem cryptic, students are overwhelmed.[40] When students receive a lot of "local-level" suggestions about phrasing, word choice, grammar, and punctuation, even those who read them all have difficulty distinguishing between major and minor issues. They tend to ignore larger issues of content and structure and simply correct minor errors. Worse, some get the idea that their job is simply to change whatever the teacher wants instead of comprehending larger principles about how to think and write well.[41]

Historian Robert E. Weir evolved as a grader. Early in his career, he cloistered himself like a medieval monk poring over manuscripts, correcting everything in a paper. "I wrote reams of commentary and marginalia, suggested alternative strategies, raised questions to consider, noted every alternative interpretation, and corrected every error of grammar and syntax. I hoped students would use all of this to launch a program of self-improvement that would send them back to grammar texts, writing guides, and history books. And, of course, I hoped they would spend hours reflecting upon the nuanced debate points I raised."[42]

Weir concluded that the payoff didn't match his investment. "First of all, I paid a heavy price. My attention to minute detail took an enormous amount of time away from my family, friends, and scholarship." He also came to believe that this hard work (so difficult he called it "martyrdom") made little pedagogical sense. Most students glanced at the grade, reacted with pleasure or disgust—usually based solely on how high or low it was—and quickly disposed of their assignments. He decided that students (not he) should be responsible for correcting certain kinds of problems. Finally, he realized that "even the best students found many of my comments beyond their comprehension, while the weaker writers were depressed by the sheer number of their 'errors.' . . . My thoroughness caused students to suffer information overload."[43]

C. Write marginal comments that are decipherable, specific, and connected to your overall comments.

In one study, a researcher recorded students as they read comments on their essays and found that they frequently misconstrued the instructor's intention.[44] I have a bad habit of underlining phrases or putting checks in the margins without telling students what those marks mean. Many of us write short but vague marginal comments that are mysterious to students. I know what I mean by "transition," but my student might not; although it takes longer for me to write, "I'm confused here; this sentence seems to contradict the previous paragraph," that's clearer. "Unclear" isn't as useful as "I can't tell if you mean ABC or XYZ." Offering these specific alternatives shows the author how a reader could misunderstand their meaning. The question, "Evidence?" isn't as useful as "A specific example from the X reading would strengthen your argument here." Ordering the student to "Introduce the speaker," isn't as useful as explaining, "I couldn't tell who the speaker was in this quotation; is she a historian, or was she someone who lived in 1730?" Even a positive comment like, "Great!" isn't as helpful as it might be; "Great example to support this point!" is more specific.

One might understandably protest, "I simply don't have time to write all those words," which is why writing instructors suggest that we mainly write marginal comments connected to our end-of-essay overall comments.[45] When we observe an important problematic pattern—such as a lack of evidence—we can write about it at the end of the paper and put marginal comments in a few places where more evidence was needed. This type of comment achieves the goal of commenting for the purpose of teaching rather than pointing out problems.[46]

D. Aim for the tone of a supportive reader who wants to coach the author to fulfill his promise.

The tone of our comments matters. We likely know this from our own experience as students or as scholars who receive reviews of our work. Receiving feedback may make us feel inadequate, vulnerable, angry, or defensive. We receive it better when we perceive the reviewer as interested and fair-minded, someone who wants to help us succeed, rather than a mean-spirited judge. Small steps make a difference in tone. It helps to make clear how a student's work affected me as a reader ("I got confused here because . . .").[47] We can direct our comments at the work performance, not the student.[48] (It's better to say, "This paragraph doesn't . . ." than to write "You failed to . . .") We should remember there is a human being reading these comments and thus avoid sarcastic, scolding, and impatient ones.[49] Writing researcher John Bean suggested we think of comments as personal correspondence with a "tone as supportive coach, someone invested in the student as a person and in the improvement of the student's powers as a writer and thinker."[50]

E. Address both positive and negative aspects of the work.

Students need to know what they are doing well, not only where they can improve, and our comments are a powerful way to reinforce good practices.[51] We know expectancy (believing one can successfully perform a task) plays a significant role in motivation. Saundra McGuire saw the research in action as director of a Center for Academic Success. She was "bowled over" by how students who had appeared lazy became willing to work hard after she explicitly expressed belief in their capabilities.[52]

When I propose that we adopt a supportive tone, I am not suggesting that we have low standards or patronize students by overpraising for mediocre work. Doing so can actually cause students (especially those from marginalized groups) to mistrust their instructors. Research about stereotype threat suggests that the most effective way to convey feedback to minoritized students is to both emphasize the high standards that were used to evaluate the work and convey the belief that the student is capable of meeting those standards. In numerous studies, students who received this form of feedback were far more motivated to opt to revise and to resubmit work that met high standards. (This practice does no harm to students from majority groups.[53])

F. Don't mark or correct all errors related to spelling, punctuation, grammar, and usage.

Resisting the urge to circle and correct all the errors doesn't mean we are unconcerned about these problems. Instead, it means that we know that research shows that the payoff of marking all of them isn't worth our effort—and doesn't help students figure out how to recognize and fix the problems for themselves. Writing experts recommend a couple of strategies for dealing with these problems. One is making "writing," or "grammar and punctuation" or "edited standard written English" one of the elements of criteria on a rubric.[54]

Excellent	Proficient	Developing
Reads very smoothly and has virtually no errors.	Reads well and has only a rare typo or error in punctuation or usage.	Contains numerous typographical, usage, or punctuation errors that distract a reader and/or obscure the author's meaning.

For a piece of work with numerous errors, after marking the "developing" level on the rubric, an instructor might mark (but not correct) all the errors on (just) one page. This practice connects comments on the paper with the rubric and alerts students to the seriousness of the problem. Another option is to set "gateway" criteria so that if students turn in a paper that doesn't meet certain criteria (related to proofreading), the instructor will return it ungraded to be revised (and receive a penalty).[55]

To help a student improve her writing, we can identify patterns of errors (such as apostrophes and comma splices) so she knows what to prioritize. If we want to go further, we can invite her to work with us on correcting a few examples or suggest she visit a campus tutoring or writing center for more assistance.

Recommendation 5:
Consider time-saving methods for communicating feedback

A good rubric saves time, but there are other tools you can use. Many learning management systems have ways to streamline the process of collecting, commenting on, and sharing the grade on a piece of work (including using an instructor-designed electronic rubric). Instructors who find themselves writing the same comments over and over often keep them in a handy document where they can copy and paste the relevant ones for an individual student. Instead of typing comments, Leah Shopkow created a "subtractive" feedback handout that listed typical problems on each component of an assignment. For example, on an assignment in which students analyzed a scholarly article, for the component "clearly explains the article's argument and its parts," the form listed:

Doesn't identify the argument in the article correctly_____
Doesn't explain it clearly_____
Doesn't recognize the argument_____
Leaves out parts of the argument_____
Doesn't do this part_____

Shopkow saved time by simply checking which (if any) of these problems were present in the work.[56]

In a similar vein, Robert Weir set up a feedback form listing positive aspects of work that he could check off when present:

Thesis/focus well-defined_____
Well-stated arguments_____
Vivid/effective examples_____
Use of specific detail_____
Good internal logic_____
Well structured/organized_____
Good intro/conclusion_____
Clear/well written_____
Creative/lively style_____
Fine command of topic_____
Superb synthesis skills_____
Well documented_____[57]

Although this list isn't as helpful as a full analytic rubric because it doesn't communicate exactly where a student's work resides on the continuum of quality for each element of the criteria, it does inform students of the main elements of good work and which ones they have achieved. In a higher-tech version, instructors can set up a digital form that allows them to simply check the buttons next to relevant comments. If using a tool like a Google form, the app automatically compiles each student's individualized feedback.

Kevin Gannon experimented with providing audio feedback. He first read a student's paper, took a few informal notes, and then recorded himself "talking through" the paper: "OK, on the third paragraph of page 2, you introduce a couple of general points, but I need to see some supporting detail. Think about how you can bring in more evidence here." Then he added a few summative comments and sent the students the file or a link to the file. (It's worth investigating a good tool/app that allows students to see the paper at the same time they hear the instructor's voice, and a way to send the file without using too much storage space.) This method saved time; it took Gannon five to eight minutes for each four- to five-page paper, which was less than half the time he spent on written comments. His students liked it, too, saying the audio feedback felt more personalized and more specific, and they felt like they "had to listen," whereas with written feedback, they usually didn't read it all.[58] Some studies confirm Gannon's perceptions.[59]

Finally, sometimes we can improve our efficiency by disciplining ourselves. We might set a timer for working on each paper to stay on track. Others use a grading sheet that limits the amount of space for comments and keeps the focus on the big picture, as in the half sheet below.[60]

Things the paper does well
Ways the paper could be better
Priority for what to work on for the next assignment

Recommendation 6:
Make returning students' work a teachable moment

The day we return a major graded assignment, we should debrief it with the whole class. Debriefing includes a quick, nondefensive description of the process used in grading (especially practices used to ensure fairness), reiteration of the characteristics of good work (even better is showing examples of it), and mentioning a few common areas where some students struggled.

Some instructors go further. Instead of worrying that some might not read their feedback, they require that each student write a brief summary of the feedback and explain how they will use it to improve on their next assignment. Instructors return this reflection to students a week before the next similar assignment is due. A variation on this theme is a "cognitive wrapper" in which students also consider the process they used when working on the assignment. As we know, there are many reasons students may perform below their potential: they may have had a limited understanding of the material, not fully understood the assignment, did not grasp the criteria, did not allocate enough time, or used ineffective study or writing strategies. In one version of a post-assignment/exam cognitive wrapper, students answer three questions: How did you prepare? What aspects of the work could have been improved? How might you prepare (similarly or differently) next time?[61]

Feedback is most effective when students are primed to hear it.[62] They might be receptive to learning about successful strategies right after they've received their first significant graded assignment. Even if we shared the criteria and suggestions for how to approach a task before the assignment, some students may not have fully appreciated them at that time. If they didn't get the grade they hoped for, they may be motivated to listen more carefully. (If they did well, they still benefit from reinforcement of successful behaviors). A short in-class metacognitive lesson about an effective studying process might inform students about research that shows it's better to anticipate potential exam questions and test themselves rather than repeatedly rereading or copying their notes.[63] Similarly, instructors who teach students without much experience in history or in writing might ask them to reflect on whether they used all the steps for writing a good take-home argumentative essay, such as in the wrapper shown in example 9.

Example 9. Wrapper for a Take-Home Essay

_____ I "tore the question apart" to make sure I understood exactly what I was being asked to do and all the parts I would need to address, and I asked the instructor about anything I wasn't sure about.

_____ I looked at the rubric to make sure I understood the criteria for evaluation and to get a sense of what a strong essay would look like.

_____ I reread and/or took better notes on the readings that I didn't understand or do a good job on.

_____ I borrowed in-class notes for any class days I was absent (and asked a student or the prof about anything I didn't understand).

_____ I reviewed all my notes on the readings and class meetings, considering which information was relevant to the essay prompt.

_____ I developed my tentative thesis, making sure it had the characteristics we discussed in class.

_____ I made a list of all the evidence to support my thesis, making sure that it came from as many sources as are relevant, including both primary and secondary sources.

_____ I considered possible counterarguments and how I might respond to them.

_____ I sketched a rough outline.

_____ I wrote my first draft.

_____ I checked the criteria in the rubric again and made sure I answered all parts of the question.

_____ I revised to strengthen my ideas and ensured that they were logically organized and clear, thanks to good transition sentences.

_____ I made sure I cited my sources correctly and double-checked that I followed all directions regarding the format.

_____ I proofread at least once and paid attention to places where Word's spell-checker and grammar-checker highlighted problems. (If I struggled, I asked a friend to read it or went to the writing center.)

Seeing this list makes it clear why it's a bad strategy to write the essay late the night before it's due.[64] Even less detailed debriefing of assignments may be beneficial, contributing to students' future learning and their ability to learn on their own, and this is especially true for underrepresented and nontraditional students.[65]

Recommendation 7:
Give additional/future assignments that use
the same criteria, so students have the chance
to show that they've learned from earlier work
and feedback

One of the reasons some students simply glance at their grade and ignore the comments is that when they see a grade on a summative assessment, which cannot change, the work is over in their minds. There's little incentive to deeply consider the comments.[66] If we don't offer an opportunity for students to use the feedback, we don't maximize the potential of the assignments to promote learning.[67] Students might use the feedback by revising their work in a new draft, a practice writing instructors strongly encourage. Alternately, students might apply the feedback in a similar kind of assignment in the future. Although it may sound interesting to give students a wide variety of types of assignments (e.g., book reviews, exams, museum exhibits, and research projects), we should remember that novices need practice to improve at difficult historical skills. As John McClymer said, "Learning is recursive. . . . We learn by going back to tasks and trying again and again."[68] Repeating a format (e.g., argumentative essay) can move (and motivate) students toward mastery. Comprehensive exams (covering material from the entire semester, some of which they were already tested on) also reward students for using past work.[69] Portfolios including revised work can serve the same purpose.[70] Regardless of what method we choose, we should explicitly explain how our feedback is relevant to future assignments, which increases its value and students' expectancy.

Individual Conversations about Grades

Even with well-thought-out standards and sound practices, a few students will raise questions about their grades. Because a student's first reaction might be emotional, I never discuss a grade immediately after handing back work; instead, I schedule an appointment, giving the student time to cool down and examine their work, the feedback, and the criteria. Following the advice of some assessment experts, I try to approach these conversations with an open mind—not assuming that this specific student is a grade-grubber (or worse). During the meeting, I listen respectfully and carefully to ascertain what the student wants from the conversation.[71] She may want me to regrade her work, better understand the reason for the grade, learn how to do better in the future, or express disappointment or frustration, all of which are different.

In his research about the characteristics and practices of excellent teachers, Ken Bain observed that they tended to have a strong sense of humility when it comes to grades, recognizing that they are fallible.[72] Therefore if a student believes he deserved a better grade, I try to quash my first reaction, which is entrenched defense of the original grade, and instead consider the possibility the student is correct. It's certainly possible that I misread the meaning of part of an essay or that I wasn't 100 percent consistent in applying my criteria. I reread the work, sometimes before the student arrives so that I feel less pressure, but also after I've listened to what they tell me. Often, I decide that the original grade should stand and that the heart of the problem is that the student doesn't fully understand the criteria. For that reason, I usually have the student read a couple of (anonymous) samples of A-worthy work. Often simply seeing excellent work (that it is different in quality from their own) allows us to spend the remainder of the meeting thinking about how they might improve.

If I adopt the role of the student's ally in learning, the conversations often become pleasant and productive. I aim to empower the student, so that by the end of the meeting, he has one or two takeaways that will help in the future. Sometimes that might be a specific thing to work on for the next assignment (e.g., answering all parts of the question, using more evidence, addressing counterarguments). I try to diagnose (or better still, have the student self-diagnose) where she might have gotten off track. How did she prepare? How effective are her class notes? How consistently and effectively is she reading? To help inculcate a learning orientation, we want students to understand that most matters related to the quality of the work are under their control.[73]

Sometimes these discussions move beyond historical thinking and morph into exploration of the meaning of grades. Some students have incorrect assumptions about how grades should be allocated, thinking they should receive a high grade simply because they worked hard; because they "need" one to do something else (e.g., attend law school or not be suspended); because they've received high grades in the past; or because they pay a lot of tuition.[74] Some confuse grades with their worth as a person, leading to great angst. Pointing out the fallacies in these assumptions can be difficult, but educational. Occasionally a student may blame me for the grade I "gave." In that case, experts suggest we try to (kindly) shift responsibility back where it belongs, stating something like, "I'm sorry that your work did not earn a higher grade," or "I know you are disappointed in the quality of your work," or "I know it's disappointing that you didn't convey everything you knew."[75] Unless students accurately attribute the reasons for their grades, they will have difficulty meeting their potential in any course.

For other students, the conversation turns to personal struggles. Some may be grappling with extraordinarily difficult issues. In these cases, providing a sympathetic ear, reflecting back what we hear, or offering information about campus resources may be valuable. Sometimes a student wants a chance to revise the assignment to earn a higher grade. This option tempts me, especially if a student's life struggles contributed to the performance. However, for the sake of fairness, I have to ask myself if I am willing to offer the opportunity to revise to all my students, some of whom also may be grappling with difficult matters or weren't able to do their best. As Walvoord and Anderson advised, "You can be sympathetic about the situation but unbending about the grade. You may change a grade because you think your original grade was not accurate, but don't have to give unmerited changes to students even though their lives are very tough."[76] In addition, it may well be wiser for an at-risk student to concentrate on the upcoming work in the course rather than risk getting behind while revising the past work. We may consider exceptions in unusual situations.[77]

If a student remains dissatisfied after we clearly and nondefensively show the reasons for the grade, we may have to let go and let the student remain frustrated. Students have the right to appeal grades, and we can point them to our institution's procedures, while keeping a paper trail that includes our criteria, comments, and actions. Clear criteria, of course, make it unlikely that students can win a grade appeal—just as they make it unlikely that students will question their grades in the first place.

■

Grading will probably never be my favorite part of teaching, but it doesn't have to be cause for despair. Setting up clear criteria (that account for distinctions in quality on important components of students' work) at the time I design the assignment helps ensure that I am consistent. I can adopt other practices to help ensure fairness. Rubrics and targeted feedback strategies can improve my efficiency. Explaining the criteria to students before they do the work not only helps avoid unpleasant grade appeals but fosters students' ability to understand historians' standards and do better work. Debriefing after the assignment also empowers students to do better in the future, especially if we make sure that they read and use our feedback and offer assignments that give them opportunities to improve.

While we correctly think of essays, exams, projects, and other major assignments as assessment of students' learning, they also provide some feedback for us as teachers about the degree to which our course is achieving its goals. There will always be differences in the degree to which students understand the material, and many factors affect how well they perform. One of those factors is the quality of our teaching—how well we chose readings, organized the course, communicated the goals and expectations, explained ideas, asked questions, knew and interacted with students, scaffolded assignments, motivated students, designed activities, facilitated discussion, lectured, engaged, and provided practice and feedback, among other things. Like all dedicated history teachers, I need feedback on how well my actions are facilitating learning.[78]

Assessing Our Teaching

Often department chairs, deans, colleagues, or other people assess the quality of our teaching. It's a reality of higher education that may be nerve-wracking, confusing, intimidating, or frustrating. Yet it also has the potential to be very useful, so we should take some ownership of the process. We should analyze the meanings of summative assessments, such as student rating forms, and seek out various opportunities for formative assessment that provide us with relevant, specific, and constructive information. That way, we'll be able to pinpoint areas for improvement, make adjustments, and deepen our practices, so that students learn better and feel satisfied with our courses. Good information lets us know what we do well, which helps us make our case to those who make decisions about hiring, continuation, tenure, promotion, or salary. Meaningful feedback also helps us recognize and feel confident about how we teach well.

Student Evaluations of Teaching

End-of-semester student rating forms administered by the institution, sometimes called student evaluations of teaching (SETs), are a complex and contested subject. Different institutions use different forms; some use questions that have been tested for reliability and validity and look at components of instruction that have been linked by research to learning, whereas others create their own forms, which may or may not be based in sound research.[79] There is a massive and evolving literature about these forms, and assessment experts disagree on some matters, so this discussion is tentative. It seems likely that some faculty concerns, such as that SETs simply reward popularity or easy courses, are myths debunked by a lot of research.[80] We should inform ourselves about the value and the limitations of these ratings, because our institution may rely on them in summative evaluations that have a substantial impact on our careers.

Student rating forms have limitations. They are not—and are not intended to be—evidence of how much students have learned, which is the most important criterion for effective teaching. Rather, they collect students' perceptions of and satisfaction with a course, instructor, and their learning.[81] Because students are not experts in our discipline, they are not in a position to evaluate certain things, such as whether the readings reflect current interpretations by historians or whether the content or assignments are appropriate for the discipline. (Our fellow historians are better suited to evaluate those matters.) Nor have most students been trained in pedagogy or research about learning, so they probably don't know the best methods for teaching historical concepts and skills. Sometimes they fill out forms very quickly. Finally, it's possible for students to have biases. There is a small number of contested—but quite troubling—studies suggesting that students judge instructors differently based on factors such as gender, race, sexual orientation, and English fluency. There is much research about the impact of implicit bias against women in higher education, and it would not be surprising for it (and other types of bias against African American, LGBTQIA, and international faculty) to appear in student evaluation ratings (and other forms of evaluation).[82] It's difficult to measure these possible biases, but some studies suggest that students evaluate instructors based partly on gendered expectations. Work by people assumed to be men is judged to be superior to that done by people assumed to be women—even when the only indicator is the author's gender-specific name.[83] Some African American faculty have received isolated comments with insulting racial connotations that make them not want to read any student comments ever again. Instructors from any group may receive irrelevant comments (on their dress, hair, voice, body) or ones where thoughtless students, emboldened by anonymity, are cruel.

Despite these important limitations, student perceptions and reactions should not be dismissed out of hand. After all, students are the object for our teaching, and if our course or instruction is not effective in their eyes, it is important to explore why this is the case. Students' ratings represent observations based on firsthand and extensive experience (and a semester of experience is different from the snapshot a dean or chair might get from observing one class period). Most experts say that students are well positioned to comment on instructor clarity, organization, and the degree to which class meetings and assignments are engaging. A well-designed exam or essay may be a more direct measure of how much students learned (although how many of us have tested our exams for reliability and validity?), but student perceptions of how much they learned should be taken seriously. Their perceptions about whether our course goals were achieved matter. In addition, student ratings are good for telling us the degree to which students found the course challenging and whether our instructional methods and materials motivated them to learn the subject.[84]

We can't ignore the possibility of some students being prejudiced against some instructors based on aspects of the instructor's identity, but we also can't ignore the experiences of the majority of our students as expressed in the ratings. Defenders of the forms assert that any identity-based biases students hold are statistically inconsequential, and even if some students enter a course with some preconceptions based on identity, the semester-long experience with their instructors can modify those views. Still it's clear that more research needs to be done, especially with regard to race.[85] Finally, it's clear that these forms should be seen as offering only one type of evidence of the quality of instruction (albeit a significant one) and should not be the sole source of evidence used to evaluate instruction. Good summative evaluation involves multiple sources of information and various methods of collecting it, which are administered at multiple moments.[86] Indeed, the developers of one of the most respected instruments recommend that student ratings should account for only 30–50 percent of an overall evaluation of teaching effectiveness.[87]

Well-designed rating forms provide a big picture or overview of student perceptions of the course and instruction. They are less helpful in providing information about specific details. For example, when students rate a course's organization, we don't know which specific practices they are thinking about. Was it the organization of typical class meetings, the ease of use of materials in the learning management system, knowing due dates in advance, or that day we forgot the essays we intended to return? When considering the data, larger sample sizes help; when we have smaller classes (fewer than ten students), the results are not as reliable. Although SETs can distinguish between very effective and not very effective courses, small differences in the numerical ratings (4.96 versus 5.12) don't tell us much. SETs can be more helpful when we have data from numerous semesters and courses to see whether our ratings are stable and generalizable. Ratings can give us comparative data—compared with other faculty teaching the same course or to others in our department or university, so that we know whether we are above average or below, and we can compare our current course to previous times we offered it, but they don't tell us what is an acceptable rating is. That is not yet a subject of research findings but is a matter that our individual institutions decide.[88]

Once we receive our SETs, we should interpret them sensibly. We should notice whether there are patterns across courses or similar items (e.g., those related to engagement, organization, materials, grading, or clarity). It's also helpful to look at them in context. For example, departmental or institutional averages help us ascertain whether we are outside the norms on specific items. Perhaps students at an institution tend to rate most instructors as higher on enthusiasm or lower on providing effective feedback. Perhaps (as at many institutions) introductory courses tend to get lower ratings than do upper-level courses. If possible, it's helpful to track our data across semesters, and look for trends (am I always high on clarity, usually lower on motivating students to learn?). We can check whether our ratings illustrate the norm that the first time an instructor teaches a course (or right after a significant revision), the ratings tend to be lower.[89]

Second, we should look for further clues about students' perceptions and the reasons for their ratings by reading their comments. We should look for patterns and suggestions mentioned by numerous students, not isolated comments. Although one harsh negative comment might upset us—I have occasionally dwelt on one for much too long—it's important to keep perspective. We should pay equal attention to both positive and negative comments. Listing them in a table and categorizing them can help us ensure we are analyzing in a rational and systematic fashion. Once we observe some patterns, we need to consider whether they address matters over which we have control.[90] We cannot change the nature of the discipline of history or the fact that historians expect students to write, for example, but we have a lot of control over the type of writing that students do and how we support them in doing it. We can't change which courses are required (and maybe not when or where they meet), but we can control how we spend class time, the clarity of our lectures, and the feedback we give.

Finally, we should distinguish between constructive and not constructive or vague comments. For example, the comment "Totally unfair" is alarming, but vague, whereas "I never felt like I knew what it took to be an excellent essay" is more constructive because it suggests a concrete matter on which the instructor could act. Similarly, "Best instructor I've ever had!" is a heart-warming comment, one that we might want to file away somewhere for when we need to be cheered up. However, it doesn't tell us which specific behaviors led to that student's conclusion. On the other hand, "I liked how the discussions helped me understand the readings better" or "I'm not usually a fan of quizzes but they did make me do the readings, so I admit I learned more because of them" supply constructive feedback, suggesting specific practices we might continue. Receiving a small number of comments should leave us eager for more information.

What should we do if we receive low student ratings? First, we need to try to be rational and recognize what they do and do not tell us. They don't reflect one's value as a person, nor one's commitment, capabilities, or potential; they are the perceptions of a group of students about a specific course.[91] It's also true that the instructor is only one of many factors affecting student learning. If less-than-desired ratings becomes a trend across semesters, it's natural to feel disappointed, hurt, upset, angry, or demoralized. We may be tempted to criticize the evaluation forms or the students or dismiss assessment of teaching as impossible; however, if we do so, our bosses may think we are making excuses. We should avoid self-defeating behaviors and should not give up the quest to teach well. It's more effective to take informed action—because ratings can be improved, even ones that have stayed the same for a long time. Informed action probably requires more information than SETs provide. It requires delving deeper into specific aspects of our course methods and materials, probably with the input of knowledgeable colleagues. As Maryellen Weimer puts it, ratings are the "first word" on instructional effectiveness, not the "last word or anything like the whole story."[92]

Formative Feedback for Instructors

No matter what our ratings are like on end-of-course ratings forms, we can all greatly benefit from gathering formative feedback. Formative feedback is shared only with us (not with department chairs or deans) and is done to promote our understanding and help us target areas for improvement (not for the purpose of a formal rating or evaluation). Formative assessment also differs from summative in its timing; it happens during our teaching rather than at the end of it, so it is much more helpful than learning about a problem after the semester when it's too late to do anything about it. Formative feedback tends to be descriptive (rather than quantitative) and can help us learn much more about specific details than more general SETs.

Inviting formative feedback usually involves some feelings of vulnerability (and therefore requires some courage), but instructors have some freedom and control over the process.[93] We decide on the timing; we might want to gather feedback three to four weeks into the term, while there's still time to make adjustments, or after a new activity, when we think things aren't going well, or around mid-semester. We decide the focus of the feedback; do we want to learn about the effectiveness of our lectures, new materials, or class climate? We decide who we want to provide the feedback and its format.

Wise and trusted colleagues can be a valuable source of formative feedback, especially when they observe our classes. However, a peer observation can be disappointing or even counterproductive, especially if the observer thinks we should do everything exactly as he does, has no sense of our goals, doesn't believe in active learning, or focuses on trivial matters. Happily, we know some practices that make peer observation beneficial. First, we should think carefully about whom to invite. Ideally, it is someone who has had some training in observation methods, such as faculty members associated with a teaching center, who not only have experience in observation but also know scholarship about effective teaching practices. We can ask a fellow historian, but the insights of faculty in other fields can be valuable on many general matters. In any case, we should choose observers who are considered strong teachers, those who can explain why they teach the way they do but also have an open mind about the various ways teaching can be done well. They should have integrity and compassion and be trustworthy regarding confidentiality. Second, we should use a three-stage process, involving a pre-observation conversation, the observation itself, and then a postobservation debriefing conversation.[94]

Before a colleague visits our class, we should explain the basic context of the course: the student learning goals, who the students are, and where the selected class meeting fits into the larger course unit. (I don't want an observer to say, "The students could have used a lecture on the background for the conflict," when I already gave that lecture the previous class period.) The observer needs to know my goals for the class meeting, how the students will prepare for it, and what strategies I will be using. We should come to agreement on how and when we will discuss how the session went—whether over coffee right after class or the next day, and whether the observer will write anything down or use a mutually agreed-on form (many are available).[95]

Observers are an additional set of eyes to notice anything that we have a hard time seeing on our own, so we should let them know exactly what areas we want feedback for. Past student comments may have made me curious about a specific aspect of teaching, such as how well I facilitate discussion. In that case, I might ask the observer to focus on how I open and close the discussion, ask questions, respond to student comments, and maintain the pace and flow. He might track how often and which students participate, and whether I talk too much or wait long enough. Some of us are interested in our overall effectiveness and might ask for comments about a few strengths (things to continue doing), a few key moments from class, the most significant areas that could be improved, and actionable recommendations.[96] If we aren't sure what to ask for, we can consult a checklist for ideas, especially ones that concentrate on instructor behaviors that research has linked to students' learning.[97]

An observer might look for whether the instructor:

- Is organized (on time; well prepared; provides an outline; transparently explains the purposes of the class meeting and the activities; relates the class to the previous one; has all materials and technology ready to go).
- Teaches appropriate content (topic, focus, and approach are significant to the discipline; material is appropriately complex and challenging but also accessible; readings are current/relevant; readings are used appropriately; multiple perspectives are explored; resources are cited).
- Uses appropriate methods of instruction (methods are aligned with goals; methods are varied; activities well introduced, timed, and facilitated; good pace of instruction; checks for student comprehension; questions are effective).
- Fosters student engagement (gets students to prepare for class; engages them during class through completing tasks, answering questions, or engaging in discussion; provides opportunities for using, extending, thinking about, or analyzing key ideas or for practicing skills; fosters positive student–student interactions; stimulates student participation).
- Is clear (defines new concepts; provides examples, evidence, and reasoning; elaborates or repeats complex information; pauses for questions; makes clear transitions; summarizes).
- Has good presentation skills (conveys enthusiasm; speaks audibly and clearly; speaks at pace that allows comprehension and note taking; varies pitch/tone for emphasis and expressiveness; makes eye contact with students all around the room; avoids simply reading; moves around the room; avoids distracting mannerisms; materials are legible, effective, and integrated).
- Has positive rapport with students (addresses students by name; notices and attends to student confusion; listens carefully and responds effectively to questions and comments; provides positive or constructive feedback when needed; invites and draws students in; students appear comfortable; instructor appears to care).[98]

Alternatively, we might ask a colleague to provide us with a detailed description of what happened during class.[99] In this ethnographic style of peer observation, every few minutes the observer fills out a log, such as the one in example 10.

One benefit of an ethnographic method is that it is purely descriptive. The observer does not rush to judgment but records specific behaviors. This approach takes seriously the scholarship showing that what students do in class is as important as what the instructor does. It provides specific data about the use of class time and the balance between instructor talking and students' active learning.[100]

After the class meeting, the observer might summarize their thoughts in a format such as the one shown in example 11.

The instructor and observer should meet to debrief while the class session is still fairly fresh in their minds. While the observer shares perceptions of what went well and what didn't, generally it's better for the instructor to mostly listen and do so with an open mind, asking for clarification when needed, and should not debate or react defensively. The instructor should explicitly thank the observer and show appreciation by acknowledging specific insights that were useful ("I had no idea . . ." or "I appreciate your confirming what I suspected about . . .").[101]

If I feel hesitant about inviting someone to observe my class, there are alternatives. Colleagues might examine my materials (syllabus or assignments) or student work, or I might ask for their thoughts about my approaches to certain topics. I can also benefit from visiting other instructors' classes, which makes me more aware of my own style and introduces me to alternatives. Class visits can be less intimidating when done with three colleagues in a "teaching square."[102] After the participants visit one another's classes, they meet to share only how their own teaching has been affected as a result of their observations (not to critique the others or offer suggestions). A final alternative is to have a class session videotaped and analyze it ourselves.

We can receive constructive formative feedback from students in ways other than SETs. If we ask for feedback earlier in the semester, students realize that we are intentionally asking their thoughts at a time when they might benefit from sharing them, so they tend to provide more and more substantive feedback. We can solicit feedback early or often, in formal or informal ways. The single prompt "minute paper"

Example 10. Ethnographic Peer Observation Form, Part A

Time	What Instructor Is Doing	What Students Are Doing
10:30	Welcomes, tells a quick story that links to the day's goals and outline	Some nods and note taking, some getting settled
10:33	Asks the question of the day (which is also on slide), then asks students to write initial thoughts on it	All but one student free-write
10:35	Asks for volunteers to share their answers	Five raise hands to volunteer; others listen
10:40	Surveys students about the previous day's class; after confusion, reviews two big concepts ...	They appeared to remember little
10:45	Begins lecture	All note taking
10:50	Lecturing, also begins moving around the left side of the room	Note taking, a few nods
10:55	Lecturing from center of room, moves to the right side	Most still taking notes, two have looked at irrelevant websites on computer
11:05	Summarizes, then asks questions (calls on random students, calls by name, checks that he has satisfactorily answered the question)	Note taking
11:05–11:15	Poses small-group discussion task: "How did the reading ... ?"; then circulates, answers question from two groups; clarifies for the whole class; circulates, refocuses one group after they got off track	Three groups get to work quickly; one dallies and discusses off-topic matters; two ask a question of the instructor. In a couple of groups there is a nonparticipator, but most seem to be contributing in some way. One group finishes faster than the others.
11:15	Asks one group's reporter to summarize their thoughts, others to jump in if drew different conclusions	Reporter is clear and concise; most other groups actively agreed, though one group disagreed sensibly
11:23	Asks students to write again on the question of the day, then summarized, linking the activity to the lecture and the reading	Brief note taking, pack up

Example 11. Ethnographic Peer Observation Form, Part B

Specific moments that were especially effective:
Specific moments that might have been more effective:
The balance of class time (teacher/student activity) and quality of engagement:
Degree to which the goals were met:

asked near the end of a class meeting may assess students' understanding of a topic while indirectly assessing whether we have taught material effectively.[103] Using the same minute paper format, we can also ask for short direct feedback on some aspect of the course (e.g., "Did that exercise help you learn? Why or why not?"). Students may share their answers on index cards or online. If we ask students to write during class, we receive a high response rate; if we use an online format, students don't worry that we recognize their handwriting. If we want to quantify results, we might ask a rating question, but to ensure we know the reasons for their answers, we should ask for some prose responses. Evaluations should be anonymous so that students know there will be no repercussions for being honest. If we don't want them to feel rushed, we might ask for feedback at the beginning of a class meeting rather than the end.[104]

Rather than questions about what students like or dislike (since enjoyment isn't the top goal), we should ask what is helping them learn and what could improve their learning. Simply asking these two open-ended prompts provides useful feedback. Alternatively, we can target specific areas, such as assignments, readings, or activities, level of challenge, inclusiveness/climate ("Are you comfortable participating in class? Why or why not?"), their understanding of expectations (a frequent source of frustration when they don't), and whether students know how they might improve their learning.

Although many instructors do a single formal mid-semester evaluation of instruction, some suggest that we come to understand student perceptions (and improve student metacognition) when we periodically ask the same few questions, such as:

- In the last few weeks, when were you most engaged? When were you least engaged?[105]
- When were you most confused?
- What action by the teacher or fellow students did you find most helpful?
- What's the most important thing you've learned recently?
- Have you been actively participating? Why or why not?

If you would rather use a questionnaire designed by someone else, there are good ones available from centers for teaching and learning.[106] One teaching consultant says that at midterm, it's "pretty close to brilliant" to use an adapted version of the university's end-of-semester form to anticipate what areas may deserve attention.[107]

Many teaching centers offer an invaluable service, sometimes called a small group instructional diagnosis (SGID) or mid-semester focus group. In this process, a trained facilitator spends about twenty minutes with students (with the instructor having left the room). The facilitator asks students in small groups to collectively fill out a form with three or four questions, which takes seven to eight minutes and may include some of the following:

- What are the goals of this course?
- Do you usually understand what is expected of you in preparing for and participating in this class? (Explain.)

- What aspects of this course and your instructor's teaching are helping you learn?
- What specific advice would you give to help your instructor improve your learning in this course?
- What steps could you take to improve your own learning in this course?
- What else do you want the instructor to know?

After they have finished, the facilitator asks the small groups to share their answers with the whole class, asks clarifying questions, and elicits matters of agreement and disagreement. Students may discover that not everyone finds the same materials or instructional strategies to be effective. In addition, sometimes a student says something that reveals a misunderstanding, which other students correct. One might say, "There's no way to know what's expected of us," and another student will point out, "Actually there's a sample essay on Blackboard that I found really useful." When there is a fair amount of consensus on an issue (e.g., "Discussions fall flat"), the facilitator may collect students' suggestions for improvement. Students might admit, for example, that if everyone did the reading, the discussions would go better, but also suggest that the instructor could ask better questions or give them more time to think before answering. At the end of the focus group, the facilitator collects the forms and types a transcript of the raw data from the small groups. They share this data and the gist of the discussion in a meeting with the instructor. The teaching center consultant helps the instructor accurately gauge trends (and not obsess about a single negative comment), consider the options for pedagogically sound adjustments, and brainstorm effective ways to talk with students about their feedback.

Whatever method we use to gather feedback from students, it's crucial that we let them know soon after that we have heard and considered their responses. I do it orally—it only takes a few moments of class—but others do it in an email or on a learning management system. I explain the changes I'll be making, and those that I can't or won't. I don't respond to each comment or suggestion, just the ones that seem most important.[108] If possible, it's beneficial to make some adjustments to the course in response to their concerns. Students often suggest a few things that are sensible and easy to accommodate (perhaps they want the take-home essay questions handed out earlier or a review session). Some things may be more of a stretch; in that case, I reject their suggestion and explain why I won't change it, but do so with sympathy. Or I may respond to their concern but use a different strategy for addressing it than what they suggested. Let's say students want me to provide a copy of my slides. If I don't think that's a good idea, I might point to research about the importance of active note taking for learning. However, to address their concern that they're not noting all the important aspects of the lectures, I agree to add more pauses and more opportunities for students to examine each other's notes. In some cases, I might agree to try their suggestion for the next few class periods and then re-assess. If I find myself unwilling to make any adjustments at all, I should consider whether I'm being inflexible. There's no point in asking for student perspectives if I'm not really interested in hearing them. In fact, probably the main way a mid-semester evaluation or focus group can backfire is if I raise expectations that I'll try to improve the course and then dismiss all student views about how to do so.[109]

While discussing students' feedback with them, I try to channel my best self and respond matter-of-factly, nondefensively, thoughtfully, and generously. I'm trying to model how I would like my students to consider and use the feedback I give them. Sometimes their comments reflect a misunderstanding of something that's on the syllabus or that I explained the first day of class. Rather than pointing that out with annoyance or sarcasm in my voice, I try to remember that sometimes people (including me) need to hear things a few times before they really understand them, so I explain it again calmly and patiently. Sometimes students raise an issue I can't do anything about at the moment (e.g., we're done with the book they found tedious), but I can let them know if I think their concerns are valid and how I'm thinking of addressing the issue next semester. Although that approach benefits future students, not the present ones, saying it demonstrates that I respect their views and care about improving the course. I conclude by thanking the students for their time, honesty, and suggestions.

Research suggests that sincerely asking for mid-semester feedback increases students' perceptions that we are interested in their learning and their satisfaction with the course and instructor. They appreciate that we care enough to ask. Instructors who regularly use a feedback mechanism like the SGID say that it deepens their understanding of their students.[110]

Finally, we shouldn't ignore our own perceptions of our courses and teaching. We are well positioned to assess certain matters, such as whether a book elicited enthusiasm or provided a suitable overview of a topic, whether students appeared confused by a specific concept or needed more practice with a certain skill, or whether an essay prompt worked the way we had hoped. We can tell whether a specific lecture or small group task worked well, especially if we make a habit of checking in with students as they do the work. Ideally, we keep track of our observations after each class meeting, noting the specific questions that stimulated great discussion (or fell flat), and whether an activity worked well and should be used again (or took longer than expected or required more explanation or other tinkering). When something didn't work the way we hoped, we don't always have an explanation for why (were students passive because of campus celebrations the night before, or were they uninspired by the subject?). Whatever the reason, the next time we offer the course—perhaps in a year or more—we will be glad for the reminder that we should try a more engaging opening to that class meeting. Unfortunately, even if something worked well one year, there is no guarantee it will work well again with different students. It takes multiple semesters of offering a course to feel confident about our strategies. Without regular reflection, we waste our valuable insights. It doesn't take long to jot down a few observations—perhaps on sticky notes, perhaps typed into the day's outline ("next time, think about . . ."), perhaps in a separate document titled "Ideas for adjusting History 333." At the end of the semester, it's also worth thinking about our overall perceptions of how the whole course went before reading students' end-of-semester ratings.

Some instructors approach assessment of their teaching in a systematic fashion. For example, Joel Sipress significantly revised his post-1877 U.S. history course around the goal of historical argumentation, emphasizing four component skills: formulating a thesis, summarizing the arguments of others, providing a well-organized argument of their own, and supplying evidence. At the end of the semester, he tabulated the results of the class on a final exam that evaluated these four skills. He found the results "startling." They revealed that one of the skills— supplying evidence—proved far more challenging than the others. Although students knew that evidence was important, the majority did not meet his expectations for providing it. None of the students exhibited mastery, 29 percent exhibited partial mastery, and 71 percent failed.

Sipress went back to the drawing board, trying to figure out why they struggled and then designed new ways to introduce and practice this skill. His efforts paid off in the next iteration of the course, when 11 percent showed mastery and 63 percent partial mastery.[111] Such improvements aren't surprising when an instructor addresses a teaching question with a scholarly approach and careful analysis of evidence. Experts on teaching agree that the habit of critical reflection enhances teaching.[112]

Demonstrating the Quality of Our Teaching

Sometimes we have to make the case that we teach effectively, such as when applying for a job or being considered for continuation, tenure, promotion, a raise, or a teaching award. The format varies depending on the context, but generally our goal should be making a clear and logical argument that is well supported by sensible evidence. This differs from what Ken Bain refers to as an ineffective "container approach," where faculty "throw everything imaginable into a box" that reflects little thought about the meaning of good teaching.[113] In making our case, we should articulate what we mean by "effective teaching." I argue in this book that effective teaching is intentional, inclusive, and rooted in knowledge about history and knowledge about teaching and that students learn thanks to what I prompt them to do.[114] Another instructor may want to argue something different, such as being engaging, innovative, passionate, thought-provoking, transformative, accessible, well organized, challenging but supportive, or continually striving to grow as an instructor. Or she may want to emphasize her excellence in teaching historical thinking, research skills, writing, or theory or in facilitating student growth or the success of average students. These different claims require different evidence.

Let's say I want to make the claim that students learned a great deal in my course. Student work (an assignment, exam, research paper, etc.) is a direct measure of learning and constitutes good evidence, but which students' work should I use? (A department chair or promotion and tenure committee probably doesn't want to read all my students' final synthetic essays.) Excellent work (that which earned an A) demonstrates great achievement, but probably represents the learning of a relatively small percentage of students in a class. Therefore I might also include an example of a B and a C essay, because although they have less sophistication than the A work, they illustrate that the majority of students learned important knowledge or skills related to the course goals. Alternatively, some instructors use pre- and post- tests to illustrate that learning occurred on a significant concept or skill (not just facts). To show growth on primary source analysis, one might ask students to analyze a document during the first week of class and then have them analyze the same document again during the last week of class. At the end of the semester, students should notice much more about the source, raise more (and smarter) questions about it, and be aware of how much more capably they approach it. In addition, one might include evidence of students' perceptions of what they learned by asking them an open-ended question on the last day of class (e.g., "What are the most important things you learned this semester?"). For those evaluating my work, I can summarize or analyze their responses (e.g., "83 percent said something related to one of my course goals, and I was only disappointed with the response of 9 percent of the students").

It's a bit trickier to show that students learned as a direct result of one's actions. However, I could show an example of an individual student's first draft, my feedback on it, and that student's final draft. I could share data I gleaned from all the students' work in a class (as Sipress did). I could report that on the first essay exam, B essays included an average of three pieces of evidence to support their thesis. Then I would describe the actions I took after the exam to improve students' understanding, which included reiterating how much historians value having a great deal of evidence from both primary and secondary sources and having students do two in-class exercises using evidence. Then I would report the results on the next exam, where B essays included an average of 5.2 pieces of evidence.

For those compiling a teaching portfolio or tenure/promotion file, the following format is useful for making a claim about teaching:

- Explain my purpose—that is, what I'm trying to do in my teaching—and why those objectives are worth achieving.[115] (E.g., I may strive to do something because of AHA/disciplinary expectations, my institutional or departmental mission, research about learning, or my individual values.)
- Explain how I try to achieve my goal—including my teaching strategies, including choices of materials, assignments, activities, and typical day-to-day methods (such as interactive lecturing, discussion, small-group active learning tasks).

- Supply evidence that I'm achieving my goal. Experts on teaching portfolios suggest considering multiple sources of evidence for my arguments, including:
  - Evidence from students—this might be examples of their completed work; pre- and post- assessments; unsolicited notes or emails from students reporting positive experiences; solicited letters from former students (who are not now and will not be in my class and therefore are not swayed by my authority); students' presentations, publications, or achievements; results of mid-semester or other surveys of students, including focus groups; data from SETs, with my analysis of items that show consistency over many semesters (or a pattern of consistent improvement).
  - Evidence from myself—this might be representative syllabi, assignments, unit plans, or class plans, especially those that show alignment with goals; assignments that illustrate my growth and development (e.g., one that became more authentic or transparent); indications of my learning and efforts I made to solicit feedback and improve, such as workshops or conference sessions I attended; narrative reflections; a statement of teaching philosophy; a video recording of class.
  - Evidence from others—this might include forms, summaries, or letters resulting from peer observations or the assessment of one's materials by colleagues at one's institution, other campuses, or a teaching and learning center; teaching honors received; presentations, publications, or invitations to share one's knowledge about teaching; reports of good work by my introductory students from faculty teaching upper-level courses or from community partners in internships, archives, or undergraduate research programs, and so on.[116]

The following example uses this format for the claim "I am an engaging history instructor."

- I strive to be an engaging instructor—and by this I don't mean "entertaining," but one whose students are thinking about or practicing history during the whole class period. I do this because research on learning tells us that gaining students' attention is the first precondition for their learning, that engagement motivates students to work harder, and that carefully chosen activities promote deeper and more lasting learning.

- I engage students in a variety of ways, including posing intriguing questions and writing prompts at the beginning of class sessions; using interactive lecturing; facilitating thoughtful discussions in which most students participate; giving students choices for research topics; and promoting regular reflections about what they are learning and how it matters to them. You can see my approach illustrated in my sample class plan on the topic of World War II.

- I have provided a number of different sources to suggest that I frequently succeed in engaging students. Two colleagues have observed my classes, and each noted that I maintained a great pace, keeping things moving but also providing time to think. They noted indications of student interest, including the high percentage of students who participated in discussions (90 percent in one class and 75 percent in the other). In addition, I asked a faculty member from the Center for Teaching Excellence to do a mid-semester focus group, and you'll see from the results that students reported that they found the class interesting and appreciated how the different activities help them stay focused and delve deeper into the material. Finally, a question on the end-of-semester evaluations asks about whether the course is engaging, and students consistently rated me above departmental and university averages (4.73).

If I were making a different argument—that in my Historical Methods course I excel at helping students develop their research skills—I might note that this goal reflects my departmental priorities and is a competency valued by the American Historical Association. To illustrate how I try to meet the goal (as evidence from myself) I could include the course outline, which demonstrated careful scaffolding of skills, frequent times when I provide formative feedback, and an assignment I designed to help students effectively search databases. To show evidence that I'm achieving the goal, I could include a variety of evidence from students and others:

- Some students' first attempts at building a list of sources and their much improved final bibliographies;

- A letter from a departmental colleague who teaches an upper-level course about how well prepared my students were for the research project in her course;
- Evidence of three mentees' achievements (those chosen to present at a regional undergraduate research conference);
- An unsolicited email from an alumnus who is attending graduate school who thanks me for the writing and research skills he developed in my course;
- A compilation of students' end-of semester reflections about what they learned in the course about doing research.

No single source of evidence conclusively proves effective teaching, but supplying numerous types in this way increases credibility.

To create an impressive portfolio, we should save course materials over a span of time (over years, if going up for promotion), collect and analyze the feedback we have received, and discuss these materials intelligently. In addition, we need to understand our audience. Faculty and administrators from different disciplines require a fuller explanation of our disciplinary goals and practices than our fellow historians do. In addition, readers of a portfolio appreciate honesty and transparency about how we use data.[117] For example, we should inform evaluators if we have chosen to include only selected (positive) student comments from a survey, or whether we transcribed all responses into a single document. Readers don't expect us to unduly criticize ourselves, but we shouldn't ignore areas that have needed improvement (which they may well notice). Portfolios should demonstrate our strengths, and hopefully those strengths include knowledge about effective teaching, self-awareness, a habit of reflection about practices, and the willingness and ability to improve.

■

For many instructors, the word "assessment" has a negative connotation. We tend to dislike or even hate grading students' work. We are frustrated by the time it takes and worry that we're not altogether consistent. We become disheartened if our feedback is misunderstood or ignored, meaning our efforts have been wasted. Rather than giving up or simply venting about the process, these strong emotions tell us that it's worth digging into exactly which aspects bother us and then taking a focused and evidence-based approach to tackling them. We can improve our effectiveness by articulating our criteria while designing the assignment, clearly communicating them, and ensuring that students engage with and understand the criteria before doing their work. We can improve the value of our feedback by being selective and smart about the comments we give and the format and tone with which we give them, and by ensuring that students respond to the feedback and can use it on future assignments. Our clarity about criteria turns assessment—and even potentially difficult conversations about grades—into an integrated and transparent part of the learning process.

We also may dislike being the subject of evaluation. In this case, too, we benefit from an intelligent and nondefensive approach to the assessment of our teaching. This includes understanding the benefits and limitations of various types of assessment (SETs, focus groups, peer observation, self-evaluation) and various types of assessors (students, peers, and colleagues from a teaching center). A thoughtful and scholarly approach to assessing teaching includes a willingness to regularly gather formative feedback and analyze evidence with an open mind, so we might investigate areas where the data are unclear or identify patterns that indicate specific areas for improvement. Then we should consult the research and talk with others about how to improve. Once we have a firm, evidence-based understanding of our strengths as instructors, we are well positioned to make a clear and persuasive case that we are doing a good job. As with assessment of students' performance, using a good approach can turn assessment into a productive process that deepens our knowledge about the noble and challenging vocation of teaching history.

5   Who We Are

Historians, by and large, are not noted for introspection. Our calling requires us to analyze past events, but we rarely turn our interpretive talents upon ourselves.

ERIC FONER

In no case is history cut off from the political economy or the personal interests and demographic characteristics of each historian. What goes on in our institutions, our polity, and our experience affects our thought. Who we are as people enters into what we see as important historically.

NELL PAINTER

Chapter 2 argued that we teach more effectively when we know our students as people with their own identities and as learners with prior knowledge, experiences, and assumptions about history and learning. This chapter makes the case that it is equally important for history faculty to know ourselves. We should, as Eric Foner suggested, turn our interpretive talents upon ourselves.[1] Our teaching benefits when we tap into what motivates us, analyze our assumptions about teaching, and carefully consider our position in the classroom and on campus. To increase the odds of a long, successful, and meaningful career, it's vital to know ourselves, understand our professional context, and follow what scholarship tells us about faculty satisfaction and engagement.

Knowing Ourselves

Our Histories

Every history instructor has an "origin story" about how we came to adopt our profession and areas of specialization. Writings by and about historians demonstrate that they emphasize different factors to explain their unique professional "causation." As Nell Painter suggested, these influences included personal experiences and characteristics, not just purely intellectual interests.[2]

Many historians found portents of their future career in the books they loved as children. Medievalist Judith Bennett came to love history through novels, as did German-born Herbert Strauss, who devoured sixty of Karl May's adventure stories set in the American Wild West. Arthur Schlesinger Jr., a fan of Robert Louis Stevenson, Alexandre Dumas, and classic fairy tales, thought those works taught important lessons for a budding historian—that human nature is not innately good, that conflict is real, and that life is harsh before it is happy.[3]

Others became fascinated by history because of places they traveled to or grew up in. H. Stuart Hughes remembered a childhood encounter with wax models of prisoners in the medieval dungeons of Mont Saint-Michel as the moment he decided to study history.[4] Janice Reiff's daily commute on the elevated train from suburban Evanston to downtown Chicago piqued her curiosity about what caused the radical differences she observed among neighborhoods, prompting her to become an urban historian.[5] U.S. historian David Hollinger studied the Nez Perce people, unsurprising because he grew up on land that was once theirs. Hollinger saw a main theme of his scholarship, the tension between cosmopolitan and provincial impulses, reflected in his past as a sheltered Anabaptist Idahoan, who was viewed as a "hick" by fellow graduate students at Berkeley.[6] Raul Hiberg grew up in a Jewish family in Vienna, and when he watched Hitler's troops entering the city in 1938, he thought, "Some day I will write about what I have seen here."[7]

As Hiberg's experience suggests, historians' choices were frequently affected by the time period in which they lived. Paul Fussell, profoundly disillusioned by his combat experiences in World War II, taught about negative aspects of the world wars, whereas veteran Charles Roland emphasized the character and patriotism of soldiers. When the well-educated John Hope Franklin volunteered for the War Department, which was desperate for educated workers, he was rejected because of his race, which led him to "the most profound questions about the sincerity of my country in rejecting bigotry."[8] After the war, he published a pioneering textbook of African American history.

"History constructs a historian," reflected Linda Gordon. Famous now for her scholarship on birth control and violence in families in the

United States, Gordon started her historical career focused on Russian history. There were no women mentioned in her dissertation. When she later encountered feminism, she became "an instant convert," astonished that she could have been so blind to the invisibility and oppression of women.[9] A whole generation of historians was transformed by a new historiographical approach, the Annales school's promotion of the study of ordinary people and openness to using social science methods. Medievalist Georges Duby said that reading *Les Annales* "made me what I am."[10] As a refugee from Hitler, Gerda Lerner experienced fascism, anti-Semitism, imprisonment, and anticommunist persecution. Through it all, she witnessed how women helped hold communities together. After she enrolled in college at age thirty-eight, she realized that in the eyes of historians, women seemed not to exist. "My commitment to women's history," she wrote, "came out of my life, not out of my head."[11]

In retrospect, certain historians' choice of vocations seemed natural given their identities. Eric Foner's father and uncle were historians; both were fired from their positions after being named members of the Communist Party. He remembered that his mother ("to my embarrassment") complained to his principal about the illustrations of slaves in his third-grade history textbook that portrayed them as happy. This background certainly makes Foner's path as a radical historian seem almost inevitable. However, as Jeremy Popkin notes, no one simply "falls into" a career in history; it takes a conscious decision and sustained effort. In fact, until midway through college, Foner intended to be an astronomer.[12] Similarly, despite being African American, female, and interested in Black identity, early in her career Darlene Clark Hine turned down an offer to write a history of Black women.[13] In historians' lives, just as with the people they study, their context affects them, but it does not determine every path they take.

Sometimes there is no apparent connection between historians' identities and their areas of expertise. Edmund Morgan, whose scholarship influenced conceptions of the Puritans, was a lifelong atheist. Mitchell Snay, a Jewish Chicago native who chose to study antebellum Southern Christianity, wanted "to write about something far removed from my personal concerns" and believed his focus was more related to historiographical trends, influential books, and his advisor.[14]

Why consider historians' personal histories as we think about teaching? As Nell Painter pointed out, "Who we are as people enters into what we see as important historically."[15] Whatever our identities, "what we see as important historically" affects not only what we choose to study but the courses we offer, the topics we include, the readings we assign, and the methods we have our students use. We needn't apologize for that. As Judith Bennett asserted, we "must not forget to share in our classrooms the pleasures that first drew us toward history."[16]

Staying connected to the historical content we are passionate about helps sustain us as teachers. (Recall what psychologists tell us about the role of value in motivation.) Motivating students must be a primary concern, but our own motivation matters, too. When Linda Gordon switched her focus from Russian to U.S. history, she noted that her studies "became more passionate," probably because they were "closer to home, in all the meanings of home: in my place, in my time, about my experience."[17] Darlene Clark Hine's shift in focus to African American women's history allowed her to "connect my biography with my profession."[18] For Gerda Lerner, building a new scholarly field and creating a women's history course when no such thing yet existed was "richly rewarding, exhilarating, and energizing."[19] Similarly, for gay professor John D'Emilio, teaching material in his "Sexuality and Community" course was highly motivating. "'Joy' and 'happiness' wildly understate the response it provoked in me every time."[20]

Many historians have reflected on how their individual values and identities influenced their teaching goals.[21] The child of Russian immigrants, Leon Litwack grew up in a working class, mostly Mexican American neighborhood that exposed him to a diversity of cultures, languages, histories, and experiences, which he found to be an "exciting, often exhilarating education." The history he encountered in school, however, "was largely the history of Anglo-Saxons and Northern Europeans. It was about Pilgrims, Puritans, and Founding Fathers. It was someone else's history, not my history, not the lives of my parents, friends, and neighbors." Litwack's teaching goals included countering the ways generations of historians had reinforced and shaped prevailing racial and ethnic biases.[22] Lillian Guerra's parents were Cuban exiles, and she experienced prejudice in her Kansas town, including from a first-grade teacher who wouldn't let her ride on a float in the Old Settlers' Day parade because Cubans weren't "old settlers." Her father comforted her by asserting that the parade celebrated those who descended from Indian killers. Guerra's otherness compelled her to study history because it was a route to social change and it was a way "to explain Big

Questions, starting with who I was and why so many other people wanted to dismiss my family and me." Not surprisingly, with her own students, she focuses on big questions.[23]

Other historians' experiences also affected their teaching goals. Gerda Lerner's experiences as a graduate student, where women lacked mentors and knowledge of how to succeed in academia, convinced her to adopt the goal of "demystifying knowledge" for her students. She focused on teaching essential skills like how to read and take notes efficiently, uncover the hidden structure of arguments, and find and use information.[24] Eileen Findlay had hated history in her younger years, but later took a course from an instructor who taught history not as facts to be memorized but as a way to understand people's pain, struggles, and hopes for a better life and as a means of explaining the contemporary world. This transformative experience caused her to adopt the same approach.[25] Michael Lewis's feminist principles—and a desire to use up-to-date SOTL and technology—informed his redesign of a women's history course "to fulfill my feminist objectives of empowering students, decentering authority in the classroom, building supportive learning communities, and effectively integrating students' subjective experiences."[26]

Historians' experiences influence their teaching methods, too. Joan Wallach Scott, who taught French history, modeled her teaching on that of U.S. intellectual historian William R. Taylor, who asked open-ended questions and sought to elicit students' reactions to texts. "He was more provocative than authoritative," she remembered. "It was not mastery, but discovery that he was after."[27] When discussing documents from feminism in the 1960s and 1970s, Estelle Freedman borrowed a teaching technique from her experiences in the feminist movement, spontaneously turning the class into a consciousness-raising session, forming a circle, and giving each participant time to talk about how a reading or idea had affected them personally.[28] Based on her experience of discovering her passion while taking the train through Chicago, urban historian Janice Reiff had her students leave the classroom and explore the neighborhoods of Los Angeles.[29]

It's important to be aware of how we can bring ourselves into the classroom in ways that enrich our teaching, but we should also consider the risks of doing so. By virtue of our position of authority in the classroom, faculty inherently bring the power to influence students in both positive and negative ways. We have more historical knowledge, educational credentials, and more experience in developing and articulating arguments. In this situation, instructors with strongly held views must constantly be aware of the dangers of pressuring students to think exactly like they do. "As an agent of social change one believes passionately and wants to share one's experiences with others," Lerner explained. "[Indoctrination] must be resisted, since that would be an abuse of the privileged position and power one holds as a teacher. I believe that I should teach my students ways of obtaining information, ways of evaluating and selecting such information, and let them experiment themselves with how to use such information for practical purposes. It is my job to demystify knowledge and to teach students how to evaluate what they are taught in light of their own experience, not of mine."[30]

Of course, as Lerner observed, students' experiences are different from those of their history professors. We cannot assume that the historical periods, events, or actors that thrill us will also thrill our students, that they will interpret the past the same way we do, or that the methods that helped us learn history will work for them. Effective teaching may be a kind of alchemy in which instructors bring the best, most appropriate, and relevant parts of their singular knowledge, experiences, identities, and skills, and blend them with those of their specific students in their specific teaching context to create deep and meaningful learning.

Our Mindsets, Assumptions, and Dispositions

Just like their students, history instructors might be hamstrung by inaccurate or problematic prior knowledge and assumptions. Probably the most dangerous problematic assumption is that teaching is a gift or talent that some people naturally have and others do not.[31] Like students who don't believe they can get better at writing, faculty with a fixed mindset toward teaching do not recognize that every aspect of teaching—including course design, lecturing, facilitating discussions, creating active learning exercises, and grading—involves learnable skills at which one can improve.

There's no question that teaching is a challenging activity. It requires using various kinds of knowledge, including that of history, pedagogy, and our students. During class, we need to (often simultaneously) pose good questions, listen carefully, respond respectfully to comments, assess how things are going, manage time, recall content, share information, transition between topics, adjust to unexpected events, and more. As the authors of *How Learning Works* observe, "Putting all these skills together is the ultimate multitask." It takes years of intelligent practice to develop expertise, and even experts have bad days. It's understandable, then, that sometimes we get frustrated. It's quite a different matter, though, to conclude that teaching is not learnable.[32]

Skepticism about the learnability of teaching becomes especially problematic when things don't go well, such as when students underperform on an exam, make negative comments, or give our course low ratings. Faculty with a fixed mindset tend to respond to these situations like others with a fixed mindset: they get defensive, give up, or blame others. Because our egos can only handle so much criticism, we look for ways to explain the causes of poor performance. Just like students who don't want to accept responsibility and instead blame poor grades on unfair exams or ineffective instructors, struggling faculty might be tempted to blame students. Harvard education researcher David Perkins described this viewpoint: "It's these kids. They just don't study. They just don't care. They really weren't very well prepared." Others blame a generation of students for their entitlement, distractedness, or reliance on technology. It's true, of course, that there are times when problems are quite clearly the fault of students, and different generations have some different characteristics, but being angry at an individual student for a specific action she took is different from casting aspersions on all students. The problematic disposition I'm referring to here is when blaming becomes an entrenched habit, the immediate explanation for times when things go poorly. It backfires on us, because students may sense and resent it if faculty paint them all with the same brush. It's understandable that when we're frustrated we're tempted to blame others, because blame relieves our guilt and puts the responsibility for change on others. It supplies an excuse for not trying anything different.[33] Without hope for changing the situation, however, faculty may develop a sense of helplessness or become bitter, cynical, dissatisfied, and/or disengaged.

In contrast, faculty with a growth mindset toward teaching tend to be more successful. Like others who see intelligence as expandable, they interpret missteps, struggles, and disappointments as a natural part of the learning process, and they view constructive criticism as an opportunity for learning how to do things better. Rather than feeling helpless, they chip away at a specific challenge, gradually making it manageable. As the authors of *How Learning Works* observe, "If we think of teaching as a set of skills one can develop and refine, it makes sense to engage in a progressive refinement."[34] Knowing ourselves means being aware of which skills we perform well and which ones need improvement.

At the other end of the spectrum from those who won't engage in efforts to improve their teaching is a history instructor with an equally problematic disposition: the perfectionist. Perfectionists imagine a perfect class meeting (universal engagement and participation, brilliant insights, etc.) and despair every time one doesn't reach that ideal. Perfectionists obsess about the one negative comment out of forty on end-of-semester evaluations and ignore the other thirty-nine. They take criticism personally, are too hard on themselves, never feel fully satisfied with a plan, or feel responsible for every individual student's lack of engagement or poor performance. They forget that although instructors can provide good material, questions, and activities, only students can do the work of learning. Excessive reflection on negative experiences leads to a vicious cycle of rumination undermining one's confidence. Maintaining a sense of perspective is a crucial part of survival for a college teacher, asserts Stephen Brookfield in *The Skillful Teacher*, so you are neither artificially inflated by your successes nor "completely demoralized by your failures."[35] The goals we set for ourselves (like those for our students) should be realistic in their number and attainability. As we know from motivation theory, expectancy is a critical component of motivation. If we have set goals that are impossible to achieve, it is difficult to sustain motivation over the long haul. Challenge is good for us as faculty, just as it is for students, but that challenge should be reasonable.

Other limiting beliefs may block our development as instructors.[36] We might think it would be a disaster if anyone found out that we're struggling or that no one is willing or able to help us. We might believe we're incapable of handling what we'll learn if our class is observed. We might think we're too busy or too set in our ways to make changes. We might believe that the quality of teaching cannot be measured definitively, so there's no point in trying to evaluate it. We might think that great teachers are mainly outgoing, funny, or charismatic, and that we simply don't have the right personality to excel.[37] Brookfield observed that in Hollywood movies, good teaching involves "charismatically charged individuals using the sheer force of their characters and personalities to wreak lifelong transformations in students' lives." Instead, he asserts, great teaching is actually about "finding ways to promote the day-to-day, incremental gains that students make as they try to understand ideas, grasp concepts, assimilate knowledge and develop new skills. All the small things you do to make this happen for students represent the real story of teaching. Helping learning is what makes you truly heroic."[38]

Some of those problematic assumptions may contain a grain of truth. For example, psychologist Dan Willingham says that working on teaching will certainly involve blows to our egos.[39] Some of those assumptions, however, may be defense mechanisms, misconceptions, or rationalizations that prevent our growth. The bottom line is that any of us, regardless of personality or background, can incrementally improve aspects of our teaching, help is available if we look for it, and we certainly won't improve if we don't take the risk of trying. Effective teachers try to uncover—and test—their assumptions, and they engage in the habit of reflection.

Our Teaching Metaphors

In *The Joy of Teaching*, teaching award–winning historian Peter Filene wrote that teaching shouldn't be like pitching a baseball toward batters and waiting to see whether they would hit it or strike out. Instead, he suggested, teaching should be more like organizing a game of Frisbee, inviting students to catch an idea and pass it on.[40] This metaphor illustrates Filene's desire to create an interactive, idea-centered, and even playful learning environment, which he hoped would be invitational and supportive rather than authoritarian or competitive. Over the years, many others have proposed metaphors for teaching. I doubt any single one can capture the complexity of teaching, much less illustrate an ideal teacher, but thinking about them helps us consider our own beliefs.

The "sage on the stage," one of the classic metaphors, portrays the teacher as a wise lecturer who weaves fascinating stories and perfect illustrations into a coherent and convincing argument, inspiring and imparting knowledge to rapt students.[41] Like the metaphors of the entertainer (an amusing instructor who makes learning fun and engaging) or broadcaster (a smooth and clear conveyor of information), this imagery posits the instructor as the focal point of what is going on in the classroom, the leading character, the one doing most of the work. The instructor is portrayed as intelligent (which makes sense, given our expertise) and transferring important information to the students in a one-way direction. Although there is always a place for information, humor, and inspiration, one limitation of these metaphors is that it's harder to understand what roles students play. They seem to occupy a passive role of audience member, note-taker, and receiver of a performance or knowledge, and we know from chapter 3 that such passivity limits their ability to learn.

Other metaphors assign students a more active part, however. In the Socrates metaphor, the (still wise) teacher listens carefully to what students say, interacts frequently and flexibly with the students, and rather than telling in a monologue, asks carefully sequenced questions that eventually lead their dialogic partners to discover smart insights. The teacher as gardener image emphasizes that students do the growing and blooming; in this metaphor, the faculty member's primary responsibility is to understand what their students need to learn so they can prepare the soil (the learning environment) and provide the right amount of water (support).[42] In the metaphor of a midwife, the student does the hard labor of learning, and the midwife brings a calm and assuring presence and expertise, knowing when to encourage, when to keep her hands off, and when to push or pull. Similarly, a travel guide sets goals, which probably include students having meaningful and memorable experiences, assists in outfitting students with the right equipment and maps, chooses a logical route to reach those destinations, and helps students understand what they are seeing. Travel guides differ from one another, of course; some jam-pack the itinerary, while others allow more time for students to stray from the schedule and discover their own adventures.[43] Teacher as architect emphasizes the importance of planning (e.g., backward design) to achieve one's goals and build appropriately for the environment, but is less clear about what happens when the plans don't go as expected.[44]

The coach of a team sport metaphor recognizes the necessity of making quick evaluations of how players are performing, giving feedback, and making adjustments to a game plan. Good coaches break down the components of the necessary skills and recognize when more practice time is needed. As with a midwife, the coach is seen by players as being part of the same team but has primarily a supportive (not starring) role. Effective coaches pay attention to team dynamics, motivations, and dispositions.[45] Coaches differ a great deal in their styles and effectiveness at the various aspects of their jobs. Some excel at making the most of the practice time, others at strategizing for the games, and still others at motivating their players; some yell, while others use more positive reinforcement. Visualizing the teacher as a conductor of a jazz symphony emphasizes many of the same aspects of coaching; the musicians play, but the conductor must find a way to direct and bring together their disparate sounds. As teaching award-winning historian Glenn McNair put it, "Every class is a new performance. I have to be enthusiastic. I have to know the music well. I have to know my musicians. The things I want to accomplish, that's kind of my score. Everybody is sort of riffing out that theme, but I have to keep it together so that at the end we've created some beautiful music together."[46]

Many metaphors do not work for teaching. English professor Rob Jenkins said that many students bring metaphors that misconstrue the appropriate faculty–student relationship. Despite the popularity of the student-as-tuition-paying-customer image, he asserted, faculty are not clerks or students' employees; nor are we their bosses (we evaluate their work, but we don't hire or fire them). We're not parents, high school teachers, an online streaming site (available on demand), or adversaries. Even though we might feel like it at certain moments, we're not warriors. Teaching may involve some nurturing and the ability to diagnose, but we're not therapists or physicians. Jenkins said he preferred to be seen as a partner or ally who cares about his students' well-being and their success in the shared educational endeavor.[47]

Although there's no perfect metaphor for teaching, we refine our thinking by considering what we find to be apt or absurd about the alternatives. What do our own metaphors say about how we see our role? (How much do we want to inhabit center stage or decenter the classroom?) What do they say about how we see the educational process? (Do we see it primarily as a process of transmission of knowledge from teacher to student, one of discovery, one of construction of knowledge by students?) What do our metaphors say about how we envision our relationship to students? (Do we want to be traveling alongside them, leading from the front, following, rooting from the sidelines?) What do our metaphors say about what we do in the classroom? (Do we aim to facilitate, inspire, encourage, correct, tell, impress, debate, ask questions, enforce, manage? Do we want to be quick with a whistle/ red pen, a tissue, an answer, an affirmation, a question?) What do they tell us about how we hope to be perceived by students? (Do we want to be seen as smart, funny, likable, inspiring, supportive, tough, interesting, understanding, amazing?) Some argue that metaphors provide a frame-work through which we interpret experiences and that they uncon-sciously influence our actions. Thus greater awareness of our "operating metaphors" allows us to analyze how they may be expanding or limiting our effectiveness.[48]

Our Teaching Personas

It may also be worth considering our "teaching persona," a loose term that encompasses the elements of our teaching style and personality, our ways of being in the classroom, and the signals we send off about who we are as instructors. "Nobody just walks into a classroom and teaches without some consideration of self-presentation," claimed Jay Parini, author of *The Art of Teaching*, "just as nobody sits down to write a poem, an essay, or a novel without considering its tone and texture, the voice behind the words."[49] When we write, we consider rhetorical matters like level of formality, tone, word choice, sentence flow, font and spacing, and openings and closings. In teaching, our rhe-torical choices also involve language: Do I use formal or informal lan-guage? What do I call students? What tone do I use in emails? How loudly do I speak? Teaching persona goes well beyond language, how-ever. How do I dress and why? Is my apparel decision affected by my culture, my taste, my gender, the impression I want to give, my income, or what's not already dirty in my laundry basket? How much do I ges-ture and move around the room? What "vibe" do I convey about my competence, approachability, or authority? Am I funny or serious? How do I want to react when students find typos in my handout, or the technology doesn't work? What about when things go badly in my life? Do I hide my political beliefs or other values, or give cues through stickers on my office door or computer? How "authentic" am I with my students?

I suspect some faculty are uncomfortable contemplating matters of style, perhaps finding it self-centered, embarrassing, or insignificant, especially when compared to history content. I do not suggest we obsess about it to the point of becoming anxious or self-conscious, but I think it would be naive not to give it some thought. After all, we know that stu-dent perceptions of us matter, and so does our own comfort. There are probably as many teaching personas as there are teachers, and while there is evidence about certain instructor characteristics that contribute to student learning, as far as I can tell there's no evidence that any single persona is superior to others. It's wise to consider a few matters as we refine our own.

As with teaching metaphors, considering a few stereotypes helps us clarify teaching personas that resonate and those that are nothing like who we want to be. There's the easy-going prof (sitting on a desk, roaming the room, wearing blue jeans, dropping allusions to pop culture, calling students by their nicknames, telling students to call him by his first name, unconcerned about late papers). There's the intellectual professor (serious tone, more formally dressed, usually standing behind a podium, calling students by "Mr." or "Ms.," frequently referring to scholarship and theory). There's the sensitive, process-oriented facilitator (speaking softly so as not to abuse his power, arranging the chairs in a circle, starting class with a free write or meditation or letting students lead discussion, who interacts with students with warmth and concern). There's the creative technological wiz (who creates amazing Prezis, seamlessly integrated memes, and a visually appealing interactive syllabus, and communicates at all hours with students via backchannels and social media). There's the tough-love Luddite (who insists on eye contact and full attention, fiercely exhorting students to turn off their technology and think, who locks the door at one minute after class begins, holding firmly to deadlines). There are many other stereotypes—and many choices for us to make about the various elements of our teaching persona.

New faculty frequently receive the advice: "Just be yourself and do what comes naturally." In general, this is a good idea. One study involving 300 students found that "authentic" instructors were perceived as approachable, passionate, attentive, capable, and knowledgeable.[50] Education writers agree that going too far outside our natural style can be ineffective, because we may come across as stilted and inauthentic or disappoint students who want to connect with us as people.[51] As Steven Volk put it, "Our students will search for and find some answers to their questions in *us*, and not just in what we teach." They want to know how we got to where we are and what keeps us committed to our work, not simply the causes of a historical phenomenon. More broadly, they are learning from us "how to have a conversation, how to investigate a complex problem, how to disagree with their peers and with us, how to live an ethical life . . . and how to do all this and still make a living."[52] Faculty often don't realize the degree to which students are looking to them as people who might help them get excited about learning, care about them as people, and encourage them to pursue their dreams—things that require faculty to be authentic human beings, not just receptacles of knowledge.[53]

The advice to "be ourselves" is misguided if it means doing things contrary to what we know works for student learning. For example, we might have a tendency to be unorganized, and we might conclude it's just "who we are." However, national studies of teaching effectiveness suggest that it is not wise to "do what comes naturally" in this case. Students might forgive a little disorganization if we are brilliant, inspiring, and caring, but if disorganization becomes a pattern, they lose patience with not knowing what tomorrow's reading is, due dates being changed, or material that we forgot to cover being included on an exam. If I regularly hear that students are frustrated by those problems, I need to work on my organization. At the other end of the spectrum, some of us are serious planners with a personality that wants to control all the details. Although organization has been correlated with positive student evaluations, a lack of flexibility might cause us to ignore a contemporary example in the news that students want to discuss, confused looks on student faces, a potentially offensive comment, or a student question that cuts at the heart of an issue, all of which could have become a valuable teachable moment.

It's worth reflecting on whether certain aspects of our personalities work in the classroom. Some of us tend to be playful, lighthearted, and funny in our day-to-day lives, and using humor in class can motivate, engage attention, and even help memory if a joke is related to course material. Instructor use of self-effacing humor can put students at ease and foster warmth. On the other hand, humor can backfire badly; a flip response to a comment may be perceived as ridicule; a joke may insult an individual or a whole group of people; and excessive use of humor may confuse students or cause them to perceive the instructor as not sufficiently serious. To avoiding offending anyone, it's safer to use self-deprecating humor—but this can reduce student perceptions of professor credibility or confidence, which is a problem especially for women faculty and those from marginalized groups.[54] Sarah Rose Cavanagh, a psychologist who studies emotions in the classroom, notes that humor can feel forced if it doesn't come naturally to an instructor. In that case, she suggests finding print cartoons or video clips to convey humor for us. Similarly, some of us are more naturally exuberant and upbeat than others, which may be beneficial, since optimism, enthusiasm, and confidence may be predictors of positive student perceptions.[55] That may be worrisome for calm introverts, but it's inaccurate to think one must be extroverted, funny, and bubbly to teach effectively.[56] Plenty of introverted historians find low-key ways to capture student attention, spur thinking, and communicate their enthusiasm for their subject matter and concern for their students.

Sometimes we really should not be our authentic selves. True, there is a cost to "faking it"—it requires brain resources and may be exhausting to control our words and body language when we are hiding irritation or pretending we are eager when we aren't. Still, there are some social norms for faculty, such as keeping calm, treating all students with the same equity and goodwill, and being enthusiastic about our subject matter.[57] Sometimes faking it makes us better teachers. (I'm not referring to pretending to know information, of course.) If we are having a bad day and feel hostile toward the world, it's probably best not to let it all hang out. When there is a course topic we're not fond of but feel obligated to cover, unless we want our apathy to spread, it's probably wise to act like we enjoy it. (Cavanagh noted that even if we're a bit bored with an article we're very familiar with, our students may not be, so it's wise to try to remember and tap into our initial excitement when we first encountered it. That's not faking so much as doing justice to our material.[58]) It's not appropriate to share the woes of our love lives or how we feel after a late night. On the other hand, sharing the fact that we are undergoing treatment for a medical condition might be appropriate, because it alerts students that we may need to cancel class at the last minute or need a little longer than usual to finish grading.

Deciding how much to reveal of who we are requires judgment. Sharing some things about ourselves helps students see us as approachable people and trustworthy, credible faculty members. Sharing signals to students that we see them as "worthy confidants" trusted with knowing aspects of our lives and that in turn we are interested in knowing them. Limited self-disclosure appears to help motivate students, improve their perceptions of the learning environment and instructor, and increase conversations between faculty and students outside of class. A personal anecdote that helps illustrate an event or an abstract concept may be very useful in improving learning. There are lines we shouldn't cross, though. Students perceive faculty as being inappropriate and distracting if they talk about themselves too much and about too many topics that seem unrelated to the course.[59]

Sharing one's past struggles in learning (so that students realize that struggle is a normal part of learning) is one of the research-based suggestions for reducing stereotype threat and promoting a positive mindset toward learning. However, some evidence suggests that when instructors engaged in a lot of sharing about their past academic mistakes, students were less likely to see their instructors as having credibility, which in turn was correlated with uncivil behavior by students.[60] Unfortunately, it may be more risky for certain faculty to share their past struggles; because women, African Americans, and international faculty are already more vulnerable to suspicions of incompetence or bias, they face a dilemma about whether they should use a teaching strategy that might benefit their students but disadvantage themselves. For them, and for those who aren't comfortable sharing personal anecdotes, using examples of real people (but not themselves) provides many of the benefits of self-disclosure.[61]

What to say about ourselves on the first day of class constitutes a dilemma that thoughtful individual faculty resolve in different ways. Some who have children don't mention them because they draw a distinct line separating the personal and the professional. Others talk about their children because they are important parts of who they are. Some male faculty do so to counteract stereotypes of uninvolved fathers; some women do so because they want their female students to know that it's possible for women to have careers and families. On the other hand, some women refrain from talking about their kids because they worry students will quickly associate them with a "mom" stereotype that makes them seem less intellectual. Some faculty talk about their spouses or partners because they think it humanizes/normalizes them in the eyes of their students. Others don't, because they think it is not relevant to the class subject matter or because they don't want to take advantage of heterosexual privilege. Some LGBTQIA faculty opt to come out to their students (to be authentic, increase visibility of these marginalized populations, and serve as potential role models, allies, or mentors). Others don't come out because of the risks (of being prejudged or stereotyped, turning off certain students, being subject to complaints to campus leaders, or receiving negative comments on evaluation forms). Still others wait until later in the semester when they have established rapport and competence, or only in courses where the topic seems relevant.

On certain matters, some of us have more choice than others. Some faculty have disabilities or medical conditions that are readily apparent, whereas others have ones that are not visible. For some of us, the nature of our appearance or name means that students can make a reasonably accurate guess about our race or ethnicity. Whether or not aspects of our identities are hidden, all faculty can choose how explicitly or under what circumstances they want to discuss their ancestry. Faculty from minority racial or ethnic groups who teach majority students may choose not to discuss it or may choose to talk in different moments in the semester about the role it plays in their lives. Because some white students think they don't "have race," it can be especially educational for white faculty to talk about their racial or ethnic identities. With regard to religious beliefs (or lack thereof) or political ideology, a case can be made for total honesty about one's values and approach as well as for being circumspect due to the risks of being seen as "other" or being suspected of bias or proselytizing. Some of us feel freer if we have seniority, tenure, or confidence in the support of our colleagues, department, or university officials. It's hard for historians to draw the lines, especially related to politics. Although many teachers strive for "balance" to give students space to explore and develop their own opinions, others argue that intellectuals have a responsibility to contextualize and analyze the causes and implications of current events and rebut mistruths.[62] Before explicitly revealing personal parts of our identity, it's wise to consider the potential benefits and the risks, as well as our comfort levels and our students.

In summary, there are no hard-and-fast, evidence-based answers about a universally "right" teaching persona. Some personas better match our individual values, personalities, and teaching contexts, however. Even if there are no absolute answers, there are good questions to ask ourselves.

Are we being ethical?

Does our individual teaching persona in any way undermine professional standards? Obviously no one condones harassing, abusing, exploiting, or discriminating against students. But we want to do better than merely meeting minimum standards. We should articulate our ethics and strive to behave consistently with them, regularly reflecting about whether we unintentionally fail to achieve them.[63] We should be vigilant that nothing in our words, tone, or actions has subtly pushed students to adopt our views, disrespected them as individuals or members of groups, intimidated them, or otherwise created a chilly climate. Furthermore, we should examine whether we have done all that we can to facilitate equal opportunity for learning.

Does our teaching persona help students learn?

Obviously the content we teach and the activities we assign are quite important in facilitating student learning, but "so is the style with which you present said content and activities."[64] We know that some instructor characteristics seem to matter a lot for learning: enthusiasm, credibility, trustworthiness, concern, immediacy, confidence, transparency, and organization. Beyond those characteristics is a whole continuum of styles that can work. One professor might choose to use informal language to try to decrease the distance between himself and the students; another might choose a more formal style and more complex vocabulary to model academic language. What's important is that both instructors have reasons for what they do that are consistent with their learning objectives. It's wise, of course, to listen carefully to the preponderance of evidence from students to see if aspects of our style appear to inhibit learning.

Is our persona authentic?

Although there are caveats to doing so, it's worth considering whether our ways of being in the classroom are true to who we are and who we want to be as an instructor. Have we found ways to feel genuine without having to "fake it" very often? Have we found a way to feel authentic without disclosing things about ourselves that put us at risk? Have we found a way to exhibit the traits of effective teachers in a way that feels comfortable and consistent with our personality?

Do we have a good reason for the way we're doing things?

Sometimes we base our actions on carefully considered reasons and evidence, but other times we are less aware. Effective teachers strive to uncover their assumptions and reflect on their motives. If we are not guided by good reasons—but instead do things one way because we've always done it that way, our mentor did it that way, it's the path of least resistance, or it strokes our ego—we should consider evidence-based alternatives. It's better to be a thoughtful, intentional instructor.

Jay Parini put it nicely, "Teachers, like writers, need to invent and cultivate a voice that serves their personal needs, their students, and the material at hand."[65]

Thriving in the Long Term

> Skillful teaching is teaching that is contextually informed.
>
> STEPHEN BROOKFIELD

> Opportunities for learning, a sense of agency to plan for and seize such opportunities, professional relationships, and a sense of community or connection, anchored in commitment, all shape the degree to which faculty make contributions to students, colleagues, institutions, and society.
>
> KERRYANN O'MEARA ET AL.

Skillful instructors know their context, Stephen Brookfield observed, and context includes one's institution, department, and career stage.[66] Understanding expectations is important for a faculty member's success. However, in their research on faculty work and careers, KerryAnn O'Meara and her colleagues concluded that we need more than that: we need a sense of personal commitment, recognition of where our goals overlap with those of our employers, a sense of agency, and professional community.[67] If we adopt the characteristics of thriving faculty, it is more likely that we will have the energy to do good, satisfying work over the long term of a career.

Context

Institutional expectations of faculty members can differ dramatically, based on mission, size, demographics, and values. Practical realities related to budget, space, and technology also affect a faculty member's daily life. Some of us juggle three or more different course preps at a time, whereas others teach just a couple courses in a whole year; these courses may be in our areas of expertise or outside our comfort zone. Some of us have a lot of choice about which courses we teach. Others learn which ones we've been assigned shortly before the semester begins. We differ in the amount of autonomy we have in determining our materials, learning objectives, assignments, and policies.

Class sizes and formats vary widely, including small face-to-face seminars, online courses or blended ones, and hundreds of students in large, impersonal lecture halls. Correspondingly, department chairs have different expectations for what should happen in those classes related to active learning, discussions, lectures, and assessment. Goals differ, too. At a community college with many first-generation students, the institution may value building students' basic academic skills and confidence and measure success by the percentage who pass the class and enroll in courses the next semester. That's very different from an institution that values building research skills and measures success in the number of history theses or students going to graduate school. Some administrators value the quality of the relationships faculty build with students or the number of students who become history majors. Some department chairs view a low class average GPA as evidence of rigor; others view it as a sign that we're not teaching very effectively; others would never check the data.

Our institutions vary in how much they value teaching compared with other professional obligations for scholarship, advising, service, and mentoring students. At many schools (though clearly not all) teaching is top priority. Sometimes what is expected of us is explicit, communicated clearly by our chairs, colleagues, deans, and/or a faculty handbook; at other times, there are mixed messages. Obviously understanding these matters is crucial to our ability to make wise decisions. How much time should we spend planning class? How generously should we offer availability for student visits and mentoring?

To understand expectations, we must seek information. New faculty should attend orientations, read official documents, and ask plenty of questions. But there's no statute of limitation on clarifying expectations, and it's smart for faculty of any status or rank to have regular conversations with those who evaluate them. Savvy new faculty invite colleagues to coffee to discuss their pedagogical style, syllabi, assignments, and practices. They observe other people's classes and ask trusted colleagues to observe their own. While it's especially important for early career faculty to build foundational knowledge about teaching, the best instructors never stop learning. They seek out resources (such as books, articles, websites, and grants), people (such as consultants, learning communities), and services (such as discussions, workshops, focus groups, observations) that are available on their campus, especially any at a teaching and learning center.[68]

As guides for new faculty attest, new faculty also should do some sleuthing to understand the unique culture of their institution and department. In addition to the visible aspects of culture related to organizational procedures and traditions, there are less visible, often unspoken, and sometimes unique norms related to collegiality and community. Those teach us expectations related to how we interact with students, peers, and administrators. It's also wise to understand our profession's standards.[69] Despite explicit standards, gray areas lead to tensions among colleagues. At a 2018 roundtable at the American Historical Association conference titled "Historians Behaving Badly," senior faculty described cases when coworkers had been selfish, petty, or entitled, and clueless or indifferent about the implications of their actions. Examples included not doing one's fair share of departmental work; not attending (or appearing bored during) meetings; not answering email promptly; thwarting initiatives one did not directly benefit from; abusing or exploiting teaching assistants, support staff, or job candidates; escalating tensions through inflammatory group emails; and not fulfilling one's obligations as mentor, advisor, reference writer, reviewer, presenter at a conference, or collaborator.[70] Clearly it's better to learn norms rather than discover after the fact that we unknowingly violated them.

Our career stage and contract status often affect us. Early career faculty tend to feel anxious about whether they have what it takes to meet expectations. Being a history professor is challenging in any career stage, but especially early on, so it's helpful to maintain perspective. Newer faculty should not lose sight of the knowledge and skills they bring. After all, in a job market with many talented historians looking for work, they were chosen by people who believed they had a lot to offer. While new faculty should strive to understand norms and build positive relationships, they should not do so at the cost of their ethics, individuality, or soul.[71] When I propose that new faculty strive to understand their institution's expectations of them, I don't mean they should unquestioningly accept all of them. They may well encounter landmines or practices they would like to change.

Departments and institutions differ in how well they tolerate significant differences of values and opinions, so it's wise for early career faculty to explore with others their options for how to navigate those, especially when disagreeing with those with more seniority or power. Twenty years ago, the *Chronicle of Higher Education*'s "Ms. Mentor" advised women faculty to stifle their concerns and keep quiet until they earned tenure. Historian Penny Gold disagreed. Gold agreed junior faculty should develop decent working relations with a variety of colleagues and collect information about how to move proposals "through—and sometimes around" the official governance structure of their institution, but she asserted that they need "tact and political savvy, not silence."[72]

Many history faculty members can't expect a long-term relationship with departmental colleagues. The often exploitative use of part-time, adjunct, and contingent faculty has been steadily growing in higher education for decades, with perhaps half of faculty positions in the United States now being part-time in nature or off the tenure track.[73] A recent study showed that the percentage of history doctorates hired who have non–tenure track positions is increasing.[74] Contingent faculty members are usually disadvantaged with regard to pay, benefits, job security, and opportunities for advancement, and this status influences their day-to-day teaching conditions (and often their morale). They often enjoy fewer resources like individual office space, computers, phone, and permanent email accounts. These problems, along with the need to travel to other campuses or jobs to make a living wage, make it more difficult for part-time faculty to be responsive to students. Mary Elizabeth Perry, an accomplished scholar and teacher, recalled that during her long career as a visiting instructor and "freeway flier," one institution neglected to give her any office at all, and she held office hours under a tree next to her classroom.[75] Research suggests that part-time faculty worry about the same issues as full-time faculty (such as keeping students engaged, dealing with unprepared or unmotivated students, grading, setting policies), but their disconnection from the other faculty constitutes an additional obstacle.[76] One study showed that even five minutes a week of interaction with full-time faculty made a difference in job satisfaction for part-timers.[77]

For adjunct faculty, it's especially important to initiate conversations about departmental expectations related to course policies, student workload, instructional style, and assessment. Before starting, it's helpful to understand what students are like, and it's crucial to know how one's teaching will be evaluated. It may feel frustrating, of course, to invest time into understanding a unique campus culture (and adapting courses) without any certainty of being rehired. But making incorrect assumptions can decrease the odds of being rehired. Not understanding an institution's norms for active learning, for example, can lead to poor evaluations. I have known part-time faculty who thought they would please students by not holding class right before spring break, not holding them accountable for plagiarism, or by giving easy multiple choice exams, only to learn later that their supervisors considered those bad decisions. History departments should provide clear information (and ideally a liaison for their adjunct faculty), but if they don't, contingent faculty should find out what information and resources are available to them. Often many of the resources, events, and services from an institution's center for teaching and learning are open to all faculty, not just full-time ones.

Not surprisingly, mid-career faculty who have long-term, full-time positions tend to feel less anxious than early career or contingent faculty. Usually they're more confident thanks to surviving a formal evaluation process, and many find they enjoy greater freedom of choice. However, some find the mid-career stage challenging, partly because they aren't sure how to proceed when the path is less prescribed. As one put it, "You reach a certain plateau and you've been aiming there a long time, and you get there, and you look around and say, 'what next?'"[78] Should my next teaching challenges involve developing new courses, experimenting incrementally with new pedagogical strategies, delving into high-impact practices like service learning, or conducting SOTL? Should my next scholarly work probe deeper in a familiar area, explore an uncharted topic, partner with new collaborators, or reach out to wider audiences? Should I explore administrative opportunities, build a program, or try to instigate change in my institution? Should I adjust the percentage of time I spend on teaching, mentoring, scholarship, and service?

Mid-career is a long stage, and research suggests that faculty describe the experience very differently from one another, with some feeling quite positive (in control, comfortable, and sensing the possibilities) and others feeling overloaded, uncertain, or at a crossroads.[79] There may well be ups and downs. Some faculty experience a mid-career "malaise" where they feel "stagnant" or "stuck."[80] Others perceive a higher workload, as their institution looks to them for more significant service or they aim for promotion. At the same time, many feel less supported because institutions tend to direct more resources toward junior faculty and because their colleagues think they no longer require mentoring. Indeed, mid-career faculty are called on to shoulder the load of mentoring and leading others. This is especially true for women and people of color, who are more frequently asked to sit on committees and do extra mentoring of students and colleagues.[81] "In addition to the usual faculty load," observed Leslie Brown, "I still play mother, sister, aunt, and cousin to too many students of color, as well as gays and lesbians. Diversity programs, women of color conferences, speaker series, and black history celebrations all take pieces of me."[82] Although some resent the extra burden, she added, "I love my job and can't think of anything I'd rather be doing." Many mid-career faculty also face challenges in their lives outside of work, due to responsibilities for child or elder care.

Although a small percentage of late career faculty (loosely defined as those five to ten years before retirement) have disengaged from their department or institution, national data suggest that as a group, late career faculty feel more satisfied than early or mid-career faculty. This may be because they have more freedom to choose which aspect of their work to spend the most time on.[83] Many late career faculty are beginning to think about their legacies and, as a result, take on important institutional service, more mentoring, or developing courses that they had long been considering. Data from the early 2000s suggests that many late career faculty dedicate more of their time to their teaching.[84] That's a good idea, because, as Brookfield observed, "As we become more and more confident in our content knowledge and ability to anticipate students' questions or reactions, it is easy to relax to the point where predictability and even boredom take over." The antidote, he asserted, is digging more deeply into teaching, listening carefully to scholarship about teaching and the observations of our students, colleagues, and selves. This critically reflective teaching "can make the difference between marking time till retirement and a genuine engagement in the classroom."[85]

Although faculty in different positions and career stages have unique experiences, most face some common challenges. Like those in other professions, faculty in higher education tend to work hard. On average, studies suggest they work fifty-five to sixty-three hours a week during the semester.[86] Many feel tired, stressed, or overwhelmed by feeling that their work is never done or could be improved. In a study of MIT faculty, 78 percent reported that "no matter how hard they work, they can't get everything done," and 62 percent reported that they "feel physically or emotionally drained at the end of the day." (More faculty felt that way than did CEOs.[87]) Every semester faculty face new challenges: new students, classrooms, technology, materials, and institutional climate. Stress results from the frequency of class meetings and their public "performances." The intangible nature of the work, combined with ambiguity in expectations and the difficulty of evaluation, means that many faculty simply don't know when they have done well enough. (The authors of *The Slow Professor* argue that faculty make the culture of busyness worse by constantly talking about how busy they are and by imposing unrealistic expectations on themselves.[88]) In addition, working with students who are struggling, worrying about whether our scholarship will be published, engaging in campus conflicts, and feeling disappointed when a class goes poorly despite our hard work can all take an emotional toll.

Given these challenges, how can we increase the odds of having a healthy, sane, satisfying, and prolonged career? Not surprisingly, given the messages in this book, I argue that we should take a two-pronged approach: first, knowing ourselves and using that knowledge wisely; second, knowing and following what the scholarship tells us about faculty satisfaction, engagement, and vitality. In addition to understanding the opportunities and resources available in our unique contexts, the literature encourages us to adopt healthy habits, anchor our work in our individual commitments, and find other people to help sustain us in our professional mission.

Emotions

Part of surviving as a college teacher, Brookfield maintained, "is developing self-awareness of your emotional extremes and how to manage them."[89] Thus our first step should be to identify those times or topics that trigger difficult emotions. For example, many introverts feel overwhelmed by the first day of class, when they encounter so many new people. To cope with that anxiety, some try a variety of strategies. These include reassuring themselves that their anxiety will abate once they get to know the students, taking five minutes before class to acknowledge their fears (and dry mouth and rapid heartbeat) and remind themselves why they want to overcome them and the skills they bring to the course, meditating to slow down the brain's flight reaction, or reinterpreting their nervousness as eagerness to do a good job.[90] Faculty with severe anxiety should seek professional help, but those whose anxiety is temporary may benefit from recognizing that many of our students are likely nervous, too, and that it's our job to focus on them. One mother advised her professor daughter, "Try thinking about yourself less, dear."[91]

Other teaching fears include public speaking, which ranks high among Americans' most common fears, up there with snakes and dying. (Of course, it is possible to improve one's skills in speaking, which may alleviate some of the fears.) Some faculty dread conflict (and might feel a little less anxious if they prepare a "pedagogical parachute" or contingency plan for handling classroom conflicts). I won't confess all the details of my recurrent teaching nightmares, but I will admit that there are two common themes: first, teaching a class where the students are out of control, and second, finding myself in a situation where I am completely unprepared. Describing these does not begin to capture how upset I feel when I wake up! When John D'Emilio first taught a course in graduate school, he remembered, "The stress of being in front of the classroom was so great that I would return home and sleep for the rest of the day." Although nothing "objectively bad" occurred during that first semester, D'Emilio was such "a wreck" that he resolved never to teach again.[92] Other common fears are of not knowing enough or that our authority will be questioned. Our fears are probably not unique. Identifying them is a prerequisite for ensuring they don't debilitate us.

The makeup of our campuses and departments can affect us, too. Research on faculty members of color illustrates that teaching on a predominantly white campus or working in a department where there are few others with the same identity may lead to feeling marginalized, lonely, and stressed. Historian Rhonda Y. Williams described the "hypervisibility and super-isolation" of being the only Black woman in the whole College of Arts and Sciences with a tenure-track job. National data from 2013-14 indicate that 57 percent of African American faculty and about 40 percent of Asian and Latino/a faculty (from all disciplines) felt that they had been discriminated against or excluded from activities because of their race/ethnicity (compared with only 6 percent of white faculty). Many faculty of color—at one predominantly white institution, 76 percent of African American professors—reported having had their competence or credibility questioned and as a result felt strong pressure not to make any mistakes. They regularly had encountered insulting stereotypes.[93] Rhonda Williams related one such incident, familiar to many women faculty, in which she was chatting with a colleague in the hallway before the first day of class, when two white students asked where they could find "Mr. Williams' class." (Her colleague asked, "You mean, Dr. Williams? She's standing right here.") Some of Barbara Ransby's senior colleagues regularly confused her with the only other African American faculty member in the history department, who was ten years younger and looked nothing like her. Along with the powerful undercurrent of stereotype threat, the constant calculus of deciding how to interpret and respond to such incidents is one more thing to exhaust faculty. "The university in many ways has always been a foreign country to me," Ransby explained, "one in which I am constantly being asked to show my passport and constantly being reminded that I am not a local."[94]

Although each identity and situation is unique, we know that it's difficult to thrive when in the minority. International faculty may feel isolated and lonely as a result of being far from some loved ones and a familiar lifestyle. At the same time, they must negotiate different cultural norms in terms of teaching methods, assessment, and student behavior in their new university. Likewise, faculty who hail from a working-class background or are the first in their families to get college degrees may feel estrangement from university culture or from their families and cultures of origin. Some feel fraudulent or as though they continually have to prove themselves. LGBTQIA faculty can feel marginalized, too. D'Emilio recalled that when he received a tenure-track position at the University of North Carolina at Greensboro in 1983, a local newspaper announced that a "fag doctor" from New York had joined the university.[95] The first generations of women faculty had a tough time in many history departments, encountering salary disparities, unequal service expectations, sexual harassment, difficulty rising in the ranks, and a chilly climate that included dirty jokes, events at male-only venues, and being asked by male colleagues to make photocopies for them. In fact, many female respondents to a 2005 AHA survey on the status of women in the profession expressed resignation, bitterness, disillusionment, and discouragement.[96] When Caroline Bynum, one of first women assistant professors at Harvard, cochaired the university's Committee on the Status of Women in the early 1970s, she received hate mail and threats. "The tremendous weight of discrimination against women came down on me like a ton of bricks," she recalled, "the isolation, the difficulties, the opposition, and yes, even the hatred." Although the numbers of women in history departments has steadily increased, history has lagged behind some other fields, and some studies suggest that women faculty continue to experience subtler types of discrimination.[97] It is difficult to be "one of just a few" of any type of person on campus or in a department: the only Jew, Muslim, evangelical Christian; the youngest in an older department or vice versa; the only one with a visible disability; the only one teaching a particular field or using a particular methodology, and so on. Being a committed instructor in a department that devalues teaching is also demoralizing.[98]

All of us experience being different from some of our students in some ways, and these differences can affect our comfort and confidence and affect how students perceive us. Students might be uncomfortable or wary if our identities don't match their own—or surprised or critical if we do not conform to what they expect. Understanding our context— however unfair or frustrating certain aspects of it may be—means we can seek situation-appropriate resources and consider possible strategies for navigating it. For example, some African American faculty use strategies to affect students' perceptions of credibility, including starting class by mentioning their credentials. D'Emilio figured out a way to name the elephant in the room (his sexual orientation) in a way that felt authentic and fun and contributed to class connectedness.[99] Despite the vulnerability some of us feel in class with students who are different from us, we still occupy a position of power in our courses, so it is incumbent on us to model intercultural knowledge and competence. Faculty who are interculturally competent know (and are comfortable with) their own identity and culture, exhibit curiosity, openness, and empathy regarding their students' cultures and identities, and communicate effectively across cultures.[100] Even students who feel discomfort with us at the beginning of a course may become more open and accepting as the semester proceeds as they witness our knowledge and love of history, the effectiveness of our teaching, and our concern for their learning.

Our differences with students also bring opportunities. Students often value the different perspectives and experiences that international faculty bring. Lisa Balabanlilar, who earned her doctorate in South Asian history at age forty-nine, believed her very presence served as "a hopeful narrative that assures [students] that everything is not based on the decisions you make when you're 20 [and] that you can reinvent yourself at any time."[101] Although literature professor Melissa Scholes

Young felt nervous about "outing" herself as a first-generation faculty member, she remembered her own confusion as an undergraduate about how to negotiate college, so she invited first-generation students to a session "where they could ask us the questions they were too afraid to ask elsewhere." She reassured faculty who worried that sharing their experiences would not hurt their credibility. In fact, "It helps build it. First-generation college students need role models who have navigated similar paths and succeeded against the odds." Faculty from marginalized groups also help students realize the benefits that come from their identities, such as resilience and the ability to cross borders.[102] "Context matters," D'Emilio noted. "In the 1980s, my presence in the classroom was at least as important as the course content." Most of his students came from small North Carolina towns for whom he "was the first gay person they had knowingly encountered." Although there were awkward moments for him and the students, he garnered enormous satisfaction. "Virtually everything we covered was something my students had never encountered before. I loved their excitement . . . and I loved the way I saw their outlooks, whatever their identities, change over the course of a semester. If anyone is skeptical of the power of history and pedagogy to change hearts and minds, I can testify that the power is real."[103]

Health, Sanity, and Happiness

Knowing ourselves also means listening to our bodies and maintaining our health. Delaying self-care is misguided, noted psychologist Susan Robison, who researched the characteristics of "peak performing professors."[104] Doing so simply increases the risks of burnout and health problems. The signs of burnout include overwhelming exhaustion, cynicism and detachment from the job, and a sense of ineffectiveness.[105] Common sense tells us that unless we take care of ourselves, we cannot attend well to our students and our work. Physiological research confirms this: sleep deprivation decreases the brain's ability to work effectively. It impairs memory formation, the ability to pay attention, and productivity. It causes irritability, increases impulsivity, slows reaction time, and depresses the immune system.[106] Prolonged and chronic stress creates even more negative health effects. Just like for our students, there is an optimal sweet spot of challenge for faculty; if we experience too much, we can become anxious, hopeless, or demoralized. When there's no chance of achieving what we hope, we might, as Parker Palmer put it, "lose heart."[107]

When we're busy, taking time for self-care seems counterintuitive, but it can make us "happier *and* a better teacher." One study of high school teachers found that their own life satisfaction was a high predictor of their students' performance.[108] Evidence shows that in addition to improving our capacity to think, sleeping well, eating well, hydrating, and exercising all improve our energy level, mood, self-discipline, and ability to bounce back when life throws us a curve ball. The takeaway is that we need to work at having a life and not just a career. We can do that by engaging in activities that bring us joy, being with people we love, deliberately doing things that help us relax, and regularly getting "outside ourselves" to keep perspective. National data from the Collaborative on Academic Careers in Higher Education survey confirm that one of the elements most critical to faculty satisfaction and success is the ability to balance one's professional life with one's personal or family time.[109] Although our institutions can encourage us with expectations, course load, policies, and an institutional culture that support faculty health and balance, ultimately no one can find the right work/life balance for us. We have to do it ourselves. That might mean learning to say no (effectively), adjusting our expectations, learning strategies for efficiency, and tearing ourselves away from the office at a reasonable time. Healthy habits should not be viewed as optional, Robison asserted. "Only by keeping . . . your systems working well will you have enough energy for a long fulfilling career and a rich satisfying life."[110]

Thriving faculty members also have a clear sense of their individual professional missions. Instead of "mission," some refer to "purpose," "goals," or "commitments," but whatever the terminology, the scholarship emphasizes that it's wise to be aware of what most drives us.[111] Academic careers are rich with possible areas for work, and not taking the time to articulate and prioritize one's commitments may lead to setting too many goals, unfocused attention, or even paralysis, so that little actually gets accomplished. For explicitly spelling out one's individual purpose statement, Robison suggests including three parts: a key verb, which indicates what we want to *do*; an object that indicates the group(s) of people to whom our efforts are directed; and the knowledge, skills, or values we hope to share or to direct our actions. Following are a few examples:

- My purpose is to engage, challenge, support, and empower students and foster their development both inside and outside the classroom through advising, mentoring, and evidence-based, inclusive teaching.
- My mission is to be an energetic and productive public historian, sharing my knowledge of how to effectively communicate history with my students, in my scholarship, and in partnerships with local museums, historical sites, and schools.
- My goals are to help students, both history majors and nonmajors, understand the relevance of history to contemporary U.S. society and help them develop skills in writing, research, and analysis.
- I aim to help people understand the many and harmful implications of ethnocentrism and imperialism through my scholarship, teaching, service, and involvement in the International Studies program.
- I strive to revitalize the history department—its community, numbers of majors, and reputation—by being a collaborative, efficient, and innovative department chair, colleague, and teacher.

A sense of purpose helps sustain us through the less inspiring or more tedious aspects of our job. A study of mid-career faculty found that those who remained engaged and excited about their work were more likely to be able to articulate specific professional goals. Those faculty were also more likely to feel a sense of control over their careers and less likely to be derailed or discouraged by challenge or failure.[112] Faculty benefit from making time to reflect on their career trajectories, opportunities for reinvention and rejuvenation, and the work they find most meaningful.

It's also important that we recognize where our individual mission overlaps with that of our department and institution. Robison warns that if our definition of "great work" doesn't intersect with that of our workplace, we may become isolated or unsupported (or even unemployed).[113] To frame that more positively, understanding how our purposes intersect with those of our institution contributes to a sense of shared vision and belonging. Indeed, one study found that the most satisfied faculty had a strong connection to their institution through finding synergy between the organization's needs and their own intellectual contributions. Those faculty who were "synergistic citizens" sought and took advantage of the opportunities presented by their institution and chose service that most aligned with their values and interests (and said "no" when necessary). They made positive contributions to their school's success and, in turn, enjoyed rewards and recognition for their achievements.[114]

Having a firm sense of our main purposes also helps us make wise decisions about where to focus our efforts. Alignment between one's goals and activities matters in our careers just as it does in our teaching.[115] We need to regularly check how we are spending our time. If teaching is our top priority, then we should spend the bulk of our time working on it; if our dean told us we need to publish more frequently, then we need to carve out quality time for scholarship. Being in tune with our sense of professional purpose can help us decide between which scholarly project to undertake next and which committee to volunteer for, so that we choose ones that motivate us.

A clear mission helps us decide how to spend our days. For busy and stressed faculty, even deciding how to most productively spend an unscheduled twenty-minute window during the day can be difficult. There's a cognitive explanation for this: having to make many small decisions can fatigue and overwhelm the brain.[116] Instead of frittering away that twenty minutes or being paralyzed by scores of decisions every day, it's better to develop efficient work habits that support our goals. We should have a sense of what our main goals are for each day and week—derived from our big-picture purpose—and build a schedule that allocates time sensibly, giving our top priorities the most time during the time of day when we are most productive. We can work efficiently by resisting multitasking and limit checking of email to just a couple of times a day. We might use backward design for our careers. (What end-of-year evidence will suggest I have met my goals? What specific activities will accomplish them?) Just as we update our goals for each course every semester, we should regularly revisit our professional mission and goals, since they are likely to change as we do.[117]

Mentors

To thrive, we also need supportive people. Research suggests that the quality of one's community and colleagues are crucial elements of faculty satisfaction.[118] Good connections with coworkers leads to more knowledge, less stress, and a better sense of belonging. Without good colleagues, autonomy may devolve into isolation, which becomes problematic when we encounter difficult situations. Personally and professionally supportive relationships help faculty at any career stage and regardless of one's identity, but women faculty and faculty of color especially appreciate them.[119]

It's useful to consider precisely what we mean by "mentoring." The traditional graduate school model—in which one senior faculty member (a "guru") serves as a single advisor in a hierarchical relationship with a more junior protégé—has limitations. Expecting a single person to serve as a mentor "will inevitably lead to disappointment, over-dependence on the advice of one person, and feelings of loneliness," noted mentoring expert Kerry Ann Rockquemore. "Gurus . . . make mistakes, and relying on one exclusively can put you at unnecessary risk and leave you with many unmet needs." Faculty have many different needs—including teaching advice, emotional support, feedback on our scholarship, role models, wisdom about campus norms and service, accountability, and sponsorship—and it's unlikely that any single person can effectively serve all those distinct needs. As Rockquemore put it, "It's probably more satisfying to meet with friends for emotional support than to expect it from your department chair. And, it's far more meaningful to join a writing group for accountability than asking your mentor to call you every week and make sure you're making progress on your writing."[120]

Scholarship on mentoring suggests that it's more useful for faculty to realize that all of us need a "mentor network," which includes a handful of people with different proficiencies who can help us in different areas. Some might be scholarly collaborators, and others might be more like friends, the kind of trusted people with whom one can laugh, cry, and safely share dreams and fears. Some of those people may be in our own department, while others reside in other fields; some may be on the same campus, while we may connect with others on different campuses or through online communities; still others (a professional coach, an editor, a therapist, a retirement consultant) may not even work in academia. Some may be senior colleagues, and others will be peers in the same career stage or junior colleagues. The concept of "mutual mentoring" recognizes that mentoring relationships do not have to be hierarchical; what matters is not a mentor's age or career stage, but their competencies. We benefit from people who have different knowledge and skills from us, even if those people have less experience. In mutual mentoring, one faculty member can share expertise in an area like using technology in teaching, and another can provide advice in a different area, such as getting published.

Some of the people in our mentor network may be similar to us in our interests, goals, experiences, or cultural traits—and thus readily understand what we are going through. Leslie Brown, for example, wrote about the delight and inspiration she felt when meeting other African American historians; after experiencing sex discrimination, Susan Groag Bell described working with other women historians as a "wide and comforting safety net of likeminded spirits."[121] However, research on mentoring suggests that it's also important that some people in our mentor network be different from us, so we have access to perspectives beyond our own.[122] For example, although Barbara Ransby remembered fondly an almost "utopian" conference of African American women in academia where she felt understood and unselfconscious, she contended that scholars do not have to be in homogeneous groups to feel secure. Her dissertation committee members were all male and "all enormously supportive and respectful" faculty who "paved different and principled career paths for themselves and made it possible for me to do the same."[123]

Faculty may wish someone would assign them a single all-knowing mentor, but research suggests a better approach. We should seek out multiple mentors to help us meet our specific needs and do this at every career stage, since our needs shift over time. Faculty who take this approach receive support, information, and encouragement, but just as importantly, they get a sense of empowerment from being proactive, intentional agents of their career development.[124]

■

I have proposed here that we should reflect on ourselves as teachers and as professionals in the academy. Indeed, much of the educational literature advises that faculty should cultivate a habit of reflection.[125] It's both enjoyable and beneficial to consider what first drew us to history and our vocation. It's useful to uncover our assumptions—especially any limiting beliefs that get in our way. Considering metaphors for teaching is one way to become aware of how we see the educational process, what we do in the classroom, and how we envision our relationship to students. It's worth reflecting on our teaching persona, too, which is based in part on our personalities, experiences, and identities. Although instructors with a wide range of styles can succeed, it's worth paying attention to which characteristics and behaviors best improve student learning, meet our goals, reflect our values, and feel authentic.

As historian Peter Filene put it, "Whether consciously or unconsciously, each of us works with some notions of what we think is good (and bad) pedagogy. So the more that you can put those notions out in front of yourself, the more likely you will design a course that fits *you*."[126] Bringing these notions to the surface helps us to make intentional and wise choices.

Some key strategies increase our chances of achieving long-term success teaching history. We must understand our context—to comprehend what is expected of us and be aware of how our work setting and career stage affect us. We should notice any difficult emotions that teaching evokes so we can develop effective ways to cope with them. We should commit to living in ways that care for our bodies, minds, and spirits. We should strive for work/life balance—because it makes it possible for us to do high-quality work and because we deserve healthy and satisfying lives. We should also consider and articulate our individual professional mission because it energizes us to tap into our sense of purpose and what we see as meaningful. Aligning our professional decisions and our daily, weekly, and yearly schedules with our mission makes us more likely to do the right work. Finally, we need good people to sustain us. Whether we call those people a mentor network or simply colleagues, collaborators, friends, role models, readers, critics, confessors, sponsors, or allies—thriving faculty tend to have a collection of people with whom they regularly connect. These people understand, respect, support, and challenge us in the different aspects of our professional work.

Conclusion

College teaching is a wonderful profession. We enjoy the opportunity to think about history during many of our waking hours. We're employed by institutions whose purpose is learning. Our profession offers autonomy and status plus challenge and variety in its daily tasks. We labor alongside smart colleagues and form long-term, warm, and supportive relationships with some of them. We do important work, teaching lessons about the past to new people each term.

We have the chance to profoundly influence students. We can transform their preconceptions that history is boring by engaging them with big questions and concepts. Instead of asking them to memorize names and dates, we can teach them about fundamental differences between political theories, cultures, religious traditions, and economic systems; the costs of war; the warning signs of despotism; and how change occurs. By introducing them to times when people have been brave, cruel, innovative, or kind, we can prompt thinking about power and agency, tyranny and freedom, and what it means to live a good life and be part of a community. Because history is not just a subject but a method and discipline, we can teach ways of thinking that last a lifetime.[1] We can help students develop the ability to read carefully, analyze evidence, understand different perspectives, observe context, create and support arguments, conduct research, and relate a complex narrative. We can help them improve their communication skills through writing essays and creating web content, making formal presentations, and participating in civil discussions. We can teach so that after they leave our classrooms, they can use their knowledge in positive ways as workers, citizens, and people.

Students do not become proficient at thinking and acting like historians in one semester. Stephen Brookfield noted that it takes time for students to learn a discipline's "epistemological grammar" and how to think critically, which involves evaluating assumptions, providing evidence for assertions, seeking out alternative perspectives, welcoming critique, and continuously appraising themselves. Although students found these intellectual habits foreign and difficult at first, they reported that certain things especially helped: when instructors eased them into critical thinking and sequenced the steps, modeled the processes, and gave them a chance to practice such thinking with specific scenarios and in discussion with others.[2]

Nor do instructors become excellent teachers in a semester. It takes time to develop critical thinking about teaching—to evaluate assumptions about it, consider evidence, seek alternative methods, welcome critique, and continually and effectively appraise ourselves. As we do for students as they learn new approaches, we should have reasonable expectations and ease ourselves into new approaches, see models in action, and practice and analyze specific situations with others. Competence comes only through conscious, goal-directed practice, and we are more likely to develop it when we receive formative feedback. After revising a course to more explicitly and consistently teach students how to think critically about history, Charles Bonwell concluded that it's important to "be patient with yourself."[3] We don't have to radically change everything about our teaching at once; instead, we can focus on and experiment with one aspect at a time. Choosing one, getting started, and doing it intentionally and reflectively can energize us and make a big difference. As James Lang observed in *Small Teaching*, just like winning the World Series is possible through stealing bases and sacrifice flies, fundamental pedagogical improvement is possible through incremental but powerful modifications.[4]

Teaching well requires a smart approach. By teaching *well*, I mean doing it in an intentional, scholarly, effective, and inclusive manner. "Intentional" means we undertake course planning and decide on our goals, materials, assignments, and daily strategies thoughtfully and with purpose, aided by backward design. "Scholarly" means we are familiar with the scholarship in our fields (about both history and teaching and learning) and that when we teach, we exhibit the characteristics of good scholars: curiosity, rigor, knowledge, clarity of expression, and a willingness to analyze evidence and adjust based on it. "Effective" means that students deeply learn meaningful (not fleeting) knowledge and skills, and they do so thanks to our methods and because we have implemented good plans with energy, organization, and flexibility. "Inclusive" means we are respectful of our students, committed to their learning, and culturally aware. Inclusive teachers intentionally teach in ways that improve the learning environment and the chances for success of all students.

This book argues that great teaching results not only from having a tool box with smart teaching techniques but from careful consideration of five interrelated and mutually reinforcing areas. One is *who we are*— our unique combination of knowledge, skills, and beliefs about teaching, our strengths and weaknesses, work context, style, values, and perspective. It's especially important to be mindful of our professional mission, that sense of purpose that motivates us and gives our work meaning.

Our content knowledge, identity, values, and "history origin story" influence *what we teach*. Deciding on our goals is a crucial step in designing an effective course. Rather than aiming for covering everything about a topic, we should focus on how we want students to be different in a lasting and meaningful way as a result of our course. We have a lush banquet of worthy goals from which to choose. Our decision about specific learning goals drives our decisions about readings, assignments/assessments, and day-to-day work. It is vital for creating an integrated course where students don't drown in a sea of facts but instead use facts for more challenging tasks and understand how everything they do is related to the big picture of the course's significant goals.

Our students are different from us—not just because they are novices at doing history but because they have their own backgrounds, interests, values, skills, and prior knowledge. Thus it's important to carefully consider *who we teach*—as learners and thinkers as well as individuals and members of cultural groups. Beyond offering us the pleasure of connecting with them, understanding our students helps us challenge and support them as they grapple with the cognitive and affective bottlenecks to learning history that scholars have uncovered. It helps us figure out how to make our content accessible and engaging, leveraging what psychologists tell us about motivation and the mindsets that encourage persistence and success. Research about students tells us about the negative effects of stereotype threat, the strikingly uneven preparation they receive in high school, and the powerful influence of classroom climate and a sense of belonging—all of which underscore the need for inclusive methods.

How we teach day to day enacts our goals and values. There's no one-size-fits-all approach or persona that ensures we will teach effectively.

Still, it's clearly important that students (not their instructors) must do the work of learning and that we should provide opportunities for low-stakes practice and (efficiently delivered) formative feedback. There is abundant research about the efficacy of active learning methods. Scholarship reveals how the brain connects new material to prior knowledge and some instructor characteristics correlated with students' learning. We know concrete ways to prompt good thinking through questions and reflections, the components of good discussions, the best ways and times to lecture, the importance of accountability, and the characteristics of good assignments. We should incorporate the relatively simple practice of teaching transparently, which increases students' success regardless of their backgrounds. Transparency helps students understand what they're learning and why. It also helps us keep our eyes on the big picture as we design integrated course units and individual class sessions and as we determine grading criteria for assignments. Our task as instructors—which requires intellect and creativity—is to figure out how to apply these principles to our specific course content in a way that feels relatively comfortable and authentic.

Our teaching is enhanced by *how we assess*. When done effectively, assessment not only evaluates how well students have learned but prompts learning by posing meaningful, clear, aligned tasks. Good feedback helps students understand standards for quality and the degree to which their performance met them, and if we get them to use it, helps them improve. When done well, the process of giving students feedback doesn't wreck or demoralize instructors either. When we assess student work, we are gathering information about how effective our materials and methods have been in achieving our goals. "Assessment of teaching begins with a careful and honest collection of evidence," asserted Ken Bain.[5] Savvy instructors recognize the advantages and limitations of various kinds of evidence and thus gather numerous kinds before carefully drawing conclusions about the quality of their teaching. Then they make evidence-based adjustments.

Paying attention to evidence empowers faculty as teachers just as it does for them as scholars and experts in the discipline of history. In this book, I synthesized some high-quality scholarship of teaching and learning, and more is available. Many topics touched on (especially those about high-impact practices) deserve deeper treatment, and many general topics deserve more exploration from scholars specifically about teaching history. The SOTL revolution shows no sign of abating, so the future will bring more exciting research findings. Instructors will be enriched if they get into the habit of looking for them, through reading good journals, attending conference sessions, subscribing to a few expert blogs, or regularly working with a center for teaching and learning.

Beyond knowledge and skills, history instructors' effectiveness lies in their dispositions and mindsets toward teaching.[6] The ideal disposition resembles the learning orientation we are looking for in our students; those who approach courses with motivation, a positive attitude, openness to feedback, and a willingness to work hard and in the right direction tend to perform best. Instructors also need intellectual modesty to realize that they don't know everything about teaching, metacognition to recognize which things to work on, and resilience to persevere when things get difficult. They need perspective—to know when to dig in and try to fix a problem and when to move on from an isolated mistake or unfortunate moment. Those with a great teaching disposition accept responsibility for their actions and are slow to get defensive or assign blame. They care. They also acknowledge and enjoy it when something goes well—and try to figure out why it worked well, so they might do it again. They are willing to take some risks and have the inclination to analyze—and have a sense of humor—when things don't go as hoped.

Although it has many benefits, our profession demands long hours and at times may be stressful, frustrating, or exhausting. Just like students, we may work hard but not in the best direction, resulting in disappointing outcomes. So it's wise to know our context and what is expected of us, seek formative feedback early and often, consider what research says about academic thriving, and build a good mentor network. That network should include colleagues who love teaching and are familiar with SOTL. We can avoid becoming demoralized or burned out by paying attention to the signs that we need to change course and by consulting experts to support us in doing so. We should heed the evidence about the importance of self-care and ways to enhance our physical and mental health. While we are fortunate to do worthwhile work, we need energy and sanity to do it well, and only we can create our appropriate work/life balance. We should show compassion for ourselves as we do our best in a challenging job.

There are many factors instructors don't control. These include students' prior life and educational experiences, genetic makeup, stresses, language skills, priorities, abilities and disabilities, and work ethic.

However, there's a lot that we do control about the teaching/learning process, such as our organization, planning, and mental and emotional readiness to teach. We determine the quality of our materials, in-class activities, and assignments. We decide on the content and timeliness of feedback, and we can convey respect and concern for students through our actions.[7] Although excellent instructors recognize the importance of reflecting on themselves, they focus intently on their students, getting to know them, attending carefully to their ideas, and imagining ways to engage their curiosity and build their understanding and skills. Excellent instructors do the incremental work of targeting where their teaching or their students' learning can improve, and then they ponder, consult resources, or talk with others to try to improve.

Intentional, effective, scholarly, and inclusive teachers—the ones with a disposition to learning and honing their craft—consistently do this work. It pays off. Teaching improves with smart, reflective practice. Along the way, the work leads to special moments, "the exciting conversations that we have, where you see the students' eyes light up when they're thinking in a new way."[8] One doesn't simply "arrive" at being a great teacher, however; there are always going to be aspects of our teaching that can be improved, new research findings to consider, and new students to get to know. We will change, too, as we move into new stages of life and new roles. "However you define yourself as a teacher now," observed Peter Filene, "you will redefine it in the course of years and courses to come."[9] Let's commit ourselves to supporting and challenging each other as we strive to grow in the noble endeavor of unleashing (as John D'Emilio put it) "the power of history and pedagogy to change hearts and minds."[10]

Acknowledgments

Great teachers transformed my life. They set my mind on fire with ideas, connected class material to the world I lived in, and taught me how to learn. Often (just as the research suggests) they made a big difference by supporting me as a person. In my first year at Knox College, medievalist Penny Gold changed my life by asking her students to explore what it means to be human, introducing us to feminism, and frankly telling me I needed to work on my writing. Then she mentored me through draft after draft of my first research project and into a great graduate program in history. Unbelievably lucky while studying at the University of North Carolina, I was assigned as a teaching assistant to Peter Filene, who modeled innovative methods and the approach of a fair-minded, respectful, and challenging professor. I encountered Ed Neal, director of the Center for Teaching and Learning, who first introduced me to backward course design, showed me many active learning techniques, and coached me through the travails of teaching my first solo course.

More good fortune led me to a job at Elon University (then Elon College), where my colleagues in the Department of History and Geography—great and committed teacher-scholars—welcomed me, offered me the chance to teach all sorts of courses, traded ideas and resources, and listened to my worries and classroom disasters. They consistently support one another with a lot of humor (and donuts). At Elon I found a whole community of faculty, staff, and administrators who care deeply about student learning. At Elon active learning is baked into the curriculum, teaching and SOTL are valued, we grapple with issues related to diversity, equity, and inclusion, and we continually strive to improve (which is both exhilarating and exhausting and the reason we contemplate work-life balance). I've benefited from Elon's really thoughtful students, who expect me to challenge and engage them, offer suggestions for how to do it better, ask tough questions, share their experiences, and reflect about what matters most.

In 2011, my career changed in exciting ways when I began working half-time as an associate director of Elon's Center for the Advancement of Teaching and Learning (CATL). At the time, I had already been promoted to full professor and enjoyed what many consider academic success as a scholar, teacher, and university citizen. Although I had always thought carefully about my teaching, working in CATL meant I had daily interactions with smart, collaborative, internationally recognized experts in SOTL who knew how to translate the research findings into action. Peter Felten, Katie King, and Deandra Little generously introduced me to proven practices and resources on the topics discussed in this book, and they inspired me. They modeled how to take intelligent risks, give students more voice, and generally teach with sensitivity and integrity. The whole CATL team of associate directors, program coordinators, student workers, and advisory board have been a joy to work with. Collaborating with these colleagues, reading thought-provoking works by leaders in educational development, and attending conferences about teaching and learning have supplied me with new pedagogical strategies and clarified why some approaches I had tried had worked and some had not. As a result of this tremendous opportunity, I learned the power of mid-career development, and I have evolved from a trial-and-error teacher to a more evidence-based, scholarly one. I'm also a braver, more inclusive, smarter, and more effective teacher.

Because I have been so enriched by this experience, I wanted to share what I have learned with my fellow instructors in history and related fields. I know that despite the amazing ability of Elon's interlibrary loan librarians, I have not synthesized all the relevant literature, and the book is far from perfect. Still, it's better than it would have been thanks to all the coworkers and friends who shared ideas and materials, especially the people who read parts or all of the manuscript and gave me helpful feedback, including Peter Filene, Charles Irons, Ed Neal, Joel Sipress, and Steven Volk. I'm grateful to those who shepherded the project from raw manuscript to actual book, including Gwen Walker, Anna Muenchrath, Adam Mehring, Laura Poole, and the whole University of Wisconsin Press production team. I appreciate the sabbatical from Elon's Faculty Research and Development Committee, which gave me the precious gift of time to think and write, and support from the Maude Sharpe Powell professorship. Jean-Paul Lavoie ably translated my ideas into illustrations. I appreciate the encouragement and perspective supplied by many friends, especially Cassie Kircher and

Pam Kiser, and family members, especially my mother, who has shown unflagging interest in my career. Barbara Z. Taylor read multiple drafts of the chapters, and through her example and countless conversations she has taught me an enormous amount about teaching, students, experiential education, and technology. Much more importantly, Barbara is my partner in everything in life, and I am grateful beyond measure for her constant presence, support, and love.

Notes

Introduction

1. Ken Bain, *What the Best College Teachers Do* (Cambridge, MA: Harvard University Press, 2004), 174; Stephen D. Brookfield, *The Skillful Teacher: On Technique, Trust, and Responsiveness in the Classroom* (Hoboken, NJ: John Wiley & Sons, 2015), 278.

2. James Grossman, "To Be a Historian Is to Be a Teacher," *Perspectives*, November 2015.

3. See, for example, Woodrow Wilson National Fellowship Foundation, "National Survey Finds Just 1 in 3 Americans Would Pass Citizenship Test," news release, October 3, 2018; William Gonch, "A Crisis in Civic Education," American Council of Trustees and Alumni, 2016, https://www.goacta.org/images/download/A_Crisis_in_Civic_Education.pdf.

4. Joan Middendorf, David Pace, Leah Shopkow, and Arlene Diaz, "Making Thinking Explicit: Decoding History Teaching," *National Teaching & Learning Forum* 16, no. 2 (February 2007): 1-2; Catherine King and Peter Felten, "Threshold Concepts in Educational Development: An Introduction," *Journal of Faculty Development* 26, no. 3 (2012): 5-7; Joel M. Sipress and David J. Voelker, "From Learning History to Doing History," in Regan A. R. Gurung, Nancy L. Chick, and Aeron Haynie, eds., *Exploring Signature Pedagogies* (Sterling, VA: Stylus, 2009), 19-35.

5. Benjamin M. Schmidt, "The History BA since the Great Recession," *Perspectives on History*, December 2018; Julia Brookins, "New Data Show Large Drop in History Bachelor's Degrees," *Perspectives on History*, March 2016.

6. James Loewen, *Lies My Teacher Told Me: Everything Your American History Textbook Got Wrong*, 2nd ed. (New York: Touchstone, 2007), 1-2.

7. Roy Rosenzweig, "How Americans Use and Think about the Past," in Peter N. Stearns, Peter Seixas, and Sam Wineburg, eds., *Knowing, Teaching, and Learning History: National and International Perspectives* (New York: New York University Press and the American Historical Association, 2000), 273-75.

8. Andrew K. Koch, "Many Thousands Failed: A Wakeup Call to History Educators," *Perspectives on History*, May 2017; Andrew K. Koch, "Big Inequity in Small Things," *National Teaching & Learning Forum* 27 (October 2018): 3-4.

9. David Pace, "The History Classroom in an Era of Crisis: A Change of Course Is Needed," *Perspectives on History*, May 2017.

10. Maryellen Weimer, "Learning More from the Wisdom of Practice," *New Directions for Teaching and Learning* 86 (Summer 2001): 45–49.

11. David Pace, "The Amateur in the Operating Room: History and the Scholarship of Teaching and Learning," *American Historical Review* 109, no. 4 (October 2004): 1172.

12. Pace, "Amateur in the Operating Room," 1172.

13. Keith A. Erekson, "Organizing and Globalizing the Scholarly Teaching of History," *Perspectives on History*, September 2007; Michael Coventry, Peter Felten, David Jaffee, Cecilia O'Leary, Tracy Weis, and Susannah McGowan, "Ways of Seeing: Evidence and Learning in the History Classroom," *Journal of American History* 92, no. 4 (March 2006): 1371–401.

14. Sam Wineburg, *Historical Thinking and Other Unnatural Acts* (Philadelphia: Temple University Press, 2001); Sam Wineburg, *Why Learn History (When It's Already on Your Phone)?* (Chicago: University of Chicago Press, 2018), 103–38; Sipress and Voelker, "From Learning History to Doing History"; Arlene Diaz, Joan Middendorf, David Pace, and Leah Shopkow, "The History Learning Project: A Department 'Decodes' Its Students," *Journal of American History* 94, no. 4 (March 2008): 1211–24; Joan Middendorf and David Pace, "Decoding the Disciplines: A Model for Helping Students Learn Disciplinary Ways of Thinking," *New Directions for Teaching and Learning* 98 (Summer 2004): 1–12; Leah Shopkow, "What Decoding the Disciplines Can Offer Threshold Concepts," in Jan H. F. Meyer, Ray Land, and Caroline Baillie, eds., *Threshold Concepts and Transformational Learning* (Rotterdam, The Netherlands: Sense Publishers, 2010), 317–31.

15. American Historical Association, "Tuning the History Discipline in the United States," https://www.historians.org/teaching-and-learning/tuning-the -history-discipline.

16. Wineburg, *Why Learn History?*, 178.

17. T. Mills Kelly, *Teaching History in the Digital Age* (Ann Arbor: University of Michigan Press, 2013), introduction; Jack Dougherty and Kristen Nawrotzki, eds., *Writing History in the Digital Age* (Ann Arbor: University of Michigan Press, 2013); John McClymer, "From Scarcity to Abundance," AHA Guide to Teaching and Learning with New Media, https://historians.org/teaching-and -learning/teaching-resources-for-historians.

18. Chad N. Loes and Ernest T. Pascarella, "The Benefits of Good Teaching Extend beyond Course Achievement," *Journal of the Scholarship of Teaching and Learning* 15, no. 2 (April 2015): 1–13; Ernest T. Pascarella and Charles Blaich, "Lessons from the Wabash National Study of Liberal Arts Education," *Change: The Magazine of Higher Learning* 45, no. 2 (2013): 6–15.

19. Mary-Ann Winkelmes, "Transparency in Teaching: Faculty Share Data and Improve Students' Learning," *Liberal Education* 99, no. 2 (Spring 2013); Mary-Ann Winkelmes, David E. Copeland, Ed Jorgensen, Alison Sloat, Anna Smedley, Peter Pizor, Katherine Johnson, and Sharon Jalene, "Benefits (Some Unexpected) of Transparent Assignment Design," *National Teaching and Learning Forum* 24, no. 4 (May 2015): 4–6. Other works interpreting multi-institutional data include Derek Bok, *Our Underachieving Colleges: A Candid Look at How Much Students Learn and Why They Should Be Learning More* (Princeton, NJ: Princeton University Press, 2006); Richard Arum and Josipa Roksa, *Academically Adrift: Limited Learning on College Campuses* (Chicago: University of Chicago Press, 2011); Doug Lederman, "Less Academically Adrift?" *Inside Higher Ed*, May 20, 2013.

20. Susan A. Ambrose, Michael W. Bridges, Michele DiPietro, Marsha C. Lovett, Marie K. Norman, and Richard E. Mayer, *How Learning Works: 7 Research-Based Principles for Smart Teaching* (San Francisco: Jossey-Bass, 2010); Claude M. Steele, *Whistling Vivaldi: How Stereotypes Affect Us and What We Can Do* (New York: Norton, 2010); Carol S. Dweck, Gregory M. Walton, and Geoffrey L. Cohen, *Academic Tenacity; Mindsets and Skills That Promote Long-Term Learning* (Gates Foundation, 2011), http://k12education.gatesfoundation.org/resource/aca demic-tenacity-mindsets-and-skills-that-promote-long-term-learning/; James M. Lang, *Small Teaching; Everyday Lessons from the Science of Learning* (San Francisco: Jossey-Bass, 2016); Benedict Carey, *How We Learn: The Surprising Truth about When, Where, and Why It Happens* (New York: Random House, 2014); Adam L. Putnam, Victor W. Sungkhasettee, and Henry L. Roediger III, "Optimizing Learning in College: Tips from Cognitive Psychology," *Perspectives on Psychological Science* 11, no. 5 (2016): 652–60; Rita Obeid, Anna Schwartz, Christina Shane-Simpson, and Patricia J. Brooks, eds., *How We Teach Now: The GSTA Guide to Student-Centered Learning* (American Psychological Association's Society for the Teaching of Psychology, 2016), http://teachpsych.org/ebooks/howwe teachnow.

21. I first encountered this framework in a webinar by Christine Stanley and Mathew Ouellett, "Four Strategies to Engage the Multicultural Classroom," Magna Online Seminar, 2012; I believe the model was created by Linda S. Marchesani and Maurianne Adams, "Dynamics of Diversity in the Teaching-Learning Process: A Faculty Development Model for Analysis and Action," *New Perspectives for Teaching and Learning* 52 (December 1992): 9–20. See also Christine A. Stanley, Shari Saunders, and Jamie M. Hart, "Multicultural Course Transformation," in Mathew Ouellett, ed., *Teaching Inclusively* (Stillwater, OK: New Forums Press, 2005), 566–83.

22. Most centers for teaching and learning use the backward design model described in detail by Jay McTighe and Grant Wiggins, *Understanding by Design*

(Alexandria, VA: Association for Supervision and Curriculum Development, 1998), and L. Dee Fink, *Creating Significant Learning Experiences: An Integrated Approach to Designing College Courses*, rev. ed. (San Francisco: Jossey-Bass, 2013).

23. For the overlap between good face-to-face and online teaching practices, see Kathryn E. Linder and Chrysanthemum Mattison Hayes, *High-Impact Practices in Online Education: Research and Best Practices* (Sterling, VA: Stylus, 2018), 215–19.

24. Patrick Blessinger and Krassie Petrova, "What the Best College Teachers Do: An HETL Interview with Dr. Ken Bain," *International Higher Education Teaching and Learning Association* 2, January 17, 2012, https://www.hetl.org/what-the-best-college-teachers-do/.

25. Jennifer Clark, "What Use Is SoTL? Using the Scholarship of Teaching and Learning to Develop a Curriculum for First Year History Courses," *Journal of University Teaching & Learning Practice* 6, no. 2 (2009).

26. Quoted in Blessinger and Petrova, "What the Best College Teachers Do."

Chapter 1. What We Teach

1. Susan A. Ambrose, Michael W. Bridges, Michele DiPietro, Marsha C. Lovett, Marie K. Norman, and Richard E. Mayer, *How Learning Works: 7 Research-Based Principles for Smart Teaching* (San Francisco: Jossey-Bass, 2010), 95–99.

2. David Perkins, *Making Learning Whole: How Seven Principles of Teaching Can Transform Education* (San Francisco: Jossey-Bass, 2009), 61.

3. The basic schema for backward design has been around a long time (sometimes attributed to Ralph Tyler in 1949), although some authors have given it different names and revised the details. Key works include Grant Wiggins and Jay McTighe, *Understanding by Design* (Alexandria, VA: Association for Supervision and Curriculum Development, 1998); L. Dee Fink, *Creating Significant Learning Experiences*, rev. ed. (San Francisco: Jossey-Bass, 2013); Edmund J. Hansen, *Idea-Based Learning: A Course Design Process to Promote Conceptual Understanding* (Sterling, VA: Stylus, 2011); John Biggs and Catherine Tang, *Teaching for Quality Learning at University: What the Student Does*, 4th ed. (Maidenhead, England: Society for Research in Higher Education and Open University Press, 2011).

4. The table adapts language about backward design from Wiggins and McTighe, *Understanding by Design*, 38, and L. Dee Fink, *A Self-Directed Guide to Designing Courses for Significant Learning* (Dee Fink and Associates, n.d.), https://www.deefinkandassociates.com/GuidetoCourseDesignAug05.pdf.

5. Sam Wineburg, "Historical Thinking and Other Unnatural Acts," *Phi Delta Kappan* 80, no. 7 (March 1999): 488–99.

6. Wiggins and McTighe, *Understanding by Design*, 7; Hansen, *Idea-Based Learning*, 5–9, 18–24.

7. Fink, *Creating Significant Learning Experiences*, 7–9; on learning as change, see also Ambrose et al., *How Learning Works*, 3.

8. Sam Wineburg, *Historical Thinking and Other Unnatural Acts* (Philadelphia: Temple University Press, 2001), 24.

9. Vicky Gunn and Leah Shopkow, "Doing SoTL in Medieval History: A Cross-Atlantic Dialogue," *Arts & Humanities in Higher Education* 6, no. 3 (2007): 255–71; Wineburg, "Historical Thinking."

10. "AHA Tuning Project: 2016 Disciplinary Core," https://www.historians.org/teaching-and-learning/tuning-the-history-discipline/2016-history-discipline-core.

11. AACU, "What Is a 21st Century Liberal Education?" https://www.aacu.org/leap/what-is-a-liberal-education; AACU Project Leap, "Essential Learning Outcomes," https://www.aacu.org/leap/essential-learning-outcomes.

12. AACU, "Inquiry and Analysis VALUE Rubric," 2009, https://www.aacu.org/value/rubrics/inquiry-analysis; AACU, "Global Learning VALUE Rubric," 2014, https://www.aacu.org/value/rubrics/global-learning; Gunn and Shopkow, "Doing SoTL in Medieval History," 255–71; see also Wineburg, "Historical Thinking."

13. Leah Shopkow, Arlene Diaz, Joan Middendorf, and David Pace, "The History Learning Project: A Department 'Decodes' Its Students," *Journal of American History* 94, no. 4 (March 2008): 1224.

14. The need to prepare students for citizenship in a democracy has furnished one of the most frequent and persuasive arguments in support of public education. Keith C. Barton and Linda S. Levstik, *Teaching History for the Common Good* (Mahwah, NJ: Lawrence Erlbaum Associates, 2004), 28, 31–39.

15. Peter Felten and Charity Johansson, *Transforming Students: Fulfilling the Promise of Higher Education* (Baltimore: Johns Hopkins University Press, 2014), 21; Maryellen Weimer, *Learner-Centered Teaching: Five Key Changes to Practice*, 2nd ed. (San Francisco: Jossey-Bass, 2013), 25; Fink, *Creating Significant Learning Experiences*, 7–9.

16. Wiggins and McTighe, *Understanding by Design*, 71.

17. Ken Bain, *What the Best College Teachers Do* (Cambridge, MA: Harvard University Press, 2004), 37, 99–102.

18. Perkins, *Making Learning Whole*, 58–62; Bain, *What the Best College Teachers Do*, 37.

19. Some of these questions were adapted from ones proposed by Bain, Perkins, and Wiggins and McTighe.

20. David A. Gerber, "Are We Giving Students Something Worthwhile to Talk About?" *Perspectives on History*, January 2018.

21. Sam Wineburg, "Teaching the Mind Good Habits," *Chronicle of Higher Education*, April 11, 2003; David Pace, "Amateur in the Operating Room: History and the Scholarship of Teaching and Learning," *American Historical Review* 109,

no. 4 (2004): 1183. On the ways expertise can be a liability in teaching novices, see Ambrose et al., *How Learning Works*, 95–99.

22. Pace, "Amateur in the Operating Room," 1179.

23. Daniel J. McInerney, "Tuning the Discipline of History in the United States: Harmony (and Dissonance) in Teaching and Learning," *Arts & Humanities in Higher Education* 6, no. 4 (October 2017): 337–57; "AHA Tuning Project: 2016 Disciplinary Core."

24. Andrews and Burke's five habits of mind included change over time, context, causality, contingency, and complexity. Thomas Andrews and Flannery Burke, "What Does It Mean to Think Historically?" *Perspectives on History*, January 2007. Lendol Calder isolated six cognitive habits: questioning, connecting, sourcing, making inferences, considering alternative perspectives, and recognizing limits to one's knowledge; Lendol Calder, "Uncoverage: Toward a Signature Pedagogy for the History Survey," *Journal of American History* 92, no. 4 (March 2006): 1358–70. Kornblith and Lasser described a "History Compass" pointing to sometimes oppositional poles (including the reasons to study history involving recovering the pastness of the past and recognizing the present-ness of the past); the contrasting tendency in exploring causation toward free will and determinism; and the divergent methodological positions of establishing historical facts and constructing interpretations. Gary J. Kornblith and Carol Lasser, *Teaching American History: Essays Adapted from the Journal of American History, 2001–2007* (New York: Bedford/St. Martin's, 2009), 1–4. T. Mills Kelly lists fifteen abilities in *Teaching History in the Digital Age* (Ann Arbor: University of Michigan Press, 2013), chap. 1. A Teagle Working Group pondered the concepts and value of history education; see National History Center, "The History Major and Liberal Education," *Liberal Education* 95, no. 2 (Spring 2009), https://www.aacu.org/publications-research/periodicals/history-major-and -liberal-education. Lendol Calder and Tracy Steffes summarized these efforts in *Measuring College Learning in History* (San Francisco: Social Science Research Council, 2016), 55–62. The History Learning Project at Indiana University research "decoded" our discipline. Joan Middendorf, David Pace, Leah Shopkow, and Arlene Diaz, "Making Thinking Explicit: Decoding History Teaching," *National Teaching & Learning Forum* 16, no. 2 (February 2007): 1211–24.

25. Catherine King and Peter Felten, "Threshold Concepts in Educational Development: An Introduction," *Journal of Faculty Development* 26, no. 3 (2012): 5–7; Ray Land, "There Could Be Trouble Ahead: Using Threshold Concepts as a Tool of Analysis," *International Journal for Academic Development* 16, no. 2 (2011): 175–78; Leah Shopkow, "What Decoding the Disciplines Can Offer Threshold Concepts," in Jan H. F. Meyer, Ray Land, and Caroline Baillie, eds., *Threshold Concepts and Transformational Learning* (Rotterdam, The Netherlands: Sense Publishers, 2010), 317–31; Linda Adler-Kassner, John Majewski, and Damian Koshnick, "The Value of Troublesome Knowledge: Transfer and

Threshold Concepts in Writing and History," *Composition Forum* 26 (Fall 2012): 12. Tona Hangen captures its essence when she says, "Effective history instruction permanently and irreversibly awakens students to the insight that history is a constructed, contestable argument, and it does so in such a way that prevents students from unlearning it." Tona Hangen, "Historical Digital Literacy, One Classroom at a Time," *Journal of American History* 101, no. 4 (March 2015): 1195–96.

26. Paulina L. Alberto and Farina Mir, "History 101: What It Is and Why We Need It Now," *Perspectives on History*, April 2018.

27. Josh Ashenmiller, "SLO Curve Ball: What I Really Want for My Students," *Perspectives on History*, January 2015.

28. Wineburg, "Teaching the Mind Good Habits."

29. Laura M. Westhoff, "Historiographic Mapping: Toward a Signature Pedagogy for the Methods Course," *Journal of American History* 98, no. 4 (March 2012): 1115. On arguments, see Barton and Levstik, *Teaching History for the Common Good*, 36–38; Joel M. Sipress and David J. Voelker, "The End of the History Survey Course: The Rise and Fall of the Coverage Model," *Journal of American History* 97, no. 4 (March 2011): 1066.

30. Wiggins and McTighe, *Understanding by Design*, 44.

31. The seven bottlenecks first identified by the History Learning Project include misunderstanding the role of facts, interpreting primary sources, maintaining appropriate emotional distance, understanding the limits of knowledge of historical actors, identifying with people in another time and place, constructing and evaluating arguments, and linking specific details in primary sources to their broader context. Middendorf et al., "Making Thinking Explicit"; Indiana University's History Learning Project, "Identifying Bottlenecks to Learning History," http://www.iub.edu/~hlp/bottlenecks.html; Weimer, *Learner-Centered Teaching*, 129.

32. Fink makes consideration of "situational factors" a key step in course design. These factors include specific context (class size, course level, whether face-to-face or online, how long and frequent class meetings are), external expectations (those of the profession, department or university, society), the nature of the subject matter, and the characteristics of the students. Fink, *Creating Significant Learning Experiences*, 74–75. Perkins mentions many worthy nondisciplinary goals. Perkins, *Making Learning Whole*, 16.

33. Ken Bain quoted in Gerber, "Are We Giving Students Something Worthwhile?"

34. Sipress and Voelker, "The End of the History Survey Course," 1066.

35. Sam Wineburg, "Crazy for History," *Journal of American History* 90, no.4 (March 2004): 1413.

36. Wiggins and McTighe, *Understanding by Design*, 15–16, 44–46; Calder, "Uncoverage," 1358–70; Perkins, *Making Learning Whole*, 57. Weimer summarized research studies about surface versus deep learning and looked at approaches

that were transmission of information-focused and teacher-focused and compared them with approaches that were focused on conceptual change and the learner. Weimer, *Learner-Centered Teaching*, 33.

37. Joel M. Sipress and David J. Voelker, "From Learning History to Doing History: Beyond the Coverage Model," in Regan A. R. Gurung, Nancy L. Chick, and Aeron Haynie, eds., *Exploring Signature Pedagogies: Approaches to Teaching Disciplinary Habits of Mind* (Sterling, VA: Stylus, 2009), 19–35.

38. Wineburg, "Teaching the Mind Good Habits." Robert Bain said that many students come to our courses with the following view of history: "The past is filled with facts, historians retrieve those facts, students memorize the facts, and all this somehow improves the present." Quoted in Kelly, *Teaching History in the Digital Age*, chap. 1.

39. Calder, "Uncoverage"; Shopkow et al., "The History Learning Project," 1211; Wiggins and McTighe, *Understanding by Design*, 227–42.

40. James Loewen, *Lies My Teacher Told Me: Everything Your American History Textbook Got Wrong*, 2nd ed. (New York: Touchstone, 2007), 3–8.

41. Lendol Calder, "Forum Introduction: Tuning History: Redirecting History Surveys for General Education," *World History Connected* 13, no. 2 (June 2016); Sipress and Voelker, "The End of the History Survey Course"; Sipress and Voelker, "From Learning History to Doing History"; Pace, "The Amateur in the Operating Room," 1174.

42. Simon quoted in Ambrose et al., *How Learning Works*, 1; on the necessity of doing and practicing for mastery, see 3–5; and Terry Doyle, *Learner-Centered Teaching; Putting the Research on Learning into Practice* (Sterling, VA: Stylus, 2011), 19.

43. Joan Middendorf and David Pace, "Decoding the Disciplines: A Model for Helping Students Learn Disciplinary Ways of Thinking," *New Directions for Teaching and Learning* 98 (Summer 2004): 7.

44. AHA Statement on Excellent Classroom Teaching of History, January 8, 2017, https://www.historians.org/jobs-and-professional-development /statements-standards-and-guidelines-of-the-discipline/statement-on-excellent -classroom-teaching-of-history.

45. Wiggins and McTighe, *Understanding by Design*, 15–16. Fink characterized facts as "foundational knowledge [that] provides the basic understanding that is necessary for other kinds of learning," *Creating Significant Learning Experiences*, 21, 35. Bloom's *Taxonomy of Educational Objectives* described a hierarchy of intellectual skills; University of Central Florida Faculty Center for Teaching and Learning, "Bloom's Taxonomy," http://www.fctl.ucf.edu/TeachingAnd LearningResources/CourseDesign/BloomsTaxonomy/.

46. Kelly, *Teaching History in the Digital Age*, chap. 3.

47. Cathy N. Davidson, *The New Education: How to Revolutionize the University to Prepare Students for a World in Flux* (New York: Basic Books, 2017), 88.

48. AHA Statement on Excellent Classroom Teaching of History.

49. David A. Sousa, *How the Brain Learns*, 3rd ed. (Thousand Oaks, CA: Corwin Press, 2006), 259; Larry Ferlazzo, "Why Is It Important for Students to Learn about Bloom's Taxonomy?" May 7, 2011, http://larryferlazzo.edublogs .org/2011/05/07/why-is-it-important-for-students-to-learn-about-blooms -taxonomy/.

50. Wiggins and McTighe pointed out that understanding requires more than knowledge and skill; it is also the ability to thoughtfully and actively "do" the work with discernment, and the ability to self-assess, justify, and critique such doings. Transfer involves "the capacity to take what we know and use it creatively, flexibly, fluently, in different situations or problems, on our own." *Understanding by Design*, 7, 40–41.

51. One of the major changes in higher education in the past few decades is the focus on the quality of the students' learning (rather than simply the teaching of the faculty). Fink, *Creating Significant Learning Experiences*, 21.

52. Charles C. Bonwell, "A Disciplinary Approach for Teaching Critical Thinking," *National Teaching & Learning Forum* 21, no. 2 (February 2012).

53. University of South Carolina Center for Teaching Excellence, "Learning Outcomes," https://www.sc.edu/about/offices_and_divisions/cte/teaching _resources/coursedevelopment/learning_outcomes/index.php.

54. This and the previous SLO were adapted from goals on the Medieval World syllabus of Kevin Gannon, http://www.thetattooedprof.com/wp -content/uploads/2014/05/HIST104A.Syllabus.Fall2014.pdf.

55. Details about the revisions are in Peter N. Stearns, "Getting Specific about Training in Historical Analysis: A Case Study in World History," in Peter N. Stearns, Peter Seixas, and Sam Wineburg, eds., *Knowing, Teaching, & Learning History: National and International Perspectives* (New York: NYU Press and the American Historical Association, 2000), 419–36.

56. John McClymer, *The AHA Guide to Teaching and Learning with New Media*, https://www.historians.org/teaching-and-learning/teaching-resources-for -historians/approaches-to-teaching/the-aha-guide-to-teaching-and-learning -with-new-media; Ambrose et al., *How Learning Works*, 3; Wiggins and McTighe, *Understanding by Design*, 250–53. Constructivist educational theory assumes "Getting students to understand . . . is a matter of getting them to undertake the appropriate learning activities. . . . It's not what *we* do but what *students* do that's the important thing." Biggs and Tang, *Teaching for Quality Learning*, 19. Grant Wiggins, "The Truth May Make You Free, but the Test May Keep You Imprisoned: Toward Assessment Worthy of the Liberal Arts," in Joan S. Stark and Alice Thomas, eds., *Assessment and Program Evaluation: An Ashe Reader* (Needham Heights, MA: Simon & Schuster), 545–56.

57. Barbara E. Walvoord and Virginia Johnson Anderson, *Effective Grading: A Tool for Learning and Assessment* (San Francisco: Jossey-Bass, 1998), 67.

58. David Boud, "Assessment and Learning: Contradictory or Complementary?" *Assessment for Learning in Higher Education* (1995): 35–48.

59. Calder and Steffes, *Measuring College Learning*, 68. This is true of other disciplines as well. Walvoord and Anderson, *Effective Grading*, 10–11.

60. Research results cited in John C. Bean, *Engaging Ideas: The Professor's Guide to Integrating Writing, Critical Thinking, and Active Learning in the Classroom*, 2nd ed. (Hoboken, NJ: John Wiley and Sons, 2001), 13; Colleen Flaherty, "When More Is Less," *Inside Higher Education*, December 4, 2015.

61. James Roth, "Student Assessment in the History Classroom: Who's in Control?" *Perspectives on History*, November 1, 2005.

62. Instead of historical reasoning, the students used factual recall, reading comprehension, and test-taking strategies. In addition, many students arrived at correct answers with little knowledge of the topic, and some showed considerable understanding of a topic but still missed the item. The researchers concluded that the questions had little cognitive validity. Mark D. Smith, "Cognitive Validity: Can Multiple-Choice Items Tap Historical Thinking Processes?" *American Educational Research Journal* (July 5, 2017): 1–32.

63. David J. Voelker, "Assessing Student Understanding in Introductory Courses: A Sample Strategy," *History Teacher* 4, no. 41 (August 2008): 505–18.

64. Joel Breakstone, Mark Smith, and Sam Wineburg, "Beyond the Bubble in History/Social Studies Assessments," *Phi Delta Kappan* 94, no. 5 (February 2013): 53–57; Stanford History Education Group, "Beyond the Bubble," http://beyondthebubble.stanford.edu/.

65. Bean, *Engaging Ideas*, 91, 102.

66. Bloom's original taxonomy of learning had synthesis as its highest level. See also Ambrose et al., *How Learning Works*, chap. 5, which stresses the importance of low-stakes practice and formative feedback, and 85–86, which note the importance of aligned objectives, assessments, and instructional strategies.

67. Grant Wiggins, *Educative Assessment: Designing Assessments to Inform and Improve Student Performance* (San Francisco: Jossey-Bass, 1998), 21–42.

68. Bean used the acronym RAFT to help faculty think rhetorically about the student's role, audience, format, and task and further specified that the task should be an "intriguing problem." Bean, *Engaging Ideas*, 97–100.

69. David A. Gerber asked students "If you were Truman, would you have used the atomic bombs?," putting them in Truman's shoes. Gerber, "Are We Giving Students Something Worthwhile?"

70. My colleague Xiaolin Duan assigned students to create small exhibits in campus spaces and host an opening event for them.

71. "Wellesley Students Write Children's Books to Explore Nontraditional Narratives from the Civil Rights Movement," Wellesley College Spotlight on Teaching, February 22, 2016, https://www.wellesley.edu/news/2016/february/node/83506.

72. National History Center, "Mock Policy Briefing Program," AHA Teaching Resources, https://www.historians.org/teaching-and-learning/teaching-re sources-for-historians/national-history-center-mock-policy-briefing-program.

73. Mary Jo Festle, "Learning and Interpreting History through Deliberative Dialogue," in Linda Nilson and Jennifer Herman, eds., *Creating Engaging Discussions: Strategies for "Avoiding Crickets" in Any Size Classroom and Online* (Sterling, VA: Stylus, 2018), 71–80.

74. Keith A. Erekson, "From Archive to Awards Ceremony: An Approach for Engaging Students in Historical Research," *Arts and Humanities in Higher Education* 10, no. 4 (July 28, 2011): 388–400.

75. Hangen, "Historical Digital Literacy," 1192–203; Martha Saxton, "Wikipedia and Women's History: A Classroom Experience," and Amanda Seligman, "Teaching Wikipedia without Apologies," both in Jack Dougherty and Kristen Nawrotzki, eds., *Writing History in the Digital Age* (Ann Arbor: University of Michigan Press, 2013), 86–93 and 121–28.

76. Hangen, "Historical Digital Literacy."

77. See Bloom's taxonomy for the ranking of creating.

78. Kenneth E. Barron and Chris S. Hulleman, "Is There a Formula to Help Understand and Improve Student Motivation?" *Essays from E-xcellence in Teaching* 6 (2006), 34–38, http://teachpsych.org/ebooks/eit.php.

79. Wiggins, "The Truth May Make You Free," 25.

80. Hangen, "Historical Digital Literacy."

81. Steven Volk, "Empathy and Engagement: Using Avatars to Bring Students into History," *Peer Review* 14, no. 3 (Summer 2012): 6–9; Edith Sheffer, "Creating Lives in the Classroom," *Chronicle of Higher Education*, November 22, 2009.

82. Wiggins and McTighe, *Understanding by Design*, 153–59. Scholars don't all agree about which characteristics are necessary for an assignment to be considered authentic. See Bruce B. Frey, Vicki L. Schmitt, and Justin P. Allen, "Defining Authentic Classroom Assessment," *Practical Research, Assessment & Evaluation* 17, no. 2 (January 2012): 1–18; Maryellen Weimer, "Authentic Assignments: What Are They?" *Teaching Professor* 25, no. 10 (December 2011). See also Fink, *Creating Significant Learning Experiences*, 96–97, on "forward-looking assessment."

83. Mary-Ann Winkelmes, David E. Copeland, Ed Jorgensen, Alison Sloat, Anna Smedley, Peter Pizor, Katherine Johnson, and Sharon Jalene, "Benefits (Some Unexpected) of Transparently Designed Assignments," *National Teaching and Learning Forum* 24, no.4 (May 2015): 4–6; "Transparency in Learning and Teaching in Education," Office of the Executive Vice President and Provost, University of Nevada–Las Vegas, https://www.unlv.edu/provost/teachingand learning.

84. I developed this assignment using the Transparency Assignment

Template at https://www.unlv.edu/sites/default/files/page_files/27/Provost -FacultyTransparentAssgntTemplate-2016.pdf.

85. Mary-Ann Winkelmes, "Transparency in Teaching: Faculty Share Data and Improve Students' Learning," AACU *Liberal Education* 99, no. 2 (Spring 2013), https://www.aacu.org/publications-research/periodicals/transparency -teaching-faculty-share-data-and-improve-students.

86. Andrew K. Koch, "Many Students Failed; A Wakeup Call to History Educators," *Perspectives on History*, May 2017; David Pace, "The History Classroom in an Era of Crisis: A Change of Course Is Needed," *Perspectives on History*, May 2017.

87. Mary-Ann Winkelmes, "Transparency in Learning and Teaching," *NEA Higher Education Advocate* 30, no. 1 (January 2013): 6–9.

88. Winkelmes et al., "Benefits (Some Unexpected)."

89. On motivation, see Ambrose et al., *How Learning Works*, 85–88. The Consortium for the Study of Writing in College research is cited in Bean, *Engaging Ideas*, 97. The five items on the Wabash Study's "instructional clarity" scale were clear explanations, good use of examples to explain difficult points, effectively reviewing and summarizing the material, interpreting abstract ideas and theories clearly, and giving assignments that help in learning the course material. Chad N. Loes and Ernest T. Pascarella, "The Benefits of Good Teaching Extend beyond Course Achievement," *Journal of the Scholarship of Teaching and Learning* 15, no. 2 (April 2015): 1–13; Ernest T. Pascarella and Charles Blaich, "Lessons from the Wabash National Study of Liberal Arts Education," *Change: The Magazine of Higher Learning* 42, no. 2 (2013): 6–15.

Chapter 2. Who We Teach

1. Elizabeth B. Moje, "'I Teach Students, Not Subjects': Teacher-Student Relationships as Contexts for Secondary Literacy," *Reading Research Quarterly* 31, no. 2 (April–June 1996): 172–95.

2. Daniel T. Willingham, *Why Don't Students Like School? A Cognitive Scientist Answers Questions about How the Mind Works and What It Means for the Classroom* (San Francisco: Jossey-Bass, 2009), 35–45; Terry Doyle, "Follow Where the Research Leads: Optimizing Learning in the Higher Education Classroom," Great Lakes Conference on Teaching and Learning Keynote Address, 2017, https://learnercenteredteaching.wordpress.com/2017/05/10/great-lakes -conference-on-teaching-and-learning-keynote-address-2017/; National Academies of Sciences, Engineering, and Medicine, *How People Learn II: Learners, Contexts, and Cultures* (Washington, DC: National Academies Press, 2018), 5, 75; Susan A. Ambrose, Michael W. Bridges, Michele DiPietro, Marsha C. Lovett, Marie K. Norman, and Richard E. Mayer, *How Learning Works: 7 Research-Based Principles for Smart Teaching* (San Francisco: Jossey-Bass, 2010), 15, 25–26.

3. Ambrose et al., *How Learning Works*, 15–17; James M. Lang, *Small Teaching: Everyday Lessons from the Science of Learning* (San Francisco: Jossey-Bass, 2016), 95–100; Doyle, "Follow Where the Research Leads."

4. Ambrose et al., *How Learning Works*, 43–46.

5. Background knowledge helps one recognize vocabulary, allows the bridging of the logical gaps that all writers leave, allows chunking (freeing up working memory), and guides the interpretation of ambiguous sentences. Willingham, *Why Don't Students Like School?*, 35–45; Lang, *Small Teaching*, 97.

6. Willingham, *Why Don't Students Like School?*, 35–45; Lang, *Small Teaching*, 97.

7. Sam Wineburg, *Historical Thinking and Other Unnatural Acts* (Philadelphia: Temple University Press, 2001), 8–10.

8. Sam Wineburg, Susan Mosborg, Dan Porat, and Ariel Duncan, "Forrest Gump and the Future of Teaching the Past," *Phi Delta Kappan* 89, no. 3 (November 2007): 168–77.

9. Cited in David Pace, "The Amateur in the Operating Room: History and the Scholarship of Teaching and Learning," *American Historical Review* 109, no. 4 (October 2004): 1178–79.

10. Lendol Calder, "The Stories We Tell," *OAH Magazine of History* 27, no. 3 (July 2013): 5–8.

11. Cited in Leah Shopkow, "How Many Sources Do I Need?" *History Teacher* 50, no. 2 (February 2017): 169–73.

12. Sam Wineburg, *Why Learn History (When It's Already on Your Phone)?* (Chicago: University of Chicago Press, 2018), 140.

13. Arlene Diaz, Joan Middendor, David Pace, and Leah Shopkow, "The History Learning Project: A Department 'Decodes' Its Students," *Journal of American History* 94, no. 4 (March 2008): 1212–16; Leah Shopkow, "What Decoding the Disciplines Can Offer Threshold Concepts," in Jan H. F. Meyer, Ray Land, and Caroline Baillie, eds., *Threshold Concepts and Transformational Learning* (Rotterdam, The Netherlands: Sense Publishers, 2010), 317–31.

14. Ambrose et al., *How Learning Works*, 163–64.

15. Mary Jo Festle, "How They Change: Students Tell Us How History Transforms Them," *Perspectives on History* (December 2015): 29–30.

16. Ambrose et al., *How Learning Works*, chap. 1 explains the implications of prior knowledge and how to activate or correct it. Using slightly different language, Lang recommends a "knowledge dump." Lang, *Small Teaching*, 98–101.

17. Ambrose et al., *How Learning Works*, 27; Willingham uses "toehold" in *Why Don't Students Like to Learn?*, 209.

18. Quote from Ambrose et al., *How Learning Works*, 27; see discussion of prior knowledge, 10–39.

19. Vicky Gunn and Leah Shopkow, "Doing SoTL in Medieval History: A

Cross-Atlantic Dialogue," *Arts & Humanities in Higher Education* 6, no. 3 (2007): 261.

20. Ambrose et al., *How Learning Works*, 27–31.

21. Wineburg, *Why Study History*, 145–59.

22. HERI data cited in Saundra Yancey McGuire with Stephanie McGuire, *Teach Students How to Learn: Strategies You Can Incorporate into Any Course to Improve Student Metacognition, Study Skills, and Motivation* (Sterling, VA: Stylus, 2015), 10; data on how few were taught to study cited in Maryellen Weimer, *Learner-Centered Teaching: Five Key Changes to Practice* (San Francisco: Jossey-Bass, 2013), 125.

23. Cathy N. Davidson and David Theo Goldberg with Zoe Marie Jones, *The Future of Thinking: Learning Institutions in a Digital Age* (Cambridge, MA: MIT Press, 2010), 7.

24. Michelle D. Miller, *Minds Online: Teaching Effectively with Technology* (Cambridge, MA: Harvard University Press, 2014), 47–48.

25. Davidson and Goldberg, *Future of Thinking*, 32.

26. National Academies, *How People Learn II*, 175; Miller, *Minds Online*, 45; Kay Hymowitz, "The Dumbest Generation by Mark Bauerlein," *Commentary*, September 2008.

27. Davidson and Goldberg, *Future of Thinking*, 54, 92–94; John Seely Brown, "Learning in the Digital Age," presentation given at the Aspen Institute, http://www.johnseelybrown.com/learning_in_digital_age-aspen.pdf, 70–71.

28. Cathy N. Davison, *The New Education: How to Revolutionize the University to Prepare Students for a World in Flux* (New York: Basic Books, 2017), 92; Davidson and Goldberg, *Future of Thinking*, 54.

29. Brown, "Learning in the Digital Age," 71.

30. Miller, *Minds Online*, 46–47; National Academies, *How People Learn II*, 231–33.

31. National Academies, *How People Learn II*, 193.

32. Elizabeth F. Barkley, *Student Engagement Techniques: A Handbook for College Faculty* (San Francisco: Jossey-Bass, 2010), 15.

33. Marilla Svinicki, "Student Goal Orientation, Motivation, and Learning," IDEA Paper no. 41, 2005, 1–4, https://www.ideaedu.org/Research/IDEA-Paper-Series.

34. Ambrose et al., *How Learning Works*, 73–74.

35. Willingham, *Why Don't Students Like School?*, 9–14; Ambrose et al., *How Learning Works*, 75.

36. Barron and Hulleman add a variable to the equation, saying M = V × E - C, with the C representing costs. Costs can be time, effort, discomfort, negative emotions, or things that someone loses by doing the activity. Because the perceived costs of an activity tend to be very individual and beyond

the instructor's control, I'm not emphasizing them in this discussion. Kenneth E. Barron and Chris S. Hulleman, "Is There a Formula to Help Understand and Improve Student Motivation?" *Essays from E-xcellence in Teaching* 6 (2006): 34–38.

37. Ambrose et al., *How Learning Works*, 80–81; Barkley, *Student Engagement Techniques*, 15.

38. Regan A. R. Gurung, "Key Aspects of Motivation in Learning," in Rita Obeid, Anna Schwartz, Christina Shane-Simpson, and Patricia J. Brooks, eds., *How We Teach Now: The GSTA Guide to Student-Centered Teaching* (Society for the Teaching of Psychology, 2017), 54, 57; Ambrose et al., *How Learning Works*, 82, 90.

39. Barron and Hulleman, "Is There a Formula?"

40. Lang, *Small Teaching*, 174–76.

41. Gerald Graff, "The Problem Problem and Other Oddities of Academic Discourse," *Arts and Humanities in Higher Education* 1, 1 (June 1, 2002): 27–42.

42. Cathy N. Davidson, "Designing Learning Outcomes to Change the World," *Inside Higher Education*, August 28, 2017.

43. Margery B. Ginsberg and Raymond Wlodkowski, "Motivation and Culture," in Janet M. Bennett, ed., *Sage Encyclopedia of Intercultural Competence* (Thousand Oaks, CA: Sage Publications, 2015), 634–37.

44. Barron and Hulleman, "Is There a Formula?"; Gurung, "Key Aspects of Motivation," 62–63.

45. Gurung, "Key Aspects of Motivation," 62.

46. Quoted in Sarah Rose Cavanagh, "Caring Isn't Coddling," *Chronicle-Vitae*, November 22, 2016, https://chroniclevitae.com/news/1621-caring-isn't -coddling. See also Barkley, *Student Engagement Techniques*, 34–35.

47. Steven A. Meyers, "Do Your Students Care Whether You Care about Them?" *College Teaching* 57, no. 4 (Fall 2009): 205–10.

48. Adrianna Kezar and Dan Maxey, "Faculty Matter: So Why Doesn't Everyone Think So?" *Thought & Action* (Fall 2014): 36; Lauren A. J. Kirby, Jessica N. Busler, and William Buskist, "Five Steps to Becoming a Student-Centered Teacher," and Janie Wilson, "Teaching Challenging Courses: Focus on Statistics and Research Methods," in Obeid et al., eds., *How We Teach Now*, 16–17 and 340–41.

49. The psychological literature distinguishes between strategies to build rapport and immediacy, but there is overlap in the advice to faculty. Meyers, "Do Your Students Care?" On positive relationships increasing value, see also Barron and Hulleman, "Is There a Formula?"; Ambrose et al., *How Learning Works*, 176–77; Svinicki, "Student Goal Orientation."

50. Gallup poll data cited in Terry Doyle, "Follow Where the Research Leads." The survey was focused on the relationship between graduates' college lives and postgraduate lives. "Great Jobs, Great Lives: The 2014 Gallup-Purdue

Index Report," Gallup, Purdue University and Lumina Foundation, 2014, https://www.luminafoundation.org/files/resources/galluppurdueindex-re port-2014.pdf.

51. Terry Doyle, *Learner-Centered Teaching: Putting the Research on Learning into Practice* (Sterling, VA: Stylus, 2011), 71, 76.

52. Ambrose et al., *How Learning Works*, 85–89.

53. Willingham, *Why Don't Students Like School?*, 9–14.

54. Doyle, "Follow Where the Research Leads."

55. Lauren Aguilar, Greg Walton, and Carl Wieman, "Psychological Insights for Improved Physics Teaching," *Physics Today* 67, no. 5 (May 2014): 49.

56. Svinicki, "Student Goal Orientation," 3–4; Barkley, *Student Engagement Techniques*, 14; Ambrose et al., *How Learning Works*, 132–33; Barbara Gross Davis, *Tools for Teaching*, 2nd ed. (San Francisco: Jossey-Bass, 2009), 279.

57. In general, easy courses are not rated as highly as courses with rigor and standards; Weimer, *Learner-Centered Teaching*, 154. John Centra, "Will Teachers Receive Higher Student Evaluations by Giving Higher Grades and Less Coursework?" *Research in Higher Education* 44, no. 5 (October 2003): 495–518.

58. Gurung, "Key Aspects of Motivation," 63; Svinicki, "Student Goal Orientation," 3.

59. Ambrose et al. use the language of "three levers."

60. Gurung, "Key Aspects of Motivation," 54; Barron and Hulleman, "Is There a Formula?"

61. Cavanagh, "Caring Isn't Coddling."

62. Gurung, "Key Aspects of Motivation," 55.

63. Doyle, *Learner-Centered Teaching*, 64.

64. Marilla Svinicki, "Motivation: An Updated Analysis," IDEA Paper no. 59, 2005, 1, https://www.ideaedu.org/Research/IDEA-Paper-Series.

65. Willingham, *Why Don't Students Like School?*, 21–22; Marilla Svinicki, "The Goldilocks Principle: 'Just Right' and Beyond," *National Teaching and Learning Forum* 24, no. 4 (May 2015): 11–12.

66. Diaz et al., "The History Learning Project."

67. Mary Jo Festle, "The Challenges of Learning History: What Students and SOTL Tell Us," *American Historian* (Summer 2016), http://tah.oah.org /content/the-challenges-of-learning-history-what-students-and-sotl-tell-us/. Students mentioned 131 different challenges (some of them mentioned more than one thing). Of those, fifty-two were related to the research and writing process, sixty to the nature of the discipline of history (other than research and writing), twelve to the amount of time it takes, and five to the department's requirements, curriculum, or professors.

68. Festle, "The Challenges of Learning History."

69. Carol S. Dweck, Gregory M. Walton, and Geoffrey L. Cohen, *Academic*

Tenacity; Mindsets and Skills That Promote Long-Term Learning (Seattle: Gates Foundation, 2011), 5–6; Doyle, "Follow the Research"; Ambrose et al., *How Learning Works*, 200–203.

70. McGuire, *Teach Students How to Learn*, 61.

71. Lang, *Small Teaching*, 195–204, Dweck quoted on 201.

72. Svinicki, "Motivation: An Updated Analysis," 3.

73. McGuire, *Teach Students How to Learn*, 60–71; Doyle, *Learner-Centered Teaching*, 64–70; Ambrose et al., *How Learning Works*, 212–13; Lang, *Small Teaching*, 206–16.

74. Claude Steele, *Whistling Vivaldi: How Stereotypes Affect Us and What We Can Do* (New York: Norton, 2010), 181–82, 208, 215–17.

75. Festle, "The Challenges of Learning History."

76. Chad Berry, Lori A. Schmied, and Josef Chad Schrock, "The Role of Emotion in Teaching and Learning History: A Scholarship of Teaching Exploration," *History Teacher* 41, no. 4 (August 2008): 437–51.

77. Mary Helen Immordino-Yang quoted in Cavanagh, "Caring Isn't Coddling."

78. Diaz et al., "The History Learning Project," 1216–17.

79. Leah Shopkow, Arlene Diaz, Joan Middendorf, and David Pace, "History Learning Project 'Decodes' a Discipline," in Kathleen McKinney, ed., *The Scholarship of Teaching and Learning in and across the Disciplines* (Bloomington: Indiana University Press, 2013), 99–110.

80. Diaz et al., "The History Learning Project," 1216–17.

81. Ambrose et al., *How Learning Works*, 167–69; Diane J. Goodman, "Dealing with Student Resistance: Sources and Strategies," AACU *Diversity and Democracy* 10, no. 2 (2007), http://www.diversityweb.org/digest/vol10no2/goodman .cfm; Lee Anne Bell and Pat Griffin refer to the "disequilibrium" students may go through when exposed to new information about injustices in "Designing Social Justice Education Courses," in Maurianne Adams, Lee Anne Bell, and Pat Griffin, eds., *Teaching for Diversity and Social Justice*, 2nd ed. (London: Routledge, 2007), 72–75.

82. Joan Middendorf, Jolante Mikute, Tara Saunders, José Najar, Andrew E. Clark-Huckstep, David Pace, with Keith Eberly and Nicole McGrath, "What's Feeling Got to Do with It? Decoding Emotional Bottlenecks in the History Classroom," *Arts and Humanities in Higher Education* 14, no. 2 (2015): 166–80.

83. Middendorf et al., "What's Feeling Got to Do with It?" 177.

84. Shopkow et al., "History Learning Project 'Decodes' a Discipline"; Middendorf et al., "What's Feeling Got to Do with It?"

85. Derald Wing Sue, *Race Talk and the Conspiracy of Silence: Understanding and Facilitating Difficult Dialogues on Race* (Hoboken, NJ: Wiley, 2015), 23–33.

86. Lee Warren, "Managing Hot Moments in the Classroom," Harvard University Derek Bok Center for Teaching and Learning, https://bokcenter .harvard.edu/managing-hot-moments-classroom.

87. Maryellen Weimer relates a similar story wherein she confronted a student who made a blatantly racist comment and another student wrote, "I don't think that student will make another racist comment in this class, but I'm pretty sure he will continue to make racist remarks." In retrospect, Weimer reflected, "When I read that, I knew the writer was correct. I may have stood up for a climate of respect in the classroom, but I hadn't done the more important thing—help the student understand that those comments are as damaging to those they target as they are to those who make them." Weimer, "Creating a Respectful Classroom Environment," Kansas State University College of Business Administration, https://cba.k-state.edu/faculty-and-staff/excellence-in -teaching/creatingarespectfulclasroomenvironment.html.

88. Christine Stanley and Mathew Ouellett, "Four Strategies to Engage the Multicultural Classroom," Magna Online Seminar, 2012; "Guidelines for Discussing Incidents of Hate, Bias, and Discrimination," University of Michigan Center for Research on Learning and Teaching, http://www.crlt.umich.edu /publinks/respondingtobias; "Making the Most of 'Hot Moments' in the Classroom," University of Michigan CRLT, https://docs.google.com/document/d /1tuMuMVnI7soHLcTNxzCTqcpkunoASHW_WvNuxphyyxA/edit.

89. Sue, *Race Talk*, 237.

90. Good resources include Warren, "Managing Hot Moments"; Diane J. Goodman, "Responding to Biased or Offensive Comments," excerpt from her book, *Promoting Diversity and Social Justice: Educating People from Privileged Groups* (London: Routledge, 2011), http://www.dianegoodman.com/documents/Re spondingToBiasedOrOffensiveCommentsexcerptarticle.pdf; "Making the Most of 'Hot Moments' in the Classroom"; Sue, *Race Talk*, 226–44.

91. Ambrose et al., *How Learning Works*, 159.

92. Sue, *Race Talk*, 238.

93. Peter Felten and Charity Johansson, *Transforming Students: Fulfilling the Promise of Higher Education* (Baltimore, MD: Johns Hopkins University Press, 2014), 20–21; Patricia Cranston, *Understanding and Promoting Transformative Learning*, 2nd ed. (San Francisco: Jossey-Bass, 2006), 23.

94. This group of students most frequently mentioned topics related to gender and sexuality, religious history, the Holocaust, U.S. foreign policy, race, the Civil War, and Chinese history.

95. Mary Jo Festle, "Do We Inspire Passion and Transformation in the Discipline of History?" unpublished presentation, International Society for the Scholarship of Teaching and Learning, Quebec City, Canada, October 24, 2014.

96. Festle, "How They Change."

97. Lang, *Small Teaching*, 98.

98. Shari Saunders and Diana Kardia, "Creating Inclusive College Classrooms," University of Michigan CRLT, http://www.crlt.umich.edu/gsis/p3 _1; the description here is one that Elon University's Center for the Advancement of Teaching and Learning based on a synthesis of others' ideas, "Inclusive Teaching," Elon Center for the Advancement of Teaching and Learning, https://www.elon.edu/u/academics/catl/inclusiveteaching/.

99. Michael S. Palmer, Lindsay B. Wheeler, and Itiya Aneece, "Does the Document Matter? The Evolving Role of Syllabi in Higher Education," *Change: The Magazine of Higher Learning* 48, no. 4 (July/August 2016): 46; the Accessible Syllabus Project from Tulane University provides examples of warmer and cooler rhetoric at https://www.accessiblesyllabus.com/rhetoric/; see also Ed Brantmeir, Andreas Broscheid, and Carl S. Moore, "Inclusion by Design: Survey Your Syllabus and Course Design," University of Virginia Center for Teaching Excellence, http://cte.virginia.edu/wp-content/uploads/2016/05/Inclusion -by-Design-Survey-Your-Syllabus-Brantmeier-Broscheid-Moore-.pdf.

100. Steele, *Whistling Vivaldi*, 135–51.

101. Gregory M. Walton and Geoffrey L. Cohen, "A Question of Belonging: Race, Social Fit, and Achievement," *Journal of Personality and Social Psychology* 92, no. 1 (2007): 94, 82–83; Kezar and Maxey, "Faculty Matter," 30.

102. "Q and A: First Generation Students," *New York Times*, June 2, 2107.

103. "Q and A: First Generation Students."

104. Brooke Lea Forster, "What Is It Like to Be Poor at an Ivy League School?" *Boston Globe Magazine*, April 9, 2015.

105. Nicholas W. Gelbar, Allison Shefcyk, and Nicholas Reichow, "A Comprehensive Survey of Current and Former College Students with Autism Spectrum Disorders," *Yale Journal of Biology and Medicine* 88, no. 1 (March 4, 2015): 45–68; Molly Sullivan, "Helping Students with Autism Thrive: College Life on the Spectrum," Madison House Autism Foundation, http://www.madisonhouse autism.org/helping-students-with-autism-thrive-college-life-on-the-spectrum/; "Going to College with Autism," https://childmind.org/article/going-to-col lege-with-autism/.

106. Shaun R. Harper, "Am I My Brother's Teacher? Black Undergraduates, Racial Socialization, and Peer Pedagogies in Predominantly White Postsecondary Contexts," *Review of Research in Education* 37, no. 1 (March 2013): 183–211.

107. Terrell L. Strayhorn, *College Students' Sense of Belonging: A Key to Educational Success for All Students* (London: Routledge, 2012). Strayhorn's book reports results of studies on first-year students, African American gay men, African American men in STEM fields, and Latino/a students.

108. There's plentiful debate about the use of laptops in college classrooms,

given how frustrated faculty are by distracted students, and some research suggested that taking notes by hand may be more effective for understanding. Often the impact on students with disabilities is ignored, as are more subtle questions about independence, effective pedagogy, and whether there are more nuanced solutions than outright bans. For a thoughtful discussion, subtitled "it's just as pointless to condemn any ban on electronic devices," see James Lang, "No, Banning Laptops Is Not the Answer," *Chronicle of Higher Education*, September 11, 2016; for a disability perspective, see Anne-Marie Womack and Rick Godden, "Making Disability Part of the Conversation," Digital Pedagogy Lab, http://www.digitalpedagogylab.com/hybridped/making-disability-part -of-the-conversation/; historian Kevin Gannon wrote a provocative blog post at http://www.thetattooedprof.com/2016/05/15/lets-ban-the-classroom-tech nology-ban/.

109. Aguilar, Walton, and Wieman, "Psychological Insights," 48.

110. Steele, *Whistling Vivaldi*, 144–47; Evava S. Pietri, India R. Johnson, and Ezgi Ozgumus, "One Size May Not Fit All: Exploring How the Intersection of Race and Gender and Stigma Consciousness Predict Effective Identity-Safe Cues for Black Women," *Journal of Experimental Social Psychology* 74 (January 2018): 291–306.

111. The Wabash longitudinal study found that engagement with diversity (especially interactions and serious conversations with those different from oneself) had positive consequences for a student's cognitive development. This was especially true for white students and those who entered college the least prepared academically. Ernest T. Pascarella and Charles Blaich, "Lessons from the Wabash National Study of Liberal Arts Education," *Change: The Magazine of Higher Learning* 42, no. 2 (2013): 6–15.

112. Steele, *Whistling Vivaldi*, 144–47 and 208–9.

113. Weimer, *Learner-Centered Teaching*, 147.

114. The National Coalition for Deliberation and Dialogue includes sample ground rules at http://ncdd.org/rc/item/1505.

115. Margery B. Ginsberg and Raymond Wlodkowski, "Motivation and Culture," in Janet M. Bennett, ed., *Sage Encyclopedia of Intercultural Competence* (Thousand Oaks, CA: Sage Publications, 2015), 635.

116. Nanda Dimitrov and Aisha Haque, "Intercultural Teaching Competence: A Multi-disciplinary Model for Instructor Reflection," *Intercultural Education* 27, no. 5 (2016): 446–47.

117. Weimer, *Learner-Centered Teaching*, 158–60.

118. Weimer, *Learner-Centered Teaching*, 158–62.

119. Sarah Rose Cavanagh, *The Spark of Learning: Energizing the College Classroom with the Science of Emotion* (Morgantown: West Virginia University Press, 2016), 198; Barron and Hulleman, "Is There a Formula?"; Gurung, "Key Aspects of Motivation."

120. Ginsberg and Wlodkowski note that respect and connectedness are essential for an inclusive learning environment. In a respectful environment, people can express themselves without threat or blame and know that their perspectives matter; connectedness is a sense of belonging, where students know that they are cared for by at least some of the group, care for others in turn, and share a common purpose. In this situation, their intrinsic motivation emerges because they feel safe, can be authentic, and can voice their opinions. "Motivation and Culture," 636–37. See also Raymond J. Wlodkowski and Margery B. Ginsberg, *Diversity & Motivation: Culturally Responsive Teaching* (San Francisco: Jossey-Bass, 1995), 62–63.

121. Peter Felten, "Confronting Prior Visual Knowledge, Beliefs, and Habits: 'Seeing' beyond the Surface," *Journal of American History* 92, no. 4 (March 2006): 1383–86.

122. Bell and Griffin, "Designing Social Justice Education Courses," 75–76.

123. Cavanagh, *Spark of Learning*, 198.

124. Ambrose et al., *How Learning Works*, 158–63.

125. Strayhorn, *College Students' Sense of Belonging*, 123.

126. Cavanagh, *Spark of Learning*, 204–6; quote on 205.

127. Doyle, *Learner-Centered Teaching*, 74–75.

128. Saundra McGuire discusses the importance of these conversations with students who may have taken on an impossible load. *Teach Students How to Learn*, 109.

129. Steele, *Whistling Vivaldi*, 209–10.

130. Steele, *Whistling Vivaldi*, 111–12, 121–25.

131. There were some differences between white and Asian students in the study, with whites falling in the middle of African American and Asian students on some of the strategies. Steele, *Whistling Vivaldi*, 99–103.

132. Weimer, *Learner-Centered Teaching*, 127–32.

133. Steele, *Whistling Vivaldi*, 8–9, 39–40, 50.

134. Steele, *Whistling Vivaldi*, 85–89.

135. Steele describes the difficulty of "identity integrating" (being one of a few type of people) in *Whistling Vivald*, chap. 8. Because we can't guarantee we can get enough students of a specific type in our courses (a "critical mass"), we have to try other strategies to lessen the impact of this difficult situation.

136. Greg Walton, Geoff Cohen, and Claude M. Steele, "Empirically Validated Strategies to Reduce Stereotype Threat," 2012, https://ed.stanford.edu/sites/default/files/interventionshandout.pdf; Steele, *Whistling Vivaldi*, 11.

137. Geoffrey L. Cohen, Claude M. Steele, and Lee D. Ross, "The Mentor's Dilemma: Providing Critical Feedback across the Racial Divide," *Personality and Social Psychology Bulletin* 25, no. 10 (October 1999): 1302–18; Aguilar et al., "Psychological Insights," 47.

138. Phillip Atiba Goff, Claude M. Steele, and Paul G. Davies, "The Space

between Us: Stereotype Threat and Distance in Interracial Contexts," *Journal of Personality and Social Psychology* 94, no. 1 (January 2008): 91–107.

139. Walton et al., "Empirically Validated Strategies." On cues, see also Sylvia Hurtado, M. Kevin Eagan, Minh C. Tran, Christopher B. Newman, Mitchell J. Chang, and Paolo Valasco, "We Do Science Here: Underrepresented Students' Interactions with Faculty in Different College Contexts," *Journal of Social Issues* 67, no. 3 (September 2011): 553–59.

140. While heterogeneous groups—based on different types of diversity, including demographics, prior experience, and skills—can be useful for learning, it's also important not to isolate women and racial or ethnic minorities. Cynthia J. Finelli, Inger Bergom, and Vilma Mesa, "Student Teams in the Engineering Classroom and Beyond," CRLT Occasional Paper no. 29, University of Michigan, 2011, http://www.crlt.umich.edu/sites/default/files/resource_files/CRLT_no29.pdf; Linda B. Nilson, *Teaching at Its Best: A Research-Based Resource for College Instructors*, 3rd ed. (Hoboken, NJ: Wiley, 2010), 160–61.

141. Gregory M. Walton and Geoffrey L. Cohen, "A Question of Belonging: Race, Social Fit, and Achievement," *Journal of Personality and Social Psychology* 92, no. 1 (January 2007): 82–96.

142. Peter Doyle provides an extensive list of things that faculty cannot control, including students' genes, family life, financial situation, work ethic, living environment, disabilities, physical habits, stress, mindset, language skills, and prior knowledge. I would add the effect of previous experiences in education and their identities (gender, race and ethnicity, sexual orientation, religious and political affiliations) and how those interact with overall campus climate. Doyle lists many things instructors do have control over: our level of preparedness, our level of planning and organization, our emotional readiness to teach, the quality of our learning activities and content delivery, and the quality and timeliness of our feedback, all which are discussed in future chapters. In addition, he points to five things alluded to here: the respect we have for students, accessibility to students, level of challenge and expectations, level of support of the learners, and quality of the learning environment. Doyle, "Follow Where the Research Leads."

143. Weimer quotes Jane Tompkins, "The classroom is a microcosm of the world; it is the chance we have to practice whatever ideals we cherish." Weimer, *Learner-Centered Teaching*, 18.

144. Robert B. Barra and John Tagg, "From Teaching to Learning: A New Paradigm for Undergraduate Education," *Change* 27, no. 6 (November–December 1995): 12–25. Maryellen Weimer's and Peter Doyle's books are two other examples.

145. Willingham, *Why Don't Students Like School?*, 209.

146. Diaz et al., "The History Learning Project," 1223.

Chapter 3. How We Teach

1. C. Roland Christensen, "The Discussion Teacher in Action," in C. Roland Christensen, David A. Garvin, and Ann Sweet, eds., *Education for Judgment: The Artistry of Discussion Leadership* (Cambridge, MA: Harvard Business School Press, 1991), 157; Maryellen Weimer, "The Art of Asking Questions," *Faculty Focus*, May 28, 2014.

2. Christensen, "The Discussion Teacher in Action," 108, 162; Carleton University Educational Development Centre, "Effective Questions for Leading Discussions," https://carleton.ca/edc/wp-content/uploads/Effective-Ques tions-for-Leading-Discussions.pdf; Stanford University Teaching Commons, "Designing Effective Discussion Questions," https://teachingcommons.stanford .edu/resources/teaching/student-teacher-communication/designing-effec tive-discussion-questions.

3. John D. W. Andrews, "The Verbal Structure of Teacher Questions: Its Impact on Class Discussion," *POD Quarterly: The Journal of the Professional and Organizational Development Network in Higher Education*, Paper 32 (1980), http:// digitalcommons.edu/podqtrly/32.

4. Christensen, "The Discussion Teacher in Action," 156–60; Barbara Gross Davis, *Tools for Teaching*, 2nd ed. (Hoboken, NJ: John Wiley and Sons, 2009), 118–26; Stephen D. Brookfield and Stephen Preskill, *Discussion as a Way of Teaching: Tools and Techniques for Democratic Classrooms*, 2nd ed. (San Francisco: Jossey-Bass, 2005), 85–89; Derek Bruff, *Teaching with Classroom Response Systems* (San Francisco: Jossey-Bass, 2009); Will Thalheimer, *Questioning Strategies for Audience Response Systems: How to Use Questions to Maximize Learning, Engage-ment, and Satisfaction* (Work-Learning Research Document, 2007), http://www .work-learning.com/catalog/; David Dean, "The Clicker Challenge: Using a Reader Response System in the (British) History Classroom," *History Teacher* 46, no. 3 (May 2013): 455–64.

5. Terry Doyle, *Learner-Centered Teaching: Putting the Research on Learning into Practice* (Sterling, VA: Stylus, 2011), 4.

6. Peter C. Brown, Henry L. Roediger III, and Mark A. McDaniel, *Make It Stick* (Cambridge, MA: Harvard University Press, 2014), 207, 227; Saundra McGuire, *Teach Students How to Learn* (Sterling, VA: Stylus, 2015), 33, 40; Bene-dict Carey, *How We Learn* (New York: Random House, 2014), 80–103; Doyle, *Learner-Centered Teaching*, 145–49.

7. Mary Bart, "Lecture vs. Active Learning: Reframing the Conversation," *Faculty Focus*, June 24, 2016.

8. Molly Worthen, "Lecture Me. Really," *New York Times Sunday Review*, October 17, 2015.

9. Josh Eyer, "Active Learning Is Not Our Enemy: A Response to Molly

Worthen," blog post, October 20, 2015, https://josheyler.wordpress.com/2015/10/20/active-learning-is-not-our-enemy-a-response-to-molly-worthen/.

10. John Barone, Cassandra Chaplinsky, Taylor Ehnle, John Heaney, Riley Jackson, Zoe Kaler, Rachael Kossy, Benjamin Lane, Thomas Lawrence, Jessica Lee, Sarah Lullo, Kevin McCammack, Daniel Seeder, Carly Smith, and Demetrius Wade, "A Lecture from the Lectured," *ChronicleVitae*, January 4, 2016, https://chroniclevitae.com/news/1235-a-lecture-from-the-lectured.

11. Bart, "Lecture vs. Active Learning"; Elizabeth F. Barkley and Claire Howell Major, *Interactive Lecturing: A Handbook for College Faculty* (San Francisco: Jossey-Bass, 2018), 7–13. Bruff observed that vociferous debaters sometimes mischaracterize one another's methods and that some "lecturers" incorporate active learning techniques. Derek Bruff, "In Defense of Continuous Exposition by the Teacher," blog post, September 15, 2015, http://derekbruff.org/?p=3126.

12. Linda B. Nilson, *Teaching at Its Best: A Research-Based Resource for College Instructors*, 3rd ed. (San Francisco: Jossey-Bass, 2010), 113; Maryellen Weimer, *Learner-Centered Teaching*, 2nd ed. (Hoboken, NJ: John Wiley and Sons, 2013), 33, 119; Spencer Kagan, "Kagan Structures, Processing, and Excellence in College Teaching," *Journal on Excellence in College Teaching* 25, no. 3 (2014): 119–38; Bruff, "In Defense of Continuous Exposition."

13. Elizabeth F. Barkley, *Student Engagement Techniques: A Handbook for College Faculty* (San Francisco: Jossey-Bass, 2010), 17.

14. Barkley, *Student Engagement Techniques*, 16–17; Barbara Millis, "Active Learning Strategies in Face-to-Face Courses," IDEA Paper no. 53, 2012, https://www.ideaedu.org; Michael Prince, "Does Active Learning Work? A Review of the Research," *Journal of Engineering Education* 93, no. 3 (July 2004): 1.

15. Barkley, *Student Engagement Techniques*, 23, and Weimer, *Learner-Centered Teaching*, 16.

16. Doyle, *Learner-Centered Teaching*, 3.

17. Prince, "Does Active Learning Work?" 3.

18. Students who received traditional lecturing were 1.5 times more likely to fail than those taught with active learning, and those in active learning sections performed about half a letter grade better on exams. Scott Freeman, Sarah L. Eddy, Miles McDonough, Michelle K. Smith, Nnadozie Okoroafor, Hannah Jordt, and Mary Pat Wenderoth, "Active Learning Increases Student Performance in Science, Engineering, and Mathematics," *Proceedings of the National Academy of Sciences* 111, no. 23 (June 2014): 8410.

19. One meta-analysis of 305 studies found that cooperative learning improved academic success, quality of relationships, self-esteem, and positive attitudes toward university. Claire Howell Major, Michael S. Harris, and Todd Zakrajsek, *Teaching for Learning: 101 Intentionally Designed Educational Activities to Put Students on the Path to Success* (London: Routledge, 2016), 8–9; see also Weimer, *Learner-Centered Teaching*, 33; Prince, "Does Active Learning Work?"

20. Eighty percent of faculty in all fields report using discussion in all or most of their courses, and 60.7 percent use cooperative learning. Kevin Egan, Ellen Bara Stolzenberg, Jennifer Berdan Lozano, Melissa C. Aragon, Maria Ramirez Suchard, and Sylvia Hurtado, *Undergraduate Teaching Faculty: The 2013–2014 HERI Faculty Survey* (Los Angeles, CA: Higher Education Research Institute, 2014), 5–6.

21. "AHA History Tuning Project: 2016 History Discipline Core," https://www.historians.org/teaching-and-learning/tuning-the-history-discipline/2016-history-discipline-core.

22. Leah Shopkow with Arlene Diaz, Joan Middendorf, and David Pace, "From Bottlenecks to Epistemology: Changing the Conversation about the Teaching of History in Colleges and Universities," in Robert J. Thompson Jr., ed., *Changing the Conversation about Higher Education* (Lanham, MD: Rowman and Littlefield Education, 2013), 17; Weimer, *Learner-Centered Teaching*, 40.

23. Quoted in Sipress and Voelker, "From Learning History to Doing History," in Regan A. R. Gurung, Nancy L. Chick, and Aeron Haynie, eds., *Exploring Signature Pedagogies: Approaches to Teaching Disciplinary Habits of Mind* (Sterling, VA: Stylus, 2009), 22. See also Jennifer Clark, "What Use Is SoTL? Using the Scholarship of Teaching and Learning to Develop a Curriculum for First Year History Courses," *Journal of University Teaching & Learning Practice* 6, no. 2 (2009).

24. Adapted from Barry K. Beyer, "What Research Tells Us about Teaching Thinking Skills," *Social Studies* 99, no. 5 (September/October 2008): 225–26; on modeling cognitive practice, see Susan A. Ambrose, Michael W. Bridges, Michele DiPietro, Marsha C. Lovett, Marie K. Norman, and Richard E. Mayer, *How Learning Works* (San Francisco: Jossey-Bass, 2010), 214.

25. Charles C. Bonwell, "A Disciplinary Approach for Teaching Critical Thinking," *National Teaching & Learning Forum* 21, no. 2 (February 2012): 3.

26. David Perkins, *Making Learning Whole: How Seven Principles of Teaching Can Transform Education* (San Francisco: Jossey-Bass, 2009), 80, 107.

27. Ambrose et al., *How Learning Works*, 128; David J. Nicol and Debra Macfarlane-Dick, "Formative Assessment and Self-Regulated Learning: A Model and Seven Principles of Good Feedback Practice," *Studies in Higher Education* 31, no. 2 (April 2006): 208–15.

28. Ambrose et al., *How Learning Works*, 124–52.

29. Ambrose et al., *How Learning Works*, 86–88.

30. Ambrose et al., *How Learning Works*, 133–34, 147; Daniel T. Willingham, *Why Don't Students Like School?* (San Francisco: Jossey-Bass, 2009), 107, 115; James Lang, *Small Teaching: Everyday Lessons from the Science of Learning* (San Francisco: Jossey-Bass, 2016), 117, 51.

31. Thomas A. Angelo and K. Patricia Cross, *Classroom Assessment Techniques: A Handbook for College Teachers*, 2nd ed. (San Francisco: Jossey-Bass, 1993), 3–5.

32. Lang, *Small Teaching*, 126–35; Ambrose et al., *How Learning Works*, 214–15; Beyer, "What Research Tells Us about Teaching Thinking Skills," 227. Some instructors have students write an outline instead of a whole paper. Shopkow et al., "From Bottlenecks to Epistemology."

33. Nilson, *Teaching at Its Best*, 218–21; Eric H. Hobson, "Getting Students to Read: Fourteen Tips," IDEA Center Paper no. 40, 2004.

34. Jay Howard uses the phrase "civil attention" for when students just give the appearance of being attentive. Jay Howard, *Discussion in the College Classroom* (San Francisco: Jossey-Bass, 2015), 19–20.

35. Howard, *Discussion in the College Classroom*, 169.

36. Nilson, *Teaching at Its Best*, 219; Karen Manarin, Miriam Carey, Melanie Rathburn, and Glen Ryland, *Critical Reading in Higher Education: Academic Goals and Social Engagement* (Bloomington: Indiana University Press, 2015), 88–90.

37. Ambrose et al., *How Learning Works*, 84–85.

38. Manarin et al., *Critical Reading in Higher Education*, 90.

39. Gregor M. Novak, "Just-in-Time Teaching," *New Directions for Teaching and Learning* 128 (Winter 2011): 63–73; "What Is Just-in-Time Teaching?" Carleton College Science Education Resource Center, https://serc.carleton.edu/introgeo/justintime/what.html.

40. Nilson, *Teaching at Its Best*, 219.

41. Elon students regularly tell me this, and one study confirmed it. In that study, large majorities agreed that regular assigned writings on the readings made them more likely to do the reading, encouraged their thinking, and were a good idea. Andrew August, "The Reader's Journal in Lower-Division History Courses: A Strategy to Improve Reading, Writing and Discussion," *History Teacher* 33, no. 3 (May 2000): 343–48.

42. Ken Bain found that the best teachers carefully chose highly provocative articles for the early readings and increased the level of difficulty in the readings over time. Ken Bain, *What the Best College Teachers Do* (Cambridge, MA: Harvard University Press, 2004), 88–89. See also Major et al., *Teaching for Learning*, 173–74; Nilson, *Teaching at Its Best*, 218.

43. "How Much Should We Assign? Estimating Out of Class Workload," Rice University Center for Teaching Excellence, http://cte.rice.edu/blogarchive/2016/07/11/workload.

44. Manarin et al., *Critical Reading in Higher Education*, 88; Maryellen Weimer, "Rethinking Rereading," *Faculty Focus*, Mary 23, 2018.

45. McGuire, *Teach Students How to Learn*, 44–50.

46. Major et al., *Teaching for Learning*, 173.

47. A good starting point is Mike Caulfield, *Web Literacy for Student Fact Checkers* (Pressbooks, 2017), https://webliteracy.pressbooks.com/.

48. John Dunlosky, Katherine A. Rawson, Elizabeth J. Marsh, Mitchell J. Nathan, and Daniel T. Willingham, "Improving Students' Learning with

Effective Learning Techniques: Promising Directions from Cognitive and Educational Psychology," *Psychological Science in the Public Interest* 14, no. 1 (2013): 4–58. McGuire, *Teach Students How to Learn*, 49–50; Doyle, *Learner-Centered Teaching*, 144–49.

49. Dee Fink generously shares resources for integrated course design. The three-column form for course alignment can be found (below the heading "Integrating the Course") at http://www.designlearning.org/resource-down loads/helpful-handouts/.

50. Fink used a "castle top" to portray the relationship. L. Dee Fink, *Creating Significant Learning Experiences*, rev. ed. (San Francisco: Jossey-Bass, 2013), 146.

51. Ernest T. Pascarella and Charles Blaich, "Lessons from the Wabash National Study of Liberal Arts Education," *Change: The Magazine of Higher Learning* 45, no. 2 (2013): 6–15.

52. In an older but influential study, participants watched thirty-second videos with no audio and rated how enthusiastic, confident, and supportive the professors were; those early ratings predicted the ratings of students who spent the entire semester in the course. Sarah Rose Cavanagh, *The Spark of Learning: Energizing the College Classroom with the Science of Emotion* (Morgantown: West Virginia University Press, 2016), 61–62. Another psychology study suggested that students form lasting impressions within two weeks of a course. Stephanie Buchert, Eric L. Laws, Jennifer M. Apperson, and Norman J. Bregman, "First Impressions and Professor Reputation: Influence on Student Evaluations of Instruction," *Social Psychology of Education* 11, no. 4 (November 2008): 404. However, a recent study suggests professors can make up for a poor first impression, and ultimately the quality of instruction matters more than first impressions. Rachel Reed, "Good First Impression of Teachers Matter Less than Lesson Quality," *University of Michigan News*, September 1, 2016, http://ns .umich.edu/new/releases/24158-good-first-impression-of-teachers-matter -less-than-lesson-quality.

53. Peter Felten, "Confronting Prior Visual Knowledge, Beliefs, and Habits: 'Seeing' beyond the Surface," *Journal of American History* 92, no. 4 (March 2006): 1383–86.

54. Mary Jo Festle, "Reading Reconstruction with Students," *Journal of American History* 84, no. 4 (March 1997): 1353–56.

55. Therese Huston, *Teaching What You Don't Know* (Cambridge, MA: Harvard University Press, 2009), 183–85, 269–70.

56. Barkley, *Student Engagement Techniques*, 103; Barron and Hulleman, "Is There a Formula?" We can find other ways to take attendance, such as sending around a sheet that students who are present sign or initial.

57. Lang, *Small Teaching*, 109; Ambrose et al., *How Learning Works*, 53–44, 61; Major et al., *Teaching for Learning*, 5.

58. Cavanagh, *Spark of Learning*, 124.

59. Stephanie Cole with Gregory Kosc, "Quit Surfing and Start 'Clicking': One Professor's Effort to Combat the Problems of Teaching the U.S. Survey in a Large Lecture Hall," *History Teacher* 43, no. 3 (May 2010): 402–3. Similarly, in a Cold War course, my colleague Jim Bissett asked students, "Which party do you think would have been more strenuously anti-communist in 1948: Democrats or Republicans?" Since the answer surprises students who base their opinion on contemporary politics, they wonder why the context was different during the Cold War.

60. Bernard Carey, quoted in Lang, *Small Teaching*, 49, 43.

61. Lilli Engle and John Engle, "Study Abroad Levels: Toward a Classification of Program Types," *Frontiers: The Interdisciplinary Journal of Study Abroad* 9 (Fall 2003): 1–20.

62. Sivasailam Thiagarajan quoted in Michael Vande Berg, R. Michael Paige, and Kris Hemming Lou, *Student Learning Abroad: What Our Students Are Learning, What They're Not, and What We Can Do about It* (Sterling, VA: Stylus, 2012), 301. Thiagarajan, an advocate of games, play, and other experiential learning, asserted that to him, all experiential learning activities (simulations, games, role plays, outdoor adventures, and other such things) merely provide an excuse for debriefing sessions, which are the key component to learning. See http://thiagi.net/archive/www/pfp/IE4H/february2004.html#Debriefing.

63. Adapted from Pamela Myers Kiser's "Integrative Processing Model," in *The Human Service Internship: Getting the Most from your Experience*, 4th ed. (Boston, MA: Cengage, 2014); Sarah L. Ash and Patti H. Clayton, "Generating, Deepening, and Documenting Learning: The Power of Critical Reflection in Applied Learning," *Journal of Applied Learning in Higher Education* 1 (Fall 2009): 34; Jennifer Moon, "Using Reflective Learning to Improve the Impact of Short Courses and Workshops," *Journal of Continuing Education in Health Professions* 24, no. 1 (2004): 4–11.

64. Major et al., *Teaching for Learning*, 6–7, 50.

65. Barkley, *Student Engagement Techniques*, 102.

66. Elizabeth F. Barkley, Claire Howell Major, and K. Patricia Cross, *Collaborative Learning Techniques: A Handbook for College Faculty* (San Francisco: Jossey-Bass, 2014), 96–97.

67. Nilson, *Teaching at Its Best*, 116.

68. Nilson, *Teaching at Its Best*, 118; Brown et al., *Make It Stick*, 40–45.

69. Angelo and Cross, *Classroom Assessment Techniques*, 120, 148–55.

70. Angelo and Cross, *Classroom Assessment Techniques*, 154–58.

71. Kiser, "Integrative Processing Model." Others emphasizing the importance of closure for different methods include Barkley, *Collaborative Learning Techniques*, 96–97; Major et al., *Teaching for Learning*, 50; Howard, *Discussion in the College Classroom*, 158.

72. Shopkow, "From Bottlenecks to Epistemology."

73. Nilson cited research that shows students can recall 62 percent of material just presented, 45 percent after three to four days, and 24 percent after eight weeks. Nilson, *Teaching at Its Best*, 113–17; Barkley, *Student Engagement Techniques*, 102; Kagan, "Kagan Structures," 120–21.

74. Willingham argued that the mind is primed to understand and remember good (short) stories using these components; *Why Don't Students Like School?*, 66–75; Lendol Calder, "The Stories We Tell," *OAH Magazine of History* 23, no. 3 (July 2013): 7–8.

75. Major et al., *Teaching for Learning*, 5–9; Nilson, *Teaching at Its Best*, 78, 113–14.

76. Stephen D. Brookfield, *The Skillful Teacher: On Technique, Trust, and Responsiveness in the Classroom*, 3rd ed. (San Francisco: Jossey-Bass, 2015), 78–79.

77. Major et al., *Teaching for Learning*, 10–12; Nilson, *Teaching at Its Best*, 114–16, 122–25.

78. Major et al., *Teaching for Learning*, 10; Barkley and Major, *Interactive Lecturing*, 7–28, 343–47.

79. Nilson, *Teaching at Its Best*, 116–22; Major et al., *Teaching for Learning*, 8–12; Kagan, "Kagan Structures," 119–38; Barkley and Howell, *Interactive Lecturing*, 274–77, 347, 352.

80. Cole, "Quit Surfing and Start 'Clicking,'" 402.

81. An excellent resource on how to use classroom response systems is Bruff, *Teaching with Classroom Response Systems*.

82. David J. Voelker, "Clicking for Clio: Using Technology to Teach Historical Thinking," *Perspectives on History*, December 2009.

83. Major et al., *Teaching for Learning*, 11; Brown et al., *Make It Stick*, 34–45.

84. This is an adaptation of one of Cole's questions in "Quit Surfing and Start 'Clicking.'"

85. One of the many books that describes this technique is Major et al., *Teaching for Learning*, 61–63. Harvard's Eric Mazur pioneered a version of think/pair/share for peer explanation of scientific concepts, which led to impressive gains in student understanding. See Catherine H. Crouch and Eric Mazur, "Peer Instruction: Ten Years of Experience and Results," *American Journal of Physics* 69, no. 9 (September 2001): 970–77; Derek Bruff, "Using Peer Instruction to Flip Your Classroom: Highlights from Eric Mazur's Recent Visit," Vanderbilt Center for Teaching blog, April 15, 2013, https://cft.vanderbilt.edu/2013/04/using-peer-instruction-to-flip-your-classroom-highlights-from-eric-mazurs-recent-visit/. Kagan asserts that equal time is important in the think/pair process, so that high achievers don't do all the talking; "Kagan Structures."

86. Howard, *Discussion in the College Classroom*, 4–7; Major et al., *Teaching for Learning*, 48–53; Nilson, *Teaching at Its Best*, 127–28; Elise J. Dallimore, Julie H. Hertenstein, and Marjorie B. Platt, "How Do Students Learn from Participation

in Class Discussion?" *Faculty Focus*, March 27, 2017; William E. Cashin, "Answering and Asking Questions," IDEA Center Paper No. 31, 1995, 1–5.

87. Brookfield and Preskill, *Discussion as a Way of Teaching*, 30.

88. Howard, *Discussion in the College Classroom*, 8; see also Brookfield and Prescott, *Discussion as a Way of Teaching*, 30–31.

89. Weimer, *Learner-Centered Teaching*, 67–72.

90. Howard, *Discussion in the College Classroom*, 166–69.

91. The six components are adapted from W. Lee Hansen, "Improving Classroom Discussion in Economics Courses," in Phillip Saunders, Arthur L. Welsh, W. Lee Hansen, eds., *Improving Classroom Discussion: Resource Manual for Teaching Training Programs in Economics* (New York: Joint Council on Economic Education, 1978), 132–33. Carnegie Mellon's Eberly Center for Teaching Excellence and Educational Innovation has an excellent resource for diagnosing and addressing problems in discussion and other aspects of instruction. "Solve a Teaching Problem," https://www.cmu.edu/teaching/solveproblem/index .html.

92. Brookfield and Preskill, *Discussion as a Way of Teaching*, 42–62; Howard, *Discussion in the College Classroom*, 21–34; Nilson, *Teaching at Its Best*, 128–30.

93. Barkley and Major, *Interactive Lecturing*, 180.

94. Robert J. Stahl, "Using 'Think-Time' and 'Wait-Time' Skillfully in the Classroom," ERIC Clearinghouse for Social Studies/Social Science Education (May 1994); Aliza A. Panjwani and Rebecca Cipollina, "The Elephant in the Room: Fostering Participation in Large Classes," in Rita Obeid, Anna Schwartz, Christina Shane-Simpson, and Patricia J. Brooks, eds., *How We Teach Now: The GSTA Guide to Student-Centered Teaching*, chapter 9.

95. Howard, *Discussion in the College Classroom*, 85.

96. Students define "large" in very different ways, so that's why their perception is what matters. Panjwani and Cipollina, "The Elephant in the Room."

97. Michelle D. Miller, *Minds Online: Teaching Effectively with Technology* (Cambridge, MA: Harvard University Press, 2014), 59.

98. Howard, *Discussion in the College Classroom*, 76; Kevin Gannon, "Creating the Space for Engaged Discussions," *Faculty Focus*, January 8, 2018.

99. Major et al., *Teaching for Learning*, 51–52.

100. Brookfield and Preskill, *Discussion as a Way of Teaching*, 83–99; Davis, *Tools for Teaching*, 118–25.

101. Christensen, "The Discussion Teacher in Action," 163–71.

102. Howard, *Discussion in the College Classroom*, 24, 35.

103. Howard reports that students can distinguish between "aggressiveness" and argumentativeness (i.e., refuting an argument) but discourages instructors from being overly eager to engage in an argument. Students know that such an argument may not be a fair fight, so the better path is to get students to

do the debating with one another, not with the instructor. *Discussion in the College Classroom*, 35–36.

104. Howard, *Discussion in the College Classroom*, 25.

105. Brookfield and Preskill, *Discussion as a Way of Teaching*, 78–79.

106. Weimer, *Learner-Centered Teaching*, 103.

107. Brookfield and Preskill, *Discussion as a Way of Teaching*, 99, 113–14.

108. Kettering Foundation National Issues Forums, https://www.nifi.org/es/home.

109. National Task Force on Civic Learning and Democratic Engagement, *A Crucible Moment: College Learning and Democracy's Future* (Washington, DC: AACU, 2012), 55; Katy J. Harriger, "Deliberative Dialogue and the Development of Democratic Dispositions," *New Directions for Higher Education* 166 (Summer 2014): 53–61. For how I have adapted the process for history classrooms, see Mary Jo Festle, "Learning and Interpreting History through Deliberative Dialogue," in Jennifer H. Herman and Linda Nilson, eds., *Creating Engaging Discussions: Strategies for "Avoiding Crickets" in Any Size Classroom and Online* (Sterling, VA: Stylus, 2018), 71–80.

110. Kelly Hogan and Viji Sathy, "Why We're 'Speaking Up' about Inclusive Teaching Strategies," *ACUE Community*, March 14, 2018; Kimberly D. Tanner, "Structure Matters: Twenty-One Teaching Strategies to Promote Student Engagement and Cultivate Classroom Equity," *CBE—Life Sciences Education* 12, no. 3 (Fall 2013): 322–31.

111. Barkley, Major, and Cross summarize evidence that collaborative learning correlates with positive learning outcomes, student engagement, positive attitudes, and persistence; that it benefits a wide range of students, including students from underrepresented groups; is good educational practice; and is valued by students and instructors. *Collaborative Learning Techniques*, 20–28. In a 2014 meta-analysis of 305 studies on cooperative learning, researchers found that cooperative learning improved academic success, the quality of relationships, self-esteem, and positive attitudes toward university experiences. Cited in Major et al., *Teaching for Learning*, 92. Nilson examines the benefits of group work and the case against it; *Teaching at Its Best*, 156–57. See also Barbara Millis and James Rhem, *Cooperative Learning in Higher Education: Across Disciplines, across the Academy* (Sterling, VA: Stylus, 2010), 1–9; Kagan, "Kagan Structures"; Weimer, *Learner-Centered Teaching*, 38–41; Panjwani and Cipollina, "The Elephant in the Room."

112. McGuire, *Teach Students How to Learn*, 56, 33.

113. Lang, *Small Teaching*, 154.

114. Cavanagh, *Spark of Emotion*, 198–201.

115. Barkley et al. have a whole chapter on avoiding and resolving common problems, and they describe the importance of orienting students to

collaborative learning. See *Collaborative Learning Techniques*, 118–36, 66–73. See also Nilson, *Teaching at Its Best*, 158–65.

116. Maryellen Weimer, "Five Things Students Can Learn through Group Work," *Faculty Focus*, March 20, 2013; on the value to employers of graduates' ability to solve problems and work in diverse teams, see Hart Research Associates and Association of American Colleges and Universities, "Key Findings from 2013 Survey of Employers," https://www.aacu.org/sites/default/files /files/LEAP/KeyFindingsfrom2013SurveyofEmployers.pdf.

117. Barkley et al., *Collaborative Learning Techniques*, 67–68.

118. Barkley et al., *Collaborative Learning Techniques*, 78; Davis, *Tools for Teaching*, 192–205; University of Texas at Austin Faculty Innovation Center, "Group Learning," https://facultyinnovate.utexas.edu/group-learning.

119. Chad Loes, Ernest Pascarella, and Paul Umbach, "Effects of Diversity Experiences on Critical Thinking Skills: Who Benefits?" *Journal of Higher Education* 83, no. 1 (January/February 2012): 1–25; Josipa Roska, Cindy Ann Kilgo, Teniell L. Trolian, Ernest T. Pascarella, Charles Blaich, and Kathleen S. Wise, "Engaging with Diversity: How Positive and Negative Diversity Interactions Influence Students' Cognitive Outcomes," *Journal of Higher Education* 88, no. 3 (2017): 297–322; Victor B. Saenz, Hoi Ning Ngai, and Sylvia Hurtado, "Factors Influencing Positive Interactions across Race for African American, Asian American, Latino, and White College Students," *Research in Higher Education* 48, no. 1 (February 2007): 31–36.

120. Nilson, *Teaching at Its Best*, 158–64; Barkley, *Collaborative Learning Techniques*, 70–72, 107.

121. Barkley et al., *Collaborative Learning Techniques*, 94–96.

122. Peter Frederick wrote of the power of active learning for the AHA more than twenty-five years ago. Frederick, "Motivating Students by Active Learning in the History Classroom," *Perspectives*, October 1993.

123. Peter Frederick recommended paired list making for relationships between texts and generating truth statements in Frederick, "The Dreaded Discussion: Ten Ways to Start," *To Improve the Academy* 1, no. 1 (June 1982): 205–15.

124. Many collaborative activities have been around a long time and adapted. This synthesis exercise sounds like what Major et al. called a "gallery walk" (*Teaching for Learning*, 103) and what Barkley called "small group stations" (*Student Engagement Techniques*, 96).

125. Invented dialogues are one of the techniques described in Angelo and Cross, *Classroom Assessment Techniques*, 203–7. They cite Richard Davis, "A Plea for the Use of Student Dialogues," *Improving College and University Teaching* 29, no. 4 (Fall 1981): 155–59.

126. Christine Nemcik introduced me to the haiku exercise.

127. Metzler designed the exercise for a religious studies course, but it could be adapted for various history courses. See Harvard's ABL (Activity-Based

Learning) Connect site, https://ablconnect.harvard.edu/book/bring-goddess
-party.

128. Nilson, *Teaching at Its Best*, 240–51.

129. Danielle Picard, "Digital Timelines," Vanderbilt University Center for Teaching, https://cft.vanderbilt.edu//cft/guides-sub-pages/digital-time lines/.

130. The timeline for Elizabeth Meadows's course is available at http://www.tiki-toki.com/timeline/entry/227613/Love-and-Marriage/.

131. Lindsey Passenger Wieck, "Blending Local and Spatial History: Using Carto to Create Maps in the History Classroom," *AHA Today*, September 25, 2017, http://blog.historians.org/2017/09/using-carto-create-maps-history -classroom/.

132. Angelo and Cross described how a memory matrix can check recall of information and is also useful for seeing the big-picture relationships. *Classroom Assessment Techniques*, 142–47.

133. Catherine Denial, "Atoms, Honeycombs, and Fabric," *History Teacher* 46, no. 3 (May 2013): 415–34.

134. Barkley summarizes the jigsaw process and its benefits in *Student Engagement Techniques*, 289–95. On the value of peer instruction, see also McGuire, *Teach Students How to Learn*, 33.

135. David Weimer, "Segregation Academies Jigsaw," https://ablconnect .harvard.edu/book/segregation-academies-jigsaw.

136. Carole Srole, Christopher Endy, and Birte Pfleger, "Active Learning in History Survey Courses: The Value of In-Class Peer Mentoring," *History Teacher* 51, no. 1 (November 2017): 89–102.

137. George D. Kuh, *High-Impact Educational Practices: What They Are, Who Has Access to Them, and Why They Matter* (Washington, DC: AACU, 2008); see also AACU, "High Impact Practices," https://www.aacu.org/resources/high -impact-practices.

138. Russell Olwell and Azibo Stevens, "'I Had to Double Check My Thoughts': How the Reacting to the Past Methodology Impacts First-Year College Student Engagement, Retention, and Historical Thinking," *History Teacher* 48, no. 3 (May 2015): 561–72; Christine L. Albright, "Harnessing Students' Competitive Spirit: Using Reacting to the Past to Structure the Introductory Greek Culture Class," *Classical Journal* 112, no. 3 (February–March 2017): 364–79.

139. Jeremiah McCall, "Teaching History with Digital Historical Games: An Introduction to the Field and Best Practices," *Simulation & Gaming* 47, no. 5 (2016): 517–42; Esther Wright, "Playing with History in Video Games," History Matters blog post, April 10, 2018, http://www.historymatters.group.shef.ac .uk/playing-history-video-games/.

140. Miller, *Minds Online*, 190–91.

141. National Academies of Sciences, Engineering, and Medicine, *How People Learn II: Learners, Contexts, and Cultures* (Washington, DC: National Academies Press, 2018), 173–76; Randy Bass and Bret Eynon, *Open and Integrative: Designing Liberal Education for the New Digital Ecosystem* (Washington, DC: AACU, 2016), 33.

142. National Academies, *How People Learn II*, 165, 196; Miller, *Minds Online*, xii, 53, 165–68.

143. Willingham, *Why Don't Students Like School?*, 191–93.

Chapter 4. How We Assess

1. Kevin Gannon, "Escape from Grading Jail: Back to School Edition," Tattooed Professor blog, August 25, 2014, http://www.thetattooedprof.com /2014/08/25/escape-from-grading-jail-back-to-school-edition/.

2. Emma J. Lapsansky-Werner, Letter to the Editor, *Journal of American History* 91, no. 2 (September 2004): 747.

3. Katherine Pickering Antonova, "Why I Hate Grading," blog, August 4, 2012, http://kpantonova.com/why-i-hate-grading/.

4. Ken Bain, *What the Best Teachers Do* (Cambridge, MA: Harvard University Press, 2004), 150.

5. Katherine Jewell, "Grading with Emojis (No, Really)," Teaching United States History blog, May 18, 2016, http://www.teachingushistory.co/2016/05 /grading-with-emojis-no-really.html.

6. Barbara E. Walvoord and Virginia Johnson Anderson, *Effective Grading: A Tool for Learning and Assessment in College*, 2nd ed. (San Francisco: Jossey-Bass, 2010), 104.

7. John C. Bean, *Engaging Ideas: The Professor's Guide to Integrating Writing, Critical Thinking, and Active Learning in the Classroom*, 2nd ed. (Hoboken, NJ: John Wiley and Sons, 2001), 313–14.

8. Emotions, ignorance of standards, and laziness are the three most common barriers to effective peer review. Linda B. Nilson, "Improving Student Peer Feedback," *College Teaching* 51, no. 1 (2003): 34–38.

9. Nilson, "Improving Student Peer Feedback"; Bean, *Engaging Ideas*, 296–98.

10. Walvoord and Anderson, *Effective Grading*, 99.

11. This is a substantially revised synthesis of things I've seen used. See also Walvoord and Anderson, *Effective Grading*, 68.

12. AHA Statement on Excellent Classroom Teaching of History (updated 2017), https://www.historians.org/jobs-and-professional-development/state ments-standards-and-guidelines-of-the-discipline/statement-on-excellent -classroom-teaching-of-history. Multiple-choice items are problematic because they do not reveal the cognitive processes behind an answer; privilege a single, right answer when historical interpretation is by nature complex, nuanced, and

multiple; and sometimes students can guess the correct response. Lendol Calder and Tracy Steffes, *Measuring College Learning in History* (San Francisco: Social Science Research Council, 2016), 71–72; Jay McTighe and Grant Wiggins, *Understanding by Design* (Alexandria, VA: Association for Supervision and Curriculum Development, 1998), 172.

13. Calder and Steffes, *Measuring College Learning in History*, 72–74; Sam Wineburg, Mark Smith, and Joel Breakstone, "New Directions in Assessment: Using Library of Congress Sources to Assess Historical Understanding," *Social Education* 76, no. 6 (November–December 2012): 290–93; Stanford History Education Group, "Beyond the Bubble," https://sheg.stanford.edu/history-assessments. On student preparation for essay exams, see Barbara Gross Davis, *Tools for Teaching*, 2nd ed. (Hoboken, NJ: John Wiley and Sons, 2009), 365.

14. Bean, *Engaging Ideas*, 211–13, 268–69; Wiggins and McTighe, *Understanding by Design*, 172; William E. Cashin, "Improving Essay Tests," IDEA Paper no. 17, January 1987.

15. Walvoord and Anderson, *Effective Grading*, 104.

16. Mary E. Huba and Jann E. Freed, *Learner-Centered Assessment on College Campuses: Shifting the Focus from Teaching to Learning* (Needham Heights, MA: Allyn and Bacon, 2000), 178; Bain, *What the Best College Teachers Do*, 152–53.

17. Huba and Freed, *Learner-Centered Assessment*, 180.

18. Wiggins and McTighe, *Understanding by Design*, 172–75.

19. I'm grateful to Joel Sipress for extolling the benefits of a straightforward rubric and sharing this one with me.

20. Walvoord and Anderson, *Effective Grading*, 40–49.

21. Mary-Ann Winkelmes, David E. Copeland, Ed Jorgensen, Alison Sloat, Anna Smedley, Peter Pizor, Katherine Johnson, and Sharon Jalene, "Benefits (Some Unexpected) of Transparent Assignment Design," *National Teaching and Learning Forum* 24, no. 4 (May 2015): 4–6.

22. Huba and Freed, *Learner-Centered Assessment*, 154, 169–70; Susan A. Ambrose, Michael W. Bridges, Michele DiPietro, Marsha C. Lovett, Marie K. Norman, and Richard E. Mayer, *How Learning Works* (San Francisco: Jossey-Bass, 2010), 231–32; Catherine Hack, "Analytical Rubrics in Higher Education: A Repository of Empirical Data," *British Journal of Educational Technology* 46, no. 5 (2015).

23. Winkelmes et al., "Benefits (Some Unexpected)."

24. Susan Ambrose, "Grading Rubric for Oral Exams in an Upper Division History Course," Eberly Center for Teaching Excellence, Carnegie Mellon University, https://www.cmu.edu/teaching/designteach/teach/rubrics.html.

25. John Rosinbum, "Before Buzzfeed: Going Viral in 19th Century America," *Perspectives on History*, March 2017; see the rubric at AHA Teaching Resources for Historians Sample Assignments, https://www.historians.org/teaching-and-learning.

26. Mary-Ann Winkelmes, "Transparency in Teaching: Faculty Share Data and Improve Students' Learning," AACU *Liberal Education* 99, no. 2 (Spring 2013).

27. Huba and Freed, *Learner-Centered Assessment*, 168.

28. Huba and Freed, *Learner-Centered Assessment*, 47, 172.

29. Leah Shopkow, "How Many Sources Do I Need?" *History Teacher* 50, no 2 (February 2017): 186.

30. Daniel J. McInerney, "Rubrics for History Courses: Lessons from One Campus," *Perspectives on History*, October 2010; Huba and Freed, *Learner-Centered Assessment*, 188.

31. Wiggins and McTighe, *Understanding by Design*, 180–82; Walvoord and Anderson, *Effective Grading*, 42.

32. Winkelmes, "Transparency in Teaching"; Ambrose et al., *How Learning Works*, 204; Walvoord and Anderson, *Effective Grading*, 103.

33. Linda B. Nilson, *Teaching at Its Best: A Research-Based Resource for College Instructors*, 3rd ed. (San Francisco: Jossey-Bass, 2010), 307; Bean, *Engaging Ideas*, 221–23.

34. Bean, *Engaging Ideas*, 288; Nilson, *Teaching at Its Best*, 303–4; John M. Malouff, Ashley J. Emmerton, and Nicola S. Schutte, "The Risk of Halo Bias as a Reason to Keep Students Anonymous during Grading," *Teaching of Psychology* 40, no. 3 (2013): 233–37.

35. Bean, *Engaging Ideas*, 221–23; Cashin, "Improving Essay Tests."

36. Davis, *Tools for Teaching*, chap. 36.

37. Ronald F. Lunsford, "When Less Is More: Principles for Responding in the Disciplines," *New Directions for Teaching and Learning* 69 (Spring 1997): 93; Eberly Center Teaching Excellence and Educational Innovation, "How Can I Effectively and Efficiently Respond to Student Writing?" Carnegie Mellon University, https://www.cmu.edu/teaching/designteach/teach/instructional strategies/writing/respond.html.

38. Lunsford, "When Less Is More," 93.

39. Bean, *Engaging Ideas*, 322–35.

40. Bean, *Engaging Ideas*, 318–20.

41. Walvoord and Anderson, *Effective Grading*, 101; Bean, *Engaging Ideas*, 336; Lunsford, "When Less Is More." 93–94, 103.

42. Robert E. Weir, "Empowering Students while Cutting Corners: Efficient Grading of History Essays," *Perspectives on History*, March 1993.

43. Weir, "Empowering Students while Cutting Corners."

44. Elizabeth Hodges, "Negotiating the Margins: Some Principles for Responding to Our Students' Writing, Some Strategies for Helping Students Read Our Comments," *New Directions for Teaching and Learning* 69 (Spring 1997): 78.

45. Hodges, "Negotiating the Margins," 82–86.

46. Bean, *Engaging Ideas*, 322.

47. Hodges, "Negotiating the Margins," 84–86; Lunsford, "When Less Is More," 103.

48. Nilson, *Teaching at Its Best*, 303–4; Huba and Freed, *Learner-Focused Assessment*, 193–96.

49. Davis, *Tools for Teaching*, 327.

50. Bean, *Engaging Ideas*, 336.

51. Peter Ferguson, "Student Perceptions of Quality Feedback in Teacher Education," *Assessment & Evaluation in Higher Education* 36, no. 1 (January 2011): 57.

52. Saundra McGuire, *Teach Students How to Learn* (Sterling, VA: Stylus, 2015), 80–81.

53. David S. Yeager, Valerie Purdie-Vaughns, Julio Garcia, Nancy Apfel, Patti Brzustoski, Allison Master, William T. Hessert, Matthew E. Williams, and Geoffrey L. Cohen, "Breaking the Cycle of Mistrust: Wise Interventions to Provide Critical Feedback across the Racial Divide," *Journal of Experimental Psychology* 143, no. 2 (2014): 804–24; David S. Yeager, Dave Paunesku, Gregory M. Walton, and Carol S. Dweck, "How Can We Instill Productive Mindsets at Scale? A Review of the Evidence and an Initial R&D Agenda," White Paper prepared for White House Meeting on Excellence in Education, 2013, https:// labs.la.utexas.edu/adrg/files/2013/12/Yeager-et-al-RD-agenda-6-10-131.pdf; "Empirically Validated Strategies to Reduce Stereotype Threat," https://ed .stanford.edu/sites/default/files/interventionshandout.pdf.

54. Walvoord and Anderson, *Effective Grading*, 56–59, 100.

55. Walvoord and Anderson, *Effective Grading*, 56, 99.

56. Shopkow, "How Many Sources Do I Need?" 172–73.

57. Weir, "Empowering Students while Cutting Corners."

58. Gannon, "Escape from Grading Jail."

59. Davis, *Tools for Teaching*, 325–26; Tanya Martini and David DiBattista, "The Transfer of Learning Associated with Audio Feedback on Written Work," *Canadian Journal for the Scholarship of Teaching and Learning* 5, no. 1, Article 8 (2014): 1–5.

60. Adapted from Sweetland Center for Writing University of Michigan College of Literature Science and the Arts, "Supplement 2—Feedback Form," https://lsa.umich.edu/sweetland/instructors/teaching-resources/giving -feedback-on-student-writing.html; see also Writing Studio, Colorado State, "Teaching in the Margins—Commenting on Student Writing," https://writing .colostate.edu/guides/teaching/commenting/index.cfm.

61. Adapted from Jose Bowen, "Cognitive Wrappers: Using Metacognition and Reflection to Improve Learning," blog, August 22, 2013, http://josebowen .com/cognitive-wrappers-using-metacognition-and-reflection-to-improve -learning/; Ambrose et al., *How Learning Works*, 251–54; Nilson, *Teaching at Its Best*, 312.

62. Ambrose et al., *How Learning Works*, 143, 149–51.

63. McGuire, *Teach Students How to Learn*, 49–50, 86.

64. On checklists, see Walvoord and Anderson, *Effective Grading*, 38–39; Ambrose et al., *How Learning Works*, 255–56; "Stylesheet and Guidelines for Written Assignments," Department of History, National University of Ireland, Galway, https://www.nuigalway.ie/media/collegeofartssocialsciencescelticstudies/schools/humanities/history/the_history_stylesheet.pdf.

65. Winkelmes, "Transparency in Teaching."

66. Quoted in Bain, *What the Best College Teachers Do*, 161.

67. Walvoord and Anderson, *Effective Grading*, 101–3; Ambrose et al., *How Learning Works*, 141; Yeager, "Breaking the Cycle of Mistrust."

68. John McClymer, "AHA Guide to Teaching and Learning with New Media," https://www.historians.org/teaching-and-learning/teaching-resources-for-historians.

69. Bain, *What the Best Teachers Do*, 161; Davis, *Tools for Teaching*, 370–71.

70. Davis, *Tools for Teaching*, 332, 369.

71. Walvoord and Anderson, *Effective Grading*, 125–30; Nilson, *Teaching at Its Best*, 212–13.

72. Bain, *What the Best Teachers Do*, 162–63.

73. McGuire, *Teach Students How to Learn*, 80–85; Huba and Freed, *Learner-Centered Assessment*, 194–95.

74. Walvoord and Anderson, *Effective Grading*, 129.

75. Walvoord and Anderson, *Effective Grading*, 129, 137.

76. Walvoord and Anderson, *Effective Grading*, 137.

77. I may consider alternative assignments for ESL learners or those with certain disabilities. On some assignments, students with certain disabilities clearly need an alternative (e.g., blind students analyzing an image). Experts often suggest the same feedback techniques for second-language learners as those for any writers, but occasionally suggest an alternative assignment. "Providing Feedback to Second Language Learners," University of Michigan Sweetland Center for Writing, https://lsa.umich.edu/sweetland/instructors/teaching-resources/providing-feedback-and-grades-to-second-language-students.html.

78. Thomas A. Angelo and K. Patricia Cross, *Classroom Assessment Techniques: A Handbook for College Teachers*, 2nd ed. (San Francisco: Jossey-Bass, 1993), 8; Bain, *What the Best Teachers Do*, 151, 164.

79. Nilson, *Teaching at Its Best*, 316–17.

80. Maryellen Weimer, *Inspired College Teaching: A Career-Long Resource for Professional Growth* (San Francisco: Jossey-Bass, 2010), 51, 57–60; Nilson, *Teaching at Its Best*, 318; Stephen L. Benton and William E. Cashin, "Student Ratings of Teaching: A Summary of Research and Literature," IDEA Paper no. 50, https://

www.ideaedu.org/Portals/o/Uploads/Documents/IDEA%20Papers/IDEA
%20Papers/PaperIDEA_50.pdf. Criticism of older research is in Linda B. Nilson,
"Time to Raise Questions about Student Ratings," in James E. Groccia and
Laura Cruz, eds., *To Improve the Academy* (San Francisco: Jossey-Bass, 2012), 31.

81. Nilson, *Teaching at Its Best*, 316–17. Students give somewhat higher
ratings to courses that require hard work. Some studies suggest a moderate
correlation between how much a student learned (e.g., on a cumulative exam)
and the ratings they give, which makes sense, because students of more effective teachers should learn more and earn higher grades. This is not necessarily
an indication of invalidity. To ensure that instructors aren't trying to win positive
ratings with easy courses, universities can have peers examine course materials,
exams, and graded work. Quoted in Benton and Cashin, "Student Ratings of
Teaching."

82. Nancy W. Gleason and Catherine S. Sanger, "Peer Observation of
Teaching: A Sourcebook for the International Liberal Arts Context," Centre for
Teaching and Learning, Yale-NUS College, Singapore, 2017, 13–16.

83. Danica Savonick and Cathy N. Davidson, "Gender Bias in Academe:
An Annotated Bibliography of Important Recent Studies," London School of
Economics and Political Science Impact blog, March 8, 2016, http://blogs.lse
.ac.uk/impactofsocialsciences/2016/03/08/gender-bias-in-academe-an-anno
tated-bibliography/; Pieter Spooren, Bert Brockx, and Dimitri Mortelmans,
"On the Validity of Student Evaluation of Teaching: The State of the Art," *Re-
view of Educational Research* 83, no. 4 (December 2013): 598–642; Joey Sprague
and Kelley Massoni, "Student Evaluations and Gendered Expectations: What
We Can't Count Can Hurt Us," *Sex Roles* 53, nos. 11/12 (December 2005): 291–
303; Patti Miles and Deanna House, "The Tail Wagging the Dog: An Overdue
Examination of Student Teaching Evaluations," *International Journal of Higher
Education* 4, no. 2 (2015): 116–26; Vanessa Lynn Ewing, Arthur Stukas, and
Eugene P. Sheehan, "Student Prejudice against Gay Male and Lesbian Lecturers,"
Journal of Social Psychology 143, no. 5 (2003): 569–79; Natascha Wagner, Matthias
Rieger, and Katherine Voorvelt, "Gender, Ethnicity, and Teaching Evaluations:
Evidence from Mixed Teaching Teams," *Economics of Education Review* 54 (Octo-
ber 2016): 79–94; Anne Boring, Kellie Ottoboni, and Philip B. Stark, "Student
Evaluations of Teaching (Mostly) Do Not Measure Teaching Effectiveness,"
Science Open Research, January 2016; Lillian MacNell, Adam Driscoll, and Andrea
N. Hunt, "What's in a Name? Exposing Gender Bias in Student Ratings of
Teachers," *Innovative Higher Education*, December 5, 2014. Some criticize the
studies about bias, including Steve Benton and Dan Li, "What's in the Study:
Exposing Validity Threats in the MacNell, Driscoll, and Hunt Study of Gender
Bias," IDEA blog, December 22, 2014, https://www.ideaedu.org/Resources
-Events/IDEA-Blog/PostId/47; Ken Ryalls, Stephen L. Benton, Dan Li, and

Jason Barr, "Response to 'Bias Against Female Instructors,'" IDEA Editorial Note no. 2, http://www.academia.edu/30838078/Response_to_Bias_Against_Female_Instructors.

84. Jared Keeley, "Course and Instructor Evaluation," in William Buskist and Victor A. Benassi, eds., *Effective College and University Teaching: Strategies and Tactics for the New Professoriate* (Thousand Oaks, CA: Sage, 2012), 175; Weimer, *Inspired College Teaching*, 51; Nilson, *Teaching at Its Best*, 321.

85. Stephen L. Benton and Kenneth R. Ryalls, "Challenging Misconceptions about Student Ratings of Instruction," IDEA Paper no. 58, April 2016, https://www.ideaedu.org/Portals/0/Uploads/Documents/IDEA%20Papers/IDEA%20Papers/PaperIDEA_58.pdf; see also Therese Huston, "Empirical Research on the Impact of Race & Gender," Center for Excellence in Teaching and Learning, Seattle University, 2005.

86. Nancy Van Note Chism, *Peer Review of Teaching: A Sourcebook*, 2nd ed. (Bolton, MA: Anker Publishing, 2002), 5–8; Keeley, "Course and Instructor Evaluation," 175; Benton and Cashin, "Student Ratings of Teaching."

87. Benton and Ryalls, "Challenging Misconceptions."

88. Weimer, *Inspired College Teaching*, 54–55; Benton and Cashin, "Student Ratings of Teaching"; Nilson, *Teaching at Its Best*, 319; Davis, *Tools for Teaching*, 544.

89. Weimer *Inspired College Teaching*, 53; Davis, *Tools for Teaching*, 543–45; Nilson, *Teaching at Its Best*, 319–20.

90. Davis, *Tools for Teaching*, 467; Weimer, *Inspired College Teaching*, 64; Nilson, *Teaching at Its Best*, 319.

91. Weimer, *Inspired College Teaching*, 58; Nilson, *Teaching at Its Best*, 316.

92. Weimer, *Inspired College Teaching*, 61.

93. Weimer, *Inspired College Teaching*, 78; Houston, *Teaching What You Don't Know*, 208.

94. Weimer, *Inspired College Teaching*, 112; Joe Bandy, "Peer Review of Teaching," Vanderbilt University Center for Teaching, https://cft.vanderbilt.edu/guides-sub-pages/peer-review-of-teaching/.

95. "Peer Observation of Teaching," Elon Center for the Advancement of Teaching and Learning, https://www.elon.edu/u/academics/catl/tlresources/assess-student-learning/peer-observation-of-teaching/.

96. C. Roland Christensen Center for Teaching and Learning, "Guidelines for Effective Observation of Case Instructors," Harvard Business School, 2005, https://www.hbs.edu/teaching/Documents/Guidelines-for-Effective-Observation-of-Case-Instructors.pdf.

97. Jared Keeley, Dale Smith, and William Buskist, "The Teacher Behaviors Checklist: Factor Analysis of Its Utility for Evaluating Teaching," *Teaching of Psychology* 33, no. 2 (April 2006): 84–91.

98. This list relies primarily on Chism, *Peer Review of Teaching*, 111–12,

although I have adapted some items to include issues discussed in this book, and I borrowed a few ideas from Bandy, "Peer Review of Teaching," and Billie Franchini, "Peer Observation and Assessment of Teaching," Institute for Teaching, Learning, and Academic Leadership, SUNY Albany (adapted from Bill Roberson for the University of Texas, El Paso), 2008.

99. Chism, *Peer Review of Teaching*, 106–7; Franchini, "Peer Observation and Assessment of Teaching"; Niki Young, "The Value of the Narrative Teaching Observation," *To Improve the Academy* 28, no. 1 (June 2010): 98–111. Coding schemes make it possible to quantify results, but these require observer training. Michelle K. Smith, Francis H. M. Jones, Sarah L. Gilbert, and Carl E. Wieman, "The Classroom Observation Protocol for Undergraduate STEM (COPUS): A New Instrument to Characterize University STEM Classroom Practices," *CBE-Life Sciences Education* 12, no. 4 (Winter 2013): 618–27.

100. I can add a column to the form for observer comments. Chism, *Peer Review of Teaching*, 106–7.

101. Franchini, "Peer Observation and Assessment of Teaching"; Davis, *Tools for Teaching*, 478.

102. BYU-Idaho Instructional Development, "Classroom Observation," http://www.byui.edu/learningandteaching; Neil Haave, "Teaching Squares Bring Cross-Disciplinary Perspectives," *Faculty Focus*, June 3, 2016.

103. Angelo and Cross, *Classroom Assessment Techniques*, xiv, 148–53; Keeley, "Course and Instructor Evaluation," 177.

104. Huston, *Teaching What You Don't Know*, 232.

105. Some of these questions are adapted from Brookfield and Preskill, "Critical Incident Questionnaires," as described in *Discussion as a Way of Teaching*, 48–50, and Wiggins and McTighe, *Understanding by Design*, 272.

106. Vanderbilt University's Center for Teaching, "Gathering Feedback from Students," https://cft.vanderbilt.edu//cft/guides-sub-pages/student-feedback/; Princeton University McGraw Center for Teaching and Learning, "Using Mid-Semester Course Evaluations," https://mcgraw.princeton.edu/node/1536; Raoul A. Arreola, *Developing a Comprehensive Faculty Evaluation System* (San Francisco: Anker, 1995), 130–41.

107. Huston, *Teaching What You Don't Know*, 215.

108. Davis, *Tools for Teaching*, 461–63.

109. Barbara J. Millis, "Three Practical Strategies for Peer Consultation," *New Directions for Teaching and Learning* 79 (September 1999): 20–21.

110. Margaret K. Snooks, Sue E. Neeley, and Lee Revere, "Midterm Student Feedback: Results of a Pilot Study," *Journal on Excellence in College Teaching* 18, no. 3 (2007): 55–73; Davis, *Tools for Teaching*, 466; Miriam Rosalyn Diamond, "The Usefulness of Structured Mid-term Feedback as a Catalyst for Change in Higher Education Classes," *Active Learning in Higher Education* 5, no. 3 (2004): 217–31; Huston, *Teaching What You Don't Know*, 229–30.

111. Joel M. Sipress, "Why Students Don't Get Evidence and What We Can Do about It," *History Teacher* 37, no. 3 (May 2004): 351–63.

112. For an example of charting student progress, see Shopkow, "How Many Sources Do I Need?"; Natasha Kenny, Carol Berenson, Nancy Chick, David Keegan, Emma Read, and Leslie Reid, "A Developmental Framework for Teaching Expertise in Postsecondary Education," International Society for the Scholarship of Teaching and Learning, Calgary, Alberta, October 11–14, 2017. On the ideal design and teaching cycle, see Wiggins and McTighe, *Understanding by Design*, 273–74.

113. Bain, *What the Best College Teachers Do*, 167–18.

114. This discussion is informed by Arreola, *Developing a Comprehensive Faculty Evaluation System*, 17–22.

115. Bain, *What the Best College Teachers Do*, 167–68.

116. Peter Seldin, J. Elizabeth Miller, and Clement A. Seldin, *The Teaching Portfolio: A Practical Guide to Improved Performance and Promotion/Tenure Decisions*, 4th ed. (San Francisco: Jossey-Bass, 2010), 10–20; Chism, *Peer Review of Teaching*, 168–85; Nilson, *Teaching at Its Best*, 321–26; Vanderbilt University Center for Teaching, "Teaching Portfolios," https://cft.vanderbilt.edu//cft/guides-sub-pages/teaching-portfolios/.

117. Bain, *What the Best College Teachers Do*, 167.

Chapter 5. Who We Are

1. Eric Foner, "My Life as a Historian," in Paul A. Cimbala and Robert F. Himmelberg, eds., *Historians and Race: Autobiography and the Writing of History* (Bloomington: Indiana University Press, 1996), 92.

2. Quoted in "The Practice of History," *Journal of American History* 90, no. 2 (September 2003): 576–611.

3. Judith Bennett, *History Matters: Patriarchy and the Challenge of Feminism* (Philadelphia: University of Pennsylvania Press, 2006), 130; Jeremy D. Popkin, *History, Historians and Autobiography* (Chicago: University of Chicago Press, 2005), 127–30. Popkin analyzed hundreds of memoirs by historians.

4. Popkin, *History, Historians and Autobiography*, 131–32.

5. Alison Hewitt, "Six Stellar Faculty Win Distinguished Teaching Award," UCLA Newsroom, May 28, 2009, http://newsroom.ucla.edu/stories/stellar-faculty-win-distinguished-93275.

6. David A. Hollinger, "Church People and Others," in James M. Banner Jr. and John R. Gillis, eds., *Becoming Historians* (Chicago: University of Chicago Press, 2009), 102, 111.

7. Popkin, *History, Historians and Autobiography*, 145.

8. Popkin, *History, Historians and Autobiography*, 194–200.

9. Linda Gordon, "History Constructs a Historian," in James M. Banner Jr.

and John R. Gillis, eds., *Becoming Historians* (Chicago: University of Chicago Press, 2009), 88, 93.

10. Popkin, *History, Historians and Autobiography*, 142.

11. Gerda Lerner, "Women among the Professors of History: The Story of a Process of Transformation," in Eileen Boris and Nupur Chaudhuri, eds., *Voices of Women Historians* (Bloomington: Indiana University Press, 1999), 1.

12. Foner, "My Life as a Historian," 91–98.

13. Darlene Clark Hine, "Reflections on Race and Gender Systems," in Paul A. Cimbala and Robert F. Himmelberg, eds., *Historians and Race: Autobiography and the Writing of History* (Bloomington: Indiana University Press, 1996), 51–60.

14. John Murrin, "Edmund Morgan," in Robert Allen Rutland, ed., *Clio's Favorites: Leading Historians of the United States, 1945–2000* (Columbia: University of Missouri Press, 2000), 126; Popkin, *History, Historians and Autobiography*, 142–43.

15. "The Practice of History," 576–611.

16. Bennett, *History Matters*, 150. O'Meara et al. observed that the field of faculty development would benefit from additional research about the person behind and in the professional role. KerryAnn O'Meara, Aimee LaPointe Terosky, and Anna Neumann, *Faculty Careers and Work Lives: A Professional Growth Perspective*, ASHE Higher Education Report 34, no. 3 (2008): 173–74.

17. Gordon, "History Constructs a Historian," 90.

18. Hine, "Reflections on Race and Gender Systems."

19. Lerner, "Women among the Professors of History," 10.

20. John D'Emilio, "Forty Years and Counting," in Leila J. Rupp and Susan K. Freeman, eds., *Understanding and Teaching U.S. Lesbian, Gay, Bisexual, and Transgender History* (Madison: University of Wisconsin Press, 2014), 44–5.

21. Popkin wrote, "Historian-autobiographers say little about the routine of teaching that does so much to define the professions because to do so would be boring," and that historians are even more reticent in discussing their work as teachers than discussing their scholarship. In this section, he posits that they might not have wanted to appear vain or were hesitant to overestimate their impact. I wonder whether there may be other explanations, such as the generation during which they were writing, which may have affected what was viewed as valuable work, or that many of the memoirists who had the opportunity to write about their lives achieved notoriety for their scholarship rather than teaching. Popkin, *History, Historians and Autobiography*, 281, 153–54.

22. Leon Litwack, "The Making of a Historian," in Paul A. Cimbala and Robert F. Himmelberg, eds., *Historians and Race: Autobiography and the Writing of History* (Bloomington: Indiana University Press, 1996), 17–18.

23. Lillian Guerra, "Why I Am a Historian: A Response to Mary Beth Norton," *Perspectives*, July 2, 2018.

24. Gerda Lerner, *Living with History/Making Social Change* (Chapel Hill: University of North Carolina Press, 2009), 12–13.

25. Alexis Doyle, "Professor Eileen Findlay: Recipient of the 2016 Outstanding Teaching in a Full-Time Appointment Award," *Her Campus at American*, October 4, 2016, https://www.hercampus.com/school/american/professor -eileen-findlay-recipient-2016-outstanding-teaching-full-time-appointment.

26. Michael Lewis Goldberg, "Redesigning the U.S. Women's History Survey Course Using Feminist Pedagogy, Educational Research and New Technologies," in Carol Berkin, Margaret S. Crocco, and Barbara Winslow, eds., *Clio in the Classroom: A Guide for Teaching U.S. Women's History* (Oxford: Oxford University Press, 2009), 209–10.

27. Joan Wallach Scott, "Finding Critical History," in James M. Banner Jr. and John R. Gillis, eds., *Becoming Historians* (Chicago: University of Chicago Press, 2009), 27.

28. Estelle Freedman, "Small Group Pedagogy: Consciousness Raising in Conservative Times," *NWSA Journal* 2, no. 4 (Autumn 1990): 603–23.

29. Hewitt, "Six Stellar Faculty."

30. Lerner, *Living with History*, 12.

31. Ken Bain, *What the Best Teachers Do* (Cambridge, MA: Harvard University Press, 2004), 174.

32. Susan A. Ambrose, Michael W. Bridges, Michele DiPietro, Marsha C. Lovett, Marie K. Norman, and Richard E. Mayer, *How Learning Works: 7 Research-Based Principles for Smart Teaching* (San Francisco: Jossey-Bass, 2010), 220–21; Daniel T. Willingham, *Why Don't Students Like School? A Cognitive Scientist Answers Questions about How the Mind Works and What It Means for the Classroom* (San Francisco: Jossey-Bass, 2009), 192.

33. Raymond J. Wlodkowski and Margery B. Ginsberg, *Diversity and Motivation: Culturally Responsive Teaching* (San Francisco: Jossey-Bass, 1995), 70–71; David Perkins, *Making Learning Whole: How Seven Principles of Teaching Can Transform Education* (San Francisco: Jossey-Bass, 2009), 103; Bain, *What the Best College Teachers Do*, 173–75.

34. Ambrose et al., *How Learning Works*, 223–24.

35. Stephen D. Brookfield, *The Skillful Teacher: On Technique, Trust, and Responsiveness in the Classroom* (Hoboken, NJ: John Wiley and Sons, 2015), 266; on rumination, see Susan Robison, *The Peak Performing Professor: A Practical Guide to Productivity and Happiness* (San Francisco: Jossey-Bass, 2013), 207.

36. One study suggested that faculty with a fixed mindset negatively affect their students, too. Elizabeth A. Canning, Katherine Muenks, Doraine J. Green, and Mary C. Murphy, "STEM Faculty Who Believe Intelligence Is Fixed Have Larger Racial Achievement Gaps," *Science Advances* 5, no. 2 (February 15, 2019): 1. Kerry Ann Rockquemore used the phrase "limiting beliefs" preventing faculty

from seeking mentoring. I've applied her term to teaching. Rockquemore, "Essay on How Mid-Career Faculty Members Can Rebrand Themselves," *Inside Higher Ed*, July 16, 2012.

37. This common misperception was noted in Ambrose et al., *How Learning Works*, 218–19.

38. Brookfield, *Skillful Teacher*, 278.

39. Willingham, *Why Don't Students Like School?*, 193.

40. Filene credits Ed Neal for the Frisbee metaphor. Peter Filene, *The Joy of Teaching: A Practical Guide for New College Instructors* (Chapel Hill: University of North Carolina Press, 2005), 3.

41. Alison King, "From Sage on the Stage to Guide on the Side," *College Teaching* 41, no. 1 (Winter 1993): 30–35.

42. I borrowed the gardening metaphor from Dennis Fox, "Personal Theories of Teaching," *Studies in Higher Education* 8, no. 2 (1983): 151–63.

43. Maryellen Weimer discusses numerous metaphors and their implications in *Learner-Centered Teaching: Five Key Changes to Practice*, 2nd ed. (San Francisco: Jossey-Bass, 2013), 59–63.

44. Wiggins and McTighe use the designer and guide metaphors in Grant Wiggins and Jay McTighe, *Understanding by Design* (Alexandria, VA: Association for Supervision and Curriculum Development, 1998), 13–15.

45. On the value of coaches, see Atul Gawande, "Personal Best: Top Athletes and Singers Have Coaches; Should You?" *New Yorker*, October 3, 2011, 44–53. David Perkins uses the coach metaphor in *Making Learning Whole*, 70.

46. "Kenyon People: Glenn McNair," http://www.kenyon.edu/middle-path/people/profile/glenn-mcnair.

47. Rob Jenkins, "Defining the Relationship," *Chronicle of Higher Education*, August 8, 2016.

48. Mary Ann Bowen, "Metaphors We Teach By: Understanding Ourselves as Teachers and Learners," *Class Action* 1, no. 4 (1998–99): 1–2.

49. Quoted in Rachel Toor, "Persona Matters," *Chronicle of Higher Education*, December 19, 2016; see also James M. Lang, "Crafting a Teaching Persona," *Chronicle of Higher Education*, February 6, 2007.

50. Colleen Flaherty, "Study on Students and 'Authenticity' in Classroom," *Inside Higher Ed*, May 26, 2017; Maryellen Weimer, "Developing a Teaching Persona," *Faculty Focus*, May 13, 2015. The "just be yourself" language comes from Linda Shadiow and Maryellen Weimer, "Six Myths about a Teaching Persona," *Faculty Focus*, October 26, 2015.

51. Brookfield, *Skillful Teacher*, 271–74; Weimer, "Developing a Teaching Persona."

52. Steven Volk, "The 'Us' in Teaching," After Class blog, 2016, https://steven-volk.blog/2016/10/31/the-us-in-teaching/.

53. Leo M. Lambert, Jason Husser, and Peter Felten, "Mentors Play a Critical Role in Quality of College Experience," *The Conversation*, https://www.elon.edu/E-Net/Article/165443.

54. Sarah Cavanagh, *The Spark of Learning: Energizing the College Classroom with the Science of Emotion* (Morgantown: West Virginia University Press, 2016), 74–81.

55. Cavanagh, *Spark of Learning*, 63.

56. Ambrose et al., *How Learning Works*, 218–19.

57. Cavanagh, *Spark of Learning*, 103–8.

58. Cavanagh, *Spark of Learning*, 96–97.

59. Cavanagh, *Spark of Learning*, 85–87; Alan K. Goodboy, Shannon T. Carton, Zachary W. Goldman, Timothy A. Gozanski, William J. C. Tyler, and Nicole R. Johnson, "Discouraging Instructional Dissent and Facilitating Students' Learning through Instructor Self-Disclosure," *Southern Communication Journal* 79, no. 2 (April–June 2014): 114–29.

60. Scott Jaschik, "TMI from Professors," *Inside Higher Ed*, October 9, 2013.

61. Cavanagh, *Spark of Learning*, 81–90, 102, 192–94. On student perceptions of marginalized faculty being less objective, including some studies where syllabi were the same except for information about the faculty member, see Kristin J. Anderson and Melinda Kanner, "Inventing a Gay Agenda: Students' Perceptions of Lesbian and Gay Professors," *Journal of Social Psychology* 41, no. 6 (June 2011): 1538–64.

62. Volk, "The 'Us' in Teaching; Kevin Gannon, "A Case for Academic Activism," Tattooed Professor blog, 2015, http://www.thetattooedprof.com/2015/03/28/a-case-for-academic-activism/.

63. Lang, "Crafting a Teaching Persona."

64. Cavanagh, *Spark of Learning*, 66. On teacher characteristics, see Zachary W. Goldman, Gregory A. Cranmer, Michael Sollitto, Sara Labelle, and Alex L. Lancaster, "What Do College Students Want? A Prioritization of Instructional Behaviors and Characteristics," *Communication Education* 66, no. 3 (2017): 280–98.

65. Quoted in Toor, "Persona Matters."

66. Brookfield, *Skillful Teacher*, 20.

67. O'Meara et al., *Faculty Careers and Work Lives*, 32.

68. O'Meara et al. conceptualize learning as being at the center of faculty work, identity, and professional growth. *Faculty Careers and Work Lives*, 167–68.

69. Christopher J. Lucas and John W. Murry Jr., *New Faculty: A Practical Guide for Academic Beginners* (New York: Palgrave Macmillan, 2007), 3–20. The American Historical Association has statements of professional standards, currently found at https://www.historians.org/jobs-and-professional-development/statements-standards-and-guidelines-of-the-discipline.

70. "Historians Behaving Badly: Intellectual Citizenship, Professional

Behavior, and the Public," Roundtable, American Historical Association annual meeting, January 4, 2018.

71. Kerry Ann Rockquemore and Tracey Laszloffy, *The Black Academic's Guide to Winning Tenure—Without Losing Your Soul* (Boulder, CO: Lynne Rienner, 2008).

72. Penny Schine Gold, "Giving Advice to Women in Academe: Where 'Ms. Mentor' Goes Wrong," *Chronicle of Higher Education*, May 1, 1998.

73. Adrianna Kezar and Daniel Maxey, *Adapting by Design: Creating Faculty Roles and Designing Faculty Work to Ensure an Intentional Future for Colleges and Universities* (Los Angeles, CA: Delphi Project on the Changing Faculty and Student Success and the University of Southern California Earl and Pauline Pullias Center for Higher Education, 2015), 5; Colleen Flaherty, "Envisioning the Faculty," *Inside Higher Education*, October 17, 2016; New Faculty Majority, "Facts about Adjuncts," http://www.newfacultymajority.info/facts-about-adjuncts/; American Association of University Professors, "Background Facts on Contingent Faculty," https://www.aaup.org/issues/contingency/background-facts; Coalition on the Academic Workforce, "A Portrait of Part-Time Faculty Members," June 2012, http://www.academicworkforce.org/CAW_portrait_2012.pdf.

74. Just over half (50.6 percent) of recently hired history PhDs held tenure-track positions at four-year colleges; almost a quarter did not work in academia, and the others either worked off tenure track or at two-year institutions. L. Maren Wood and Robert B. Townsend, "The Many Careers of History PhDs: A Study of Job Outcomes," American Historical Association, https://www.historians.org/jobs-and-professional-development/career-diversity-for-historians/career-diversity-resources/the-many-careers-of-history-phds; Robert B. Townsend, "Underpaid and Underappreciated: A Portrait of Part-Time Faculty," *Perspectives on History*, September 2012.

75. Mary Elizabeth Perry, "Clio on the Margins," in Eileen Boris and Nupur Chaudhuri, eds., *Voices of Women Historians* (Bloomington: Indiana University Press, 1999), 249. A historian's "Invisible Adjunct" blog criticized the absurdities of academia and advised people not to get a PhD in the humanities due to the poor chances of finding full-time employment. See Popkin, *History, Historians and Autobiography*, 151; Christopher Shea, "The Case of the Invisible Adjunct," *Boston Globe*, May 9, 2004.

76. Cara Meixner, S. E. Kruck, and Laura T. Madden, "Inclusion of Part-Time Faculty for the Benefit of Faculty and Students," *College Teaching* 58, no. 4 (October 2010): 141–47; Jean Waltman, Inger Bergom, Carol Honnenshead, Jeanne Miller, and Louise August, "Factors Contributing to Job Satisfaction and Dissatisfaction among Non-Tenure Track Faculty," *Journal of Higher Education* 83, no. 3 (May/June 2012): 411–34.

77. Meixner et al., "Inclusion of Part-Time Faculty."

78. Roger Baldwin, Deborah DeZure, Allyn Shaw, and Kristin Moretto, "Mapping the Terrain of Mid-Career Faculty at a Research University: Implications for Faculty and Academic Leaders," *Change* (September/October 2008): 46–55.

79. Roger G. Baldwin, "Making Mid-Career Meaningful," *Department Chair* 16, no. 2 (Fall 2005): 14–16.

80. Ellen L. West, "What Are You Doing the Rest of Your Life? Strategies for Fostering Faculty Vitality and Development Mid-Career," *Journal of Learning in Higher Education* 8, no. 1 (Spring 2012): 59–66; Amy Strage and Joan Merdinger, "Professional Growth and Renewal for Mid-Career Faculty," *New Forums Press* 28, no. 3 (September 2014): 41–43; Anne Marie Canale, Cheryl Herdklotz, and Lynn Wild, "Mid-Career Faculty Support: The Middle Years of the Academic Profession," Rochester Institute of Technology Faculty Career Development Services, October 23, 2013.

81. Canale et al., "Mid-Career Faculty Support"; Baldwin et al., "Mapping the Terrain of Mid-Career Faculty." The HERI faculty survey indicates that women faculty spend more time advising students than do male faculty. Kevin Egan, Ellen Bara Stolzenberg, Jennifer Berdan Lozano, Melissa C. Aragon, Maria Ramirez Suchard, and Sylvia Hurtado, "Undergraduate Teaching Faculty: The 2013–14 HERI Faculty Survey," Higher Education Research Institute, https://www.heri.ucla.edu/monographs/HERI-FAC2014-monograph.pdf.

82. Leslie Brown, "How a Hundred Years of History Tracked Me Down," in Deborah G. White, ed., *Telling Histories: Black Women Historians in the Ivory Tower* (Chapel Hill: University of North Carolina Press, 2008), 268.

83. Therese A. Huston, Marie Norman, and Susan A. Ambrose, "Expanding the Discussion of Faculty Vitality to Include Productive but Disengaged Senior Faculty," *Journal of Higher Education* 78, no. 5 (September–October 2007): 493–522; Colleen Flaherty, "Midcareer Professors Need Love, Too," *Inside Higher Ed*, January 26, 2017.

84. Roger G. Baldwin, Christina J. Lunceford, and Kim E. Vanderlinden, "Faculty in the Middle Years: Illuminating an Overlooked Phase of Academic Life," *Review of Higher Education* 29, no. 1 (Fall 2005): 97–118; Peter Seldin, "Tailoring Professional Development Programs to Faculty Career Stages," POD Conference presentation, Dallas, TX, November 2014.

85. Brookfield, *Skillful Teacher*, 22; Baldwin et al., "Mapping the Terrain of Mid-Career Faculty."

86. The Faculty Survey of Student Engagement indicated that faculty nationally (all disciplines) work an average of fifty-five to sixty-three hours a week, and that those in the arts and humanities spend 64 percent of their time on teaching. "2006 Faculty Time," http://fsse.indiana.edu/html/FSSE_2006_Faculty_Time.cfm. A time study at Boise State indicated that faculty worked an

average of sixty-one hours a week during the semester. John Ziker, "The Long, Lonely Job of Homo academicus," *Blue Review*, March 31, 2014, https://theblue review.org/faculty-time-allocation/. Jerry Jacobs, "The Faculty Time Divide," *Sociological Forum* 19, no. 1 (March 2004): 3–27.

87. Maggie Berg and Barbara K. Seeber, *The Slow Professor: Challenging the Culture of Speed in the Academy* (Toronto: University of Toronto Press, 2016), 16–17.

88. Berg and Seeber, *Slow Professor*, 3, 7, 31–32.

89. Brookfield, *Skillful Teacher*, 266.

90. Robison, *Peak Performing Professor*, 194; Erika Vause, "Beyond First-Day Jitters: Teaching while Introverted, Shy, or Both," *Perspectives on History*, March 2016.

91. Berg and Seeber, *Slow Professor*, 41–42.

92. D'Emilio, "Forty Years and Counting," 33.

93. Many faculty of color feel they have to work harder than their colleagues to be perceived as a serious scholar. Egan et al., "2013–14 HERI Faculty Survey"; Christine A. Stanley, ed., *Faculty of Color: Teaching in Predominantly White Colleges and Universities* (Bolton, MA: Anker, 2006), 5–13; Rockquemore and Laszloffy, *Black Academic's Guide to Winning Tenure*, 12–23; Roxanna Harlow's study of black faculty having their credibility questioned was cited in Cavanagh, *Spark of Learning*, 192–94.

94. Rhonda Y. Williams, "Teaching Black Women's History and Other Stories: Ruminations of a Young Black Female History Professor," Howard University Archives, http://www.huarchivesnet.howard.edu/0005huarnet/womenhis1.htm; Barbara Ransby, "Dancing on the Edges of History, but Never Dancing Alone," in Deborah G. White, ed., *Telling Histories: Black Women Historians in the Ivory Tower* (Chapel Hill: University of North Carolina Press, 2008), 246–49.

95. Research on international geography faculty seems to capture the situation in other disciplines as well. Heike C. Alberts, "The Challenges and Opportunities of Foreign-Born Instructors in the Classroom," *Journal of Geography in Higher Education* 32, no. 2 (May 2008): 189–203; Jennifer M. Collins, "Coming to America: Challenges for Faculty Coming to United States' Universities," *Journal of Geography in Higher Education* 32, no. 2 (May 2008): 179–88; Nick Tingle, "Working Class Academics," presentation at Conference on Working Class Studies, Youngstown, Ohio, May 2005, http://www.writing.ucsb.edu/faculty/tingle/firstpage/Working%20Class%20Academics.htm; D'Emilio, "Forty Years and Counting," 37.

96. Elizabeth Lunbeck for the AHA Committee on Women Historians, "The Status of Women in the Historical Profession," American Historical Association, 2005, 4–16; *Gender Equity in the Academic History Workplace: A Guide to Best*

Practices (American Historical Association, 2005), https://www.historians.org/about-aha-and-membership/governance/reports-of-committees-and-divisions/gender-equity-in-the-academic-history-workplace-(2005).

97. In a small investigation, Nicholas L. Syrett discovered that students in history courses believed that being a woman influences how a female professor teaches more than being a man influences the way a male professor teaches, and that the professor being a man (teaching women's history) lent more objectivity and more significance to the subject matter. Syrett, "Who Is Teaching Women's History? 'Insight,' 'Objectivity,' and Identity," in Carol Berkin, Margaret S. Crocco, and Barbara Winslow, eds., *Clio in the Classroom: A Guide for Teaching U.S. Women's History* (Oxford: Oxford University Press, 2009), 267–73; Robert B. Townsend, "What the Data Reveals about Women Historians," *Perspectives*, May 2010; Bynum quoted in Popkin, *History, Historians and Autobiography*, 182.

98. Ambrose et al., *How Learning Works*, 222.

99. Cited in Cavanagh, *Spark of Learning*, 192–94; D'Emilio, "Forty Years and Counting," 38–39.

100. Association of American Colleges and Universities, "Intercultural Knowledge and Competence VALUE Rubric," https://www.aacu.org/value/rubrics/intercultural-knowledge; Nanda Dimitrov and Aisha Haque, "Intercultural Teaching Competence: A Multi-disciplinary Model for Instructor Reflection," *Intercultural Education* 27, no. 5 (2016): 437–45.

101. Jeff Falk, "Balabanlilar Wins Rice's Top Teaching Award," Rice University News and Media, 2016, http://news.rice.edu/2016/04/25/balabanlilar-wins-rices-top-teaching-award/; Collins, "Coming to America."

102. Melissa Scholes Young, "Navigating Campus Together," *The Atlantic*, May 6, 2016; Stefanie Stiles, "Blue-Collar Advantage: How Working-Class Academics Can Bring Us Together," *Times Higher Education*, April 25, 2017.

103. D'Emilio, "Forty Years and Counting," 45.

104. Robison, *Peak Performing Professor*, 177.

105. Allison Boye, "Mattering to Ourselves: Confronting Burnout and Compassion Fatigue for Educational Developers," POD Conference presentation, Montreal, Quebec, October 2017.

106. Terry Doyle, "Follow Where the Research Leads: Optimizing Learning in the Higher Education Classroom," Great Lakes Conference on Teaching and Learning Keynote Address, 2017, https://learnercenteredteaching.wordpress.com/2017/05/10/great-lakes-conference-on-teaching-and-learning-keynote-address-2017/.

107. Parker J. Palmer, *The Courage to Teach: Exploring the Inner Landscape of a Teacher's Life* (San Francisco: Jossey-Bass, 1998), 17.

108. Cavanagh, *Spark of Learning*, 66, 98.

109. Cathy Ann Trower, *Success on the Tenure Track: Five Keys to Faculty Job*

Satisfaction (Baltimore, MD: Johns Hopkins University Press, 2012), 3. Chapter 4 describes policies institutions can adopt to improve faculty work/life balance.

110. Robison, *Peak Performing Professor*, 179, 181–85, 194, 208, 211, 5, 10.

111. Robison, *Peak Performing Professor*, xvi–xvii, 212; O'Meara et al., *Faculty Careers and Work Lives*, 175–78. Robison distinguishes between purpose, mission, vision, and goals; I have simplified her discussion of these driving forces.

112. Strage and Merdinger, "Professional Growth and Renewal," 41–50; Robison, *Peak Performing Professor*, 194–98, 212. The absence of concrete, motivating goals can lead to a loss of momentum or disengagement. Baldwin et al., "Mapping the Terrain of Mid-Career Faculty."

113. Robison, *Peak Performing Professor*, 11–12.

114. The research by Tamara Beauboeuf, Jan Thomas, and Karla Erickson contrasts "synergistic citizens" with "weary citizens," "independent agents," and "disgruntled and discouraged." Cited in Colleen Flaherty, "Research on Midcareer Professors Makes Case for Support after Tenure," *Inside Higher Education*, January 26, 2017.

115. Robison, *Peak Performing Professor*, xv–xviii; Kerry Ann Rockquemore, "Essay on Need for Tenured Faculty Members to Have Mentoring," *Inside Higher Ed*, November 28, 2011.

116. Robison, *Peak Performing Professor*, 3.

117. Robison explicitly encourages a form of backward design for project management, *Peak Performing Professor*, 91–95.

118. Trower, *Success on the Tenure Track*, 122; Robison, *Peak Performing Professor*, 213.

119. Canale et al., "Mid-Career Faculty Support"; Jung H. Yun, Brian Baldi, and Mary Deane Sorcinelli, "Mutual Mentoring for Early-Career and Underrepresented Faculty: Model, Research, and Practice," *Innovative Higher Education* (online January 22, 2016); Strage and Merdinger, "Professional Growth and Renewal"; O'Meara et al., *Faculty Careers and Work Lives*, 86, 178.

120. Kerry Ann Rockquemore, "There Is No Guru," *Inside Higher Ed*, April 19, 2010; Kerry Ann Rockquemore, "Why Mentor Matches Fail," *Inside Higher Ed*, February 3, 2016; Rockquemore, "Essay on How Mid-Career Faculty Members Can Rebrand Themselves."

121. Barbara Gelpi, "Remembering Susan Groag Bell," Stanford University Gender News, August 12, 2015, http://gender.stanford.edu/news/2015/remem bering-susan-groag-bell; Brown, "How a Hundred Years of History," 264; quoted in Popkin, *History, Historians and Autobiography*, 182. Popkin observed that male historians' memoirs tended to tell stories of individual career success rather than referring to the importance of networks of women scholars as women did.

122. Yun et al., "Mutual Mentoring"; Jung H. Yun and Mary Dean Sorcinelli, "When Mentoring Is the Medium: Lessons Learned from Mutual Mentoring as a

Faculty Development Initiative," *To Improve the Academy* 27, no. 1 (June 2009): 365–84.

123. Ransby, "Dancing on the Edges of History," 242.

124. Yun et al., "Mutual Mentoring"; Strage and Merdiger, "Professional Growth and Renewal."

125. Natasha Kenny, Carol Berenson, Nancy Chick, David Keegan, Emma Read, and Leslie Reid, "A Developmental Framework for Teaching Expertise in Postsecondary Education," International Society for the Scholarship of Teaching and Learning, October 11–14, 2017, Calgary, Alberta; Stephen D. Brookfield, *Becoming a Critically Reflective Teacher*, 2nd ed. (San Francisco: Jossey-Bass, 2017), 2–4; Barbara Larrivee, "Transforming Teaching Practice: Becoming the Critically Reflective Teacher," *Reflective Practice* 1, no. 3 (2000): 293–307.

126. Filene, *Joy of Teaching*, 11.

Conclusion

1. Robert B. Bain, "Into the Breach: Using Research and Theory to Shape History Instruction," in Peter N. Stearns, Peter Seixas and Sam Wineburg, eds., *Knowing, Teaching and Learning History: National and International Perspectives* (New York: New York University Press, 2000), 332; "Becoming Square with History: Jill Lepore CN '93," *Fellowship: The Newsletter of the Woodrow Wilson National Fellowship Foundation* (Fall/Winter 2018): 8.

2. Stephen D. Brookfield, *The Skillful Teacher: On Technique, Trust, and Responsiveness in the Classroom*, 3rd ed. (San Francisco: Jossey-Bass, 2015), 155–57.

3. Charles C. Bonwell, "A Disciplinary Approach for Teaching Critical Thinking," *National Teaching & Learning Forum* 21, no. 2 (February 2012): 1–6.

4. James M. Lang, *Small Teaching: Everyday Lessons from the Science of Learning* (San Francisco: Jossey-Bass, 2016), 4–5.

5. Ken Bain, *What the Best Teachers Do* (Cambridge, MA: Harvard University Press, 2004), 167.

6. *How Learning Works* emphasizes the importance of faculty dispositions and that teaching is a long-term process of adaptation, incremental progressive refinement, and development. Susan A. Ambrose, Michael W. Bridges, Michele DiPietro, Marsha C. Lovett, Marie K. Norman, and Richard E. Mayer, *How Learning Works: 7 Research-Based Principles for Smart Teaching* (San Francisco: Jossey-Bass, 2010), 219–22.

7. I've adapted Terry Doyle's list of those aspects of teaching faculty control and those they do not. Terry Doyle, "Follow Where the Research Leads: Optimizing Learning in the Higher Education Classroom," Great Lakes Conference on Teaching and Learning Keynote Address, 2017, https://learnercentered teaching.wordpress.com/2017/05/10/great-lakes-conference-on-teaching -and-learning-keynote-address-2017/.

8. Quoted in Alexis Doyle, "Professor Eileen Findlay: Recipient of the 2016 Outstanding Teaching in a Full-Time Appointment Award," *Her Campus at American*, October 4, 2016, https://www.hercampus.com/school/american/professor-eileen-findlay-recipient-2016-outstanding-teaching-full-time-appointment.

9. Peter Filene, *The Joy of Teaching: A Practical Guide for New College Instructors* (Chapel Hill: University of North Carolina Press, 2005), 12.

10. John D'Emilio, "Forty Years and Counting," in Leila J. Rupp and Susan K. Freeman, eds., *Understanding and Teaching U.S. Lesbian, Gay, Bisexual, and Transgender History* (Madison: University of Wisconsin Press, 2014), 45.

Index

active learning, 92–96. *See also* clickers; discussions; games; graphic organizers; groups, small; interactive lecturing; jigsaw; list making; peer instruction, student; primary sources, analyzing; synthesizing; think/pair/share; writing

AHA. *See* American Historical Association

alignment: example of aligned course, 103–5; of goals with assessments and assignments, 9, 29–32; of teaching and learning activities with assessments, 34–35, 103–6

American Historical Association (AHA): disciplinary core and learning outcomes, 20, 95; professional ethics, 212; Tuning Project, 7, 20, 22, 95

Andrews, Thomas, 242n24

Antonova, Katherine, 142, 143

Ashenmiller, Josh, 21

assessment of student work: characteristics of effective, 143; criteria for, 157–58; efficiency of, 164–65; rubrics, 146–57. *See also* grading

assessment of student work, types of: essays, 148–64; formative, 118, 129–32, 143–48; ID questions, 23, 33, 45; multiple choice questions, 32–33, 121, 122, 148; peer assessment, 145–46; quizzes, 100–101; short answer questions, 33, 100, 148; student self-evaluation, 146–48; summative, 148–49

assessment of teaching: demonstrating effectiveness, 186–90; gathering formative feedback on, 176–84; peer observation, 176–78, 180–81;

self-evaluation, 185–86; student evaluation of teaching forms (SETs), 172–76

assignments: aligned, 29–32, 34–35; authentic, 39–40; designing good, 14–15, 28–45; digital, 38–39; engaging, 35–40; feasible, 32–35; transparent, 40–45. *See also* assessment of student work, types of

attention, 55, 59–60, 62, 94, 115, 119, 140, 220

authenticity. *See* assignments: authentic; instructors: authenticity

backward course design, 14–22, 25–29, 46, 103–10

Bain, Ken, 12, 19, 143, 169, 186, 230

Balabanlilar, Lisa, 219

beginnings, 59, 110, 112–16

Bell, Susan Groag, 225

belonging, student sense of, 41, 73–74, 78–79, 83–84

big questions, 18–22, 195–96

Bonwell, Charles, 25, 96, 228

boredom, 5, 59

bottlenecks, 50–52, 63, 67–68, 86

Brookfield, Stephen, 127, 199, 210, 215, 216, 227

Brown, Leslie, 215, 225

Burke, Flannery, 242n24

Bynum, Catherine, 218

Calder, Lendol, 23, 51, 53, 242n24

challenge, 18, 19, 29, 40, 44, 61–66, 70–71

class participation: discussions, 123–28; evaluation of, 146–48; setting up norms, 76–78; small group, 129–31 classroom response system. *See* clickers

clickers, 116, 122

climate. *See* inclusive teaching

closure. *See* endings

Collaborative on Academic Careers in Higher Education, 221

content, 13–28, 58–59

coverage vs. uncoverage, 23–25, 46, 229

cues, 66, 73, 83, 112, 203

decoding the discipline. *See* bottlenecks

Deliberative Dialogue, 38, 128–29

D'Emilio, John, 195, 217, 218, 219, 220, 232

Denial, Catherine, 137

disabilities. *See* faculty: with disabilities; students: identities of

discussions: benefits of, 123; common problems of, 123–25; components of effective, 124–25; Deliberative Dialogue, 38, 128–29; facilitating, 125–28

dispositions. *See* mindsets, student

dissonance, 70–71

document analysis. *See* primary sources, analyzing

Duby, Georges, 194

Dweck, Carol, 65

effective teaching, 8–9, 11, 84, 110, 169, 178, 197–98, 204–5, 209, 228–29, 231

emotions: of instructors, 175–56; of students, 66–71, 78–80

endings, 116–18

essays. *See* assessment of student work, types of

ethics, 208–9, 212–13

evaluation of teaching. *See* assessment of teaching

evidence-based teaching, 6, 8–9, 12, 186, 191, 229, 230

expectancy. *See* motivation, student

experiential learning, 138–40

facts, 23–26, 51, 229

faculty: of color, 172–73, 207, 215, 217–19, 223–24, 225, 275n83; contexts, 210–11;

contingent, part-time, or adjunct, 213–14; with disabilities, 208; first-generation, 218–19, 220; health and well-being, 215–16, 220–21, 223–26; identities, 192–97, 219, 203–10; international, 172–73, 207, 218, 219; late career, 215; LGBTQIA, 207–8, 215, 218, 220; mid-career, 214–15; new, 211–12; origin stories, 192–97; promotion and tenure, 171–72; purpose, 221–23; satisfaction, 216, 222–23; women, 205, 206–7, 213, 215, 218–19, 225, 223–25, 275n83; workload, 215–16. *See also* instructors

feedback on student work, 97–98, 129, 131–32, 144–46, 166–68

feedback on teaching. *See* assessment of teaching

Felten, Peter, 77, 113, 114, 234

Filene, Peter, 102, 200, 226, 232, 233, 224

Findlay, Eileen, 196

Fink, Dee, 17, 103, 107

first day of class, 110, 112–15, 207–8

Foner, Eric, 192, 194

Franklin, John Hope, 193

Freedman, Estelle, 196

games, 139

Gannon, Kevin, 142, 165

Gardner Institute study of introductory U.S. history courses, 5

goals for students' learning: AHA disciplinary core and learning outcomes, 20, 22, 95; Association of American Colleges and Universities, 17; list of possible, 17–22, 25–28, 242n24; skills, 17, 18, 21–22; thinking/habits of mind, 16–22, 25, 29

Gold, Penny, 213, 233

Gordon, Linda, 193, 194, 195

grading: characteristics of effective, 143; checklists, 164–65; conversations with students about, 168–71; criteria, 149–58, 163, 168; efficiency, 143, 144–46, 153, 164–65; fairness, 151, 158–59; instructor hatred of, 142–43; rubrics,

150–57; transparency of expectations, 157–58; writing comments, 160–66. *See also* assessment of student work, types of
graphic organizers, 135–37
Grossman, James, 3
groups, small, 99, 129–32
Guerra, Lillian, 195

halo effect, 159
Hiberg, Raul, 193
Higher Education Research Institute study, 54
high-impact practices, 138–39
Hine, Darlene Clark, 194, 195
historians. *See* faculty; instructors; *and individual names*
history: benefits of understanding, 17–18; big questions for, 18–22, 195–96; bottlenecks for students, 50–52, 63, 67–68, 86; content, 3–4, 6, 13–25; digital revolution impact on, 7; goals and outcomes, 17–22, 25–28, 242n24; perception as boring, 5, 59; skills, 17, 18, 21–22; threshold concepts, 4, 21, 51; ways of thinking, 7, 16–22, 25, 29, 96–98, 227–28
History Learning Project, 51, 63, 67, 85–86
Hollinger, David, 193
hot moments, 68–71
Howard, Jay, 99, 123, 124, 127
How Learning Works, 53, 100, 198
humor, 205–6, 231
Huston, Therese, 114–15

illusions of fluency, 97
inclusive teaching: definition, 8–9, 71–72, 228–29, 257n120; fairness, 34, 60–61, 84, 140, 143, 151, 158–60, 170; hot moments, 68–71; practices to avoid, 75–76; stereotype threat, 80–84, 162–63, 207, 229, 273n53; strategies to promote, 72–80, 157, 162–63, 182; transparency, 40–45, 96, 115, 130, 157–58, 209, 230
indoctrination, dangers of, 196–97, 208–9

instructors: authenticity, 203, 210; characteristics and behavior of effective, 110, 169, 178, 197–98, 204–5, 209, 228–29, 231; contexts, 210–11; demoralized, 175–76, 231; differences with students, 197, 219–20, 229; as disciplinary experts, 13, 49, 54, 85, 102, 172; emotions, 216–20; factors they can control, 47–48, 74, 84, 175, 176, 231–32, 258n142; health, stress, and well-being, 220; identities, 192–97, 207–9; and identity-related biases, 172–74; metacognition, 16–17, 231; mindsets, dispositions, and limiting beliefs, 197–200, 231; motivation, 195, 199, 221–23, 231; purpose, 221–23; self-disclosure and authenticity, 203–9; style, 203–10; success over the long term, 206–26; teaching persona, 203–10
intentional teaching, 9, 11, 106–7, 140–41, 209–10, 225–26, 228, 232
interactive lecturing, 120–22
intercultural knowledge and competence, 17, 219

Jenkins, Rob, 202
jigsaw, 137–38

Lang, James, 71, 117, 228
Lapsansky-Werner, Emma, 142
learning and neurological networks, 48–49, 85, 94, 116
learning-centeredness, 84–86
lectures, 119–22
Lerner, Gerda, 194, 195, 196, 197
Lewis, Michael, 196
list making, 92, 132
Litwack, Leon, 195

matrix, 136–37
McClymer, John, 28, 29, 168
McGuire, Saundra, 64, 102, 162
McNair, Glenn, 202
McTighe, Jay, 22
mentors for faculty, 223–25, 226

metacognition, student, 8, 16–17, 40–41, 92, 115, 116–18, 129–30, 146, 153, 166–67, 182
metaphors for teaching, 200–203
Middendorf, Joan, 24
mid-semester focus groups, 182–84
mindsets, student, 63–66
minute papers, 118, 180
Morgan, Edmund, 194
motivation, student, 44, 56–63, 67, 73, 79, 83, 97, 100, 115, 131, 139, 162, 168
muddiest point, 118

Neal, Ed, 233, 234, 281n40

objectives. See goals for students' learning
O'Meara, KerryAnn, 210
outcomes, student learning (SLOs). See goals for students' learning
over-efforting, 81

Pace, David, 6, 20, 24
Painter, Nell, 192, 193, 194
Parini, Jay, 203, 210
peer evaluation of student work, 145–46
peer instruction, student, 137–38
peer observation of teaching, 176–78, 180–81
Perkins, David, 13, 14, 19, 198
Perry, Mary Elizabeth, 213
Perry, William, 51–52
personas, teaching, 203–10
perspective taking, 135
portfolios, teaching. See assessment of teaching
practice, 96–97
preparation for class and student accountability, 99–102
Preskill, Stephen, 127
primary sources, analyzing, 21, 22, 27, 31–32, 97–98, 106–7, 113–14, 134–35
prior knowledge, 48–54, 84, 85, 90, 112
promotion and tenure. See assessment of teaching

questions: big and meaningful, 18–22, 195–96; effective, 88–89, 121–22, 126;

examples, 89–92; importance of, 87–88; problematic, 88; types, 89–92
quizzes, 99

race. See faculty: of color; students: identities of
Ransby, Barbara, 218, 225
rapport, 59–60
Reacting to the Past pedagogy, 139
readings, 99–102, 124
reflection: faculty, 225, 232; student, 116–17
Reiff, Janice, 193, 196
Robison, Susan, 220, 221, 222
Roland, Charles, 193
rubrics: benefits of, 150–51; description of, 149–50; examples, 146–47, 151–56, 163

scaffolding of learning, 97–99, 134
Schlesinger, Arthur, Jr., 193
scholarly teaching, 8–9, 186, 191, 229, 230
scholarship of teaching and learning (SOTL), 6–8, 230
Scott, Joan Wallach, 196
Shopkow, Leah, 18, 53, 95, 157, 164
significant learning, 16–21
Sipress, Joel, 150, 185–86, 187, 234
Slow Professor, 216
small group collaborative activities. See groups, small
Small Group Instructional Diagnosis. See mid-semester focus groups
Snay, Mitchell, 194
SOTL. See scholarship of teaching and learning
sources. See primary sources, analyzing
Stanford History Education Group, 33
stereotype threat, 80–84, 162–63, 207, 229, 273n53
Strauss, Herbert, 193
student-centeredness, 48, 84–86
student evaluation of teaching ratings (SETs), 172–76
student learning outcomes (SLOs). See goals for students' learning
students: challenging, 61–64; common misunderstandings of, 50–52, 63, 67–68,

86, 169–70; as digital natives, 55–56; emotions of, 66–71, 78–80; freeloading and social loafing, 99, 130; identities of, 71–85, 89, 256n108, 274n77; importance of knowing, 47–48, 52–56, 73–75, 85–86; mindsets and dispositions of, 63–66; motivation of, 44, 56–63, 67, 73, 79, 83, 97, 100, 115, 131, 139, 162; as novices, 49; prior knowledge and assumptions of, 48–56; personal struggles of, 79–80, 170; supporting, 61–62, 71, 101, 98–99, 101, 162–63, 169–70
student-student interactions, 68–71, 76–79, 83
studying, 54
"sweet spot" of challenge, 61–63, 101, 220
syllabus, 72, 113–14
synthesizing, 34–35, 61, 132–34

teachers. See faculty; instructors
teaching squares, 179
teaching techniques. See clickers; discussions; games; graphic organizers; groups, small; jigsaw; list making; peer instruction, student; primary sources, analyzing; synthesizing; think/pair/share; writing
technology: banning, 256n108; benefits, 7, 140; digital assignments, 27, 28, 34, 38–39, 154–56; digital natives, 55–56; and grading, 164–65; impact on learning, 56; student access to tools and literacy, 56; student difficulty with evaluating information on the web, 7, 51, 54, 55, 102

think/pair/share, 122
threshold concepts, 4, 21, 51
timelines. See graphic organizers
transfer, 22, 25, 56, 78
transformation, 70–71, 85, 199, 227
transparency, 40–45, 96, 115, 130, 157–58, 209, 230
Transparency in Teaching and Learning Project, 8, 40–45, 157–58
Tuning Project, 7, 20, 22, 95

understanding by design. See backward course design
unit plan, 107–12

value. See motivation, student
Voelker, David, 33, 122

Wabash Institute National Study of Liberal Arts Education, 8, 44, 110, 248n89, 256n111
Weir, Robert E., 160–61, 164
Wiggins, Grant, 22, 28, 29, 39
Williams, Rhonda Y., 217–18
Willingham, Daniel, 85, 200
Wineburg, Sam, 7, 20, 23, 50, 51, 54
wrappers, exam or cognitive, 166–67
writing: as active learning, 92, 134; as bottleneck, 63–64; commenting on, 160–65; drafts, 145, 168; peer review of, 145–46; quality vs. quantity, 32; scaffolding of research papers, 98–99; types of assignments, 35–40. See also feedback on student work; grading

Young, Melissa Scholes, 219–20